Get the eBook FREE!

(PDF, ePub, Kindle, and liveBook all included)

We believe that once you buy a book from us, you should be able to read it in any format we have available. To get electronic versions of this book at no additional cost to you, purchase and then register this book at the Manning website.

Go to https://www.manning.com/freebook and follow the instructions to complete your pBook registration.

That's it!
Thanks from Manning!

Machine Learning
for Business

USING AMAZON SAGEMAKER AND JUPYTER

DOUG HUDGEON
AND RICHARD NICHOL

MANNING
SHELTER ISLAND

For online information and ordering of this and other Manning books, please visit www.manning.com. The publisher offers discounts on this book when ordered in quantity. For more information, please contact

    Special Sales Department
    Manning Publications Co.
    20 Baldwin Road
    PO Box 761
    Shelter Island, NY 11964
    Email: orders@manning.com

Manning Publications Co.
20 Baldwin Road
PO Box 761
Shelter Island, NY 11964

Development editor:	Toni Arritola
Technical development editor:	Arthur Zubarev
Review editor:	Ivan Martinović
Production editor:	Deirdre Hiam
Copy editor:	Frances Buran
Proofreader:	Katie Tennant
Technical proofreader:	Karsten Strøbæk
Typesetter:	Dennis Dalinnik
Cover designer:	Marija Tudor

ISBN: 9781617295836
Printed in the United States of America

brief contents

iii

contents

preface

This book shows you how to apply machine learning in your company to make your business processes faster and more resilient to change. This book is for people beginning their journey in machine learning or for those who are more experienced with machine learning but want to see how it can be applied in practice.

Based on our experiences with automating business processes and implementing machine learning applications, we wanted to write a book that would allow anyone to start using machine learning in their company. The caveat to *anyone* isn't that you need to have a certain technical background, it's that you're willing to put in the time when you run the code to understand what's happening and why.

We look at a variety of different functions within various companies ranging across accounts payable (supplier invoices), facilities management (power consumption forecasting), customer support (support tickets), and sales (customer retention). The intent is that this will give you some insight into the range and scale of potential applications of machine learning and encourage you to discover new business applications on your own.

A secondary focus of this book is to demonstrate how you can use the Amazon SageMaker cloud service to rapidly and cost effectively bring your business ideas to life. Most of the ideas we present can be implemented using other services (such as Google Cloud or Microsoft Azure); however, the differences are significant enough that to cover multiple providers would be beyond the scope of this book.

We hope you enjoy our book and that you're able to dramatically improve the productivity of your company by applying the techniques inside. Please hit us up in liveBook if you have questions, comments, suggestions, or examples of how you've tackled certain problems. See page xxi for access to the liveBook site. We'd love to hear from you.

acknowledgments

Writing this book was a lot of work but would have been a lot more without Richie cranking out the notebook code and contributing to chapter ideas. My advice to anyone looking to write a technical book is to find a coauthor and break up the work. Richie and I have different coding styles, and I learned to appreciate his way of tackling certain problems during my documentation of his code.

I'd like to acknowledge the team at Manning for their help and guidance through the process, and Toni Arritola, in particular, for accommodating the different time zones and having the flexibility to deal with two very busy people in putting this book together.

Thank you to everyone at Manning: Deirdre Hiam, our production editor, Frances Buran, our copy editor, Katie Tennant, our proofreader, Arthur Zubarev, our technical development editor, Ivan Martinović, our review editor, and Karsten Strøbæk, our technical proofreader. To all of our reviewers—Aleksandr Novomlinov, Arpit Khandelwal, Burkhard Nestmann, Clemens Baader, Conor Redmond, Dana Arritola, Dary Merckens, Dhivya Sivasubramanian, Dinesh Ghanta, Gerd Klevesaat, James Black, James Nyika, Jeff Smith, Jobinesh Purushothaman Manakkattil, John Bassil, Jorge Ezequiel Bo, Kevin Kraus, Laurens Meulman, Madhavan Ramani, Mark Poler, Muhammad Sohaib Arif, Nikos Kanakaris, Paulo Nuin, Richard Tobias, Ryan Kramer, Sergio Fernandez Gonzalez, Shawn Eion Smith, Syed Nouman Hasany, and Taylor Delehanty—thank you, your suggestions helped make this a better book.

And, of course, I'd like to thank my spouse and family for their patience and understanding.

—Doug Hudgeon

I'm very grateful to Doug for asking me to join him as coauthor in writing this book, but also for his creativity, positivity, friendship, and sense of humor. Although it was a lot of work, it was also a pleasure.

I'd also like to offer my special thanks to my parents, family, and friends for putting up with the long hours and lost weekends. Most of all, I'd like to thank my wife, Xenie, who could not have been more supportive and understanding during the years I completed my studies as well as this book. No husband could hope for a better wife, and I can't believe how lucky I am to be spending my days beside her.

—Richard Nichol

about this book

Companies are on the cusp of a massive leap in productivity. Today, thousands of people are involved in process work, where they take information from one source and put it into another place. For example, take procurement and accounts payable:

- Procurement staff help a customer create a purchase order, and then send it to a supplier.
- The supplier's order-processing staff then take the purchase order and enter it into the order-processing system, where it's fulfilled and shipped to the customer that placed the order.
- Staff on the customer's loading dock receive the goods, and the finance staff enters the invoice into the customer's finance system.

Over the next decade, all of these processes will be completely automated in almost every company, and machine learning will play a big part in automating the decision points at each stage of the process. It will help businesses make the following decisions:

- Does the person approving the order have the authority to do so?
- Is it OK to substitute a product for an out-of-stock item?
- If a supplier has substituted a product, will the receiver accept it?
- Is the invoice OK to pay as is or should it be queried?

The real benefit of machine learning for business is that it allows you to build decision-making applications that are resilient to change. Instead of programming dozens or hundreds of rules into your systems, you feed in past examples of good and bad decisions, and then let the machine make a determination based on how similar the current scenario is to past examples.

The benefit of this is that the system doesn't break when it comes across novel input. The challenge is that it takes a different mindset and approach to deliver a machine learning project than it does to deliver a normal IT project.

In a normal IT project, you can test each of the rules to ensure they work. In a machine learning project, you can only test to see whether the algorithm has responded appropriately to the test scenarios. And you don't know how it will react to novel input. Trusting in safeguards that catch it when it's not reacting appropriately requires you and your stakeholders to be comfortable with this uncertainty.

Who should read this book

This book is targeted at people who may be more comfortable using Excel than using a programming language such as Python. Each chapter contains a fully working Jupyter notebook that creates the machine learning model, deploys it, and runs it against a dataset prepared for the chapter. You don't need to do any coding to see the code in action.

Each chapter then takes you through the code step by step so that you understand how it works. With minor modifications, you can apply the code directly to your own data. By the end of the book, you should be able to tackle a wide range of machine learning projects within your company.

How this book is organized: A roadmap

This book has three parts:

Part 1 starts with a description of why businesses need to become a lot more productive to remain competitive, and it explains how effective decision-making plays a role in this. You'll then move on to why machine learning is a good way to make business decisions, and how, using open source tools and tools from AWS, you can start applying machine learning to making decisions in your business.

In part 2, you'll then work through six scenarios (one scenario per chapter) that show how machine learning can be used to make decisions in your business. The scenarios focus on how an ordinary company can use machine learning, rather than on how Facebook or Google or Amazon use machine learning.

Finally, in part 3, you'll learn how to set up and share your machine learning models on the web so your company can make decisions using machine learning. You'll then go through some case studies that show how companies manage the change that comes along with using machine learning to make decisions.

About the code

In each chapter in part 2, we provide you a Jupyter notebook and one or more sample datasets that you can upload to AWS SageMaker and run. In part 3, we provide the code to set up a serverless API to serve your predictions to users across the web.

You run and write the code used in part 2 of the book on AWS SageMaker. You don't need to install anything locally. You can use any type of computer with internet access for this code—even a Google Chromebook. To set up the serverless API in part 3 of the book, you need to install Python on a laptop running macOS, Windows, or Linux operating systems.

This book contains many examples of source code both in numbered listings and in line with normal text. In both cases, source code is formatted in a `fixed-width font like this` to separate it from ordinary text.

In many cases, the original source code has been reformatted; we've added line breaks and reworked indentation to accommodate the available page width in the book. Code annotations (comments) accompany many of the listings, highlighting important concepts. Additionally, comments in the source code have often been removed from the listings when the code is described in the text.

The code for the examples in this book is available for download from the Manning website at https://www.manning.com/books/machine-learning-for-business?query =hudgeon and from GitHub at https://git.manning.com/agileauthor/hudgeon/tree/master/manuscript.

liveBook discussion forum

The purchase of *Machine Learning for Business* includes free access to a private web forum run by Manning Publications, where you can make comments about the book, ask technical questions, and receive help from the authors and from other users. To access the forum, go to https://livebook.manning.com/book/machine-learning-for-business/welcome/v-6/. You can also learn more about Manning's forums and the rules of conduct at https://livebook.manning.com/#!/discussion.

Manning's commitment to our readers is to provide a venue where a meaningful dialog between individual readers and between readers and authors can take place. It is not a commitment to any specific amount of participation on the part of the authors, whose contribution to the forum remains voluntary (and unpaid). We suggest you try asking them some challenging questions lest their interest stray! The forum and the archives of previous discussions will be accessible from the publisher's website as long as the book is in print.

about the authors

Richard (Richie) and Doug worked together at a procurement software company. Doug became CEO not long after Richie was hired as a data engineer to help the company categorize millions of products.

After leaving the company, Doug built Managed Functions (https://managedfunctions .com), an integration/machine learning platform that uses Python and Jupyter notebooks to automate business processes. Richie went on to complete a Master of Data Science at the University of Sydney, Australia, and is now working as Senior Data Scientist for Faethm (http://www.faethm.ai).

about the cover illustration

The figure on the cover of *Machine Learning for Business* is captioned "*Costumes civils actuels de tous les peuples connus*," meaning "current civilian costumes of all known peoples." The illustration is taken from a collection of dress costumes from various countries by Jacques Grasset de Saint-Sauveur (1757-1810), titled *Costumes de Différents Pays*, published in France in 1797.

Each illustration is finely drawn and colored by hand. The rich variety of Grasset de Saint-Sauveur's collection reminds us vividly of how culturally apart the world's towns and regions were just 200 years ago. Isolated from each other, people spoke different dialects and languages. In the streets or in the countryside, it was easy to identify where they lived and what their trade or station in life was just by their dress.

The way we dress has changed since then, and the diversity by region, so rich at the time, has faded away. It is now hard to tell apart the inhabitants of different continents, let alone different towns, regions, or countries. Perhaps we have traded cultural diversity for a more varied personal life—certainly for a more varied and fast-paced technological life.

At a time when it is hard to tell one computer book from another, Manning celebrates the inventiveness and initiative of the computer business with book covers based on the rich diversity of regional life of two centuries ago, brought back to life by Grasset de Saint-Sauveur's pictures.

Part 1

Machine learning for business

The coming decade will see a massive surge in business productivity as companies automate tasks that are important but time consuming for people to do. Examples of such tasks include approving purchase orders, evaluating which customers are at risk of churning, identifying support requests that should be escalated immediately, auditing invoices from suppliers, and forecasting operational trends, such as power consumption.

Part one looks at why this trend is occurring and the role of machine learning in creating the surge. Companies that are not able to accelerate to catch this surge will quickly find themselves outdistanced by their competitors.

How machine learning applies to your business

1

This chapter covers

- Why our business systems are so terrible
- What machine learning is
- Machine learning as a key to productivity
- Fitting machine learning with business automation
- Setting up machine learning within your company

Technologists have been predicting for decades that companies are on the cusp of a surge in productivity, but so far, this has not happened. Most companies still use people to perform repetitive tasks in accounts payable, billing, payroll, claims management, customer support, facilities management, and more. For example, all of the following small decisions create delays that make you (and your colleagues) less responsive than you want to be and less effective than your company needs you to be:

- To submit a leave request, you have to click through a dozen steps, each one requiring you to enter information that the system should already know or to make a decision that the system should be able to figure out from your objective.

- To determine why your budget took a hit this month, you have to scroll through a hundred rows in a spreadsheet that you've manually extracted from your finance system. Your systems should be able to determine which rows are anomalous and present them to you.
- When you submit a purchase order for a new chair, you know that Bob in procurement has to manually make a bunch of small decisions to process the form, such as whether your order needs to be sent to HR for ergonomics approval or whether it can be sent straight to the financial approver.

We believe that you will soon have much better systems at work—machine learning applications will automate all of the small decisions that currently hold up processes. It is an important topic because, over the coming decade, companies that are able to become more automated and more productive will overtake those that cannot. And machine learning will be one of the key enablers of this transition.

This book shows you how to implement machine learning, decision-making systems in your company to speed up your business processes. "But how can I do that?" you say. "I'm technically minded and I'm pretty comfortable using Excel, and I've never done any programming." Fortunately for you, we are at a point in time where any technically minded person can learn how to help their company become dramatically more productive. This book takes you on that journey. On that journey, you'll learn

- How to identify where machine learning will create the greatest benefits within your company in areas such as
  - Back-office financials (accounts payable and billing)
  - Customer support and retention
  - Sales and marketing
  - Payroll and human resources
- How to build machine learning applications that you can implement in your company

1.1   Why are our business systems so terrible?

"The man who goes alone can start today; but he who travels with another must wait till that other is ready."

Henry David Thoreau

Before we get into how machine learning can make your company more productive, let's look at why implementing systems in your company is more difficult than adopting systems in your personal life. Take your personal finances as an example. You might use a money management app to track your spending. The app tells you how much you spend and what you spend it on, and it makes recommendations on how you could increase your savings. It even automatically rounds up purchases to the nearest dollar and puts the spare change into your savings account. At work, expense management is a very different experience. To see how your team is tracking against their budget, you send a request to the finance team, and they get back to you the following week. If you want to drill down into particular line items in your budget, you're out of luck.

There are two reasons why our business systems are so terrible. First, although changing our own behavior is not easy, changing the behavior of a group of people is really hard. In your personal life, if you want to use a new money management app, you just start using it. It's a bit painful because you need to learn how the new app works and get your profile configured, but still, it can be done without too much effort. However, when your company wants to start using an expense management system, everyone in the company needs to make the shift to the new way of doing things. This is a much bigger challenge. Second, managing multiple business systems is really hard. In your personal life, you might use a few dozen systems, such as a banking system, email, calendar, maps, and others. Your company, however, uses hundreds or even thousands of systems. Although managing the interactions between all these systems is hard for your IT department, they encourage you to use their *end-to-end enterprise software system* for as many tasks as possible.

The end-to-end enterprise software systems from software companies like SAP and Oracle are designed to run your entire company. These end-to-end systems handle your inventory, pay staff, manage the finance department, and handle most other aspects of your business. The advantage of an end-to-end system is that everything is integrated. When you buy something from your company's IT catalog, the catalog uses your employee record to identify you. This is the same employee record that HR uses to store your leave request and send you paychecks. The problem with end-to-end systems is that, because they do everything, there are better systems available for each thing that they do. Those systems are called *best-of-breed systems*.

Best-of-breed systems do one task particularly well. For example, your company might use an expense management system that rivals your personal money management application for ease of use. The problem is that this expense management system doesn't fit neatly with the other systems your company uses. Some functions duplicate existing functions in other systems (figure 1.1). For example, the expense management system has a built-in approval process. This approval process duplicates the approval process you use in other aspects of your work, such as approving employee leave. When your company implements the best-of-breed expense management system, it has to make a choice: does it use the expense management approval workflow and train you to use two different approval processes? Or does it integrate the expense management system with the end-to-end system so you can approve expenses in the end-to-end system and then pass the approval back into the expense management system?

To get a feel for the pros and cons of going with an end-to-end versus a best-of-breed system, imagine you're a driver in a car rally that starts on paved roads, then

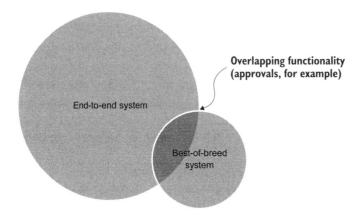

Figure 1.1   Best-of-breed approval function overlaps the end-to-end system approval function.

goes through desert, and finally goes through mud. You have to choose between putting all-terrain tires on your car or changing your tires when you move from pavement to sand and from sand to mud. If you choose to change your tires, you can go faster through each of the sections, but you lose time when you stop and change the tires with each change of terrain. Which would you choose? If you could change tires quickly, and it helped you go much faster through each section, you'd change tires with each change of terrain.

Now imagine that, instead of being the driver, your job is to support the drivers by providing them with tires during the race. You're the Chief Tire Officer (CTO). And imagine that instead of three different types of terrain, you have hundreds, and instead of a few drivers in the race, you have thousands. As CTO, the decision is easy: you'll choose the all-terrain tires for all but the most specialized terrains, where you'll reluctantly concede that you need to provide specialty tires. As a driver, the CTO's decision sometimes leaves you dissatisfied because you end up with a system that is clunkier than the systems you use in your personal life.

We believe that over the coming decade, machine learning will solve these types of problems. Going back to our metaphor about the race, a machine learning application would automatically change the characteristics of your tires as you travel through different terrains. It would give you the best of both worlds by rivaling best-of-breed performance while utilizing the functionality in your company's end-to-end solution.

As another example, instead of implementing a best-of-breed expense management system, your company could implement a machine learning application to

- Identify information about the expense, such as the amount spent and the vendor name
- Decide which employee the expense belongs to
- Decide which approver to submit the expense claim to

Returning to the example of overlapping approval functions, by using machine learning in conjunction with your end-to-end systems, you can automate and improve your company's processes without implementing a patchwork of best-of-breed systems (figure 1.2).

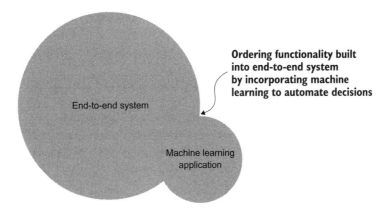

Figure 1.2   Machine learning enhances the functionality of end-to-end systems.

Is there no role for best-of-breed systems in the enterprise?

There is a role for best-of-breed systems in the enterprise, but it is probably different than the role these systems have filled over the past 20 years or so. As you'll see in the next section, the computer era (1970 to the present) has been unsuccessful in improving the productivity of businesses. If best-of-breed systems were successful at improving business productivity, we should have seen some impact on the performance of businesses that use best-of-breed systems. But we haven't.

So what will happen to the best-of-breed systems? In our view, the best-of-breed systems will become

- More integrated into a company's end-to-end system
- More modular so that a company can adopt some of the functions, but not others

Vendors of these best-of-breed systems will base their business cases on the use of problem-specific machine learning applications to differentiate their offerings from those of their competitors or on solutions built in-house by their customers. Conversely, their profit margins will get squeezed as more companies develop the skills to build machine learning applications themselves rather than buying a best-of-breed solution.

1.2   *Why is automation important now?*

We are on the cusp of a dramatic improvement in business productivity. Since 1970, business productivity in mature economies such as the US and Europe has barely moved, compared to the change in the processing power of computers, and this trend has been clearly visible for decades now. Over that period of time, business productivity has merely doubled, whereas the processing power of computers is 20 million times greater!

If computers were really helping us become more productive, why is it that much faster computers don't lead to much greater productivity? This is one of mysteries of modern economics. Economists call this mystery the *Solow Paradox*. In 1987, Robert Solow, an American economist, quipped:

> *"You can see the computer age everywhere but in the productivity statistics."*

Is the failure of businesses to become more productive just a feature of business? Are businesses at maximum productivity now? We don't think so. Some companies have found a solution to the Solow Paradox and are rapidly improving their productivity. And we think that they will be joined by many others—hopefully, yours as well.

Figure 1.3 is from a 2017 speech on productivity given by Andy Haldane, Chief Economist for the Bank of England.[1] It shows that since 2002, the top 5% of companies

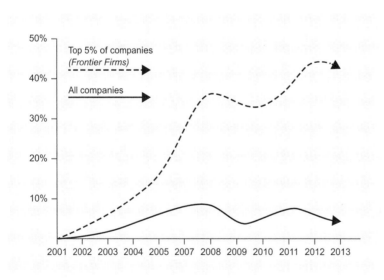

Figure 1.3   Comparison of productivity across frontier firms (the top 5%) versus all companies

---

[1]   Andy Haldane, "Productivity Puzzles," https://www.bis.org/review/r170322b.pdf.

have increased productivity by 40%, while the other 95% of companies have barely increased productivity at all.[2] This low-growth trend is found across nearly all countries with mature economies.

1.2.1 *What is productivity?*

Productivity is measured at a country level by dividing the annual Gross Domestic Product (GDP) by the number of hours worked in a year. The GDP per hour worked in the UK and the US is currently just over US$100. In 1970, it was between US$45 and US$50. But the GDP per hour worked by the top 5% of firms (the frontier firms) is over US$700 and rising.

The frontier firms were able to hit such a high GDP per hour by minimizing human effort to generate each dollar of revenue. Or, to put it another way, these firms *automate* everything that can be automated. We predict that productivity growth will improve rapidly as more companies figure out how to replicate what the top companies are doing and will make the jump from their current level of productivity to the top levels of productivity.

We believe that we're at the end of the Solow Paradox; that machine learning will enable many companies to hit the productivity levels we see in the top 5% of companies. And we believe that those companies that do not join them, that don't dramatically improve their productivity, will wither and die.

1.2.2 *How will machine learning improve productivity?*

In the preceding sections, we looked at why companies struggle to become more automated and the evidence showing that, while company productivity has not improved much over the past 50 years, there is a group of frontier firms becoming more productive by automating everything that can be automated. Next we'll look at how machine learning can help your company become a frontier firm before showing you how you can help your company make the shift.

For our purposes, *automation* is the use of software to perform a repetitive task. In the business world, repetitive tasks are everywhere. A typical retail business, for example, places orders with suppliers, sends marketing material to customers, manages products in inventory, creates entries in their accounting system, makes payments to their staff, and hundreds of other things.

Why is it so hard to automate these processes? From a higher level, these processes look pretty simple. Sending marketing material is just preparing content and emailing it to customers. Placing orders is simply selecting product from a catalog, getting it approved, and sending the order to a supplier. How hard can it be?

The reason automation is hard to implement is because, even though these processes look repetitive, there are small decisions that need to be made at several steps along the way. This is where machine learning fits in. You can use machine learning to

---

[2] Andy Haldane dubbed the top 5% of companies *frontier firms*.

make these decisions at each point in the process in much the same way a human currently does.

1.3   *How do machines make decisions?*

For the purposes of this book, think of machine learning as a way to arrive at a decision, based on patterns in a dataset. We'll call this *pattern-based decision making*. This is in contrast to most software development these days, which is *rules-based decision making*—where programmers write code that employs a series of rules to perform a task.

When your marketing staff sends out an email newsletter, the marketing software contains code that queries a database and pulls out only those customers selected by the query (for example, males younger than 25 who live within 20 kilometers of a certain clothing outlet store). Each person in the marketing database can be identified as being in this group or not in this group.

Contrast this with machine learning where the query for your database might be to pull out all users who have a purchasing history similar to that of a specific 23-year-old male who happens to live close to one of your outlet stores. This query will get a lot of the same people that the rules-based query gets, but it will also return those who have a similar purchasing pattern and are willing to drive further to get to your store.

1.3.1   *People: Rules-based or not?*

Many businesses rely on people rather than software to perform routine tasks like sending marketing material and placing orders with suppliers. They do so for a number of reasons, but the most prevalent is that it's easier to teach a person how to do a task than it is to program a computer with the rules required to perform the same task.

Let's take Karen, for example. Her job is to review purchase orders, send them to an approver, and then email the approved purchase orders to the supplier. Karen's job is both boring and tricky. Every day, Karen makes dozens of decisions about who should approve which orders. Karen has been doing this job for several years, so she knows the simple rules, like IT products must be approved by the IT department. But she also knows the exceptions. For example, she knows that when Jim orders toner from the stationery catalog, she needs to send the order to IT for approval, but when Jim orders a new mouse from the IT catalog, she does not.

The reason Karen's role hasn't been automated is because programming all of these rules is hard. But harder still is maintaining these rules. Karen doesn't often apply her "fax machine" rule anymore, but she is increasingly applying her "tablet stylus" rule, which she has developed over the past several years. She considers a tablet stylus to be more like a mouse than a laptop computer, so she doesn't send stylus orders to IT for approval. If Karen really doesn't know how to classify a particular product, she'll call IT to discuss it; but for most things, she makes up her own mind.

Using our concepts of rules-based decision making versus pattern-based decision making, you can see that Karen incorporates a bit of both. Karen applies rules most of the time but occasionally makes decisions based on patterns. It's the pattern-based part of Karen's work that makes it hard to automate using a rules-based system. That's why, in the past, it has been easier to have Karen perform these tasks than to program a computer with the rules to perform the same tasks.

1.3.2 *Can you trust a pattern-based answer?*

Lots of companies have manual processes. Often this is the case because there's enough variation in the process to make automation difficult. This is where machine learning comes in.

Any point in a process where a person needs to make a decision is an opportunity to use machine learning to automate the decision or to present a restricted choice of options for the person to consider. Unlike rules-based programming, machine learning uses examples rather than rules to determine how to respond in a given situation. This allows it to be more flexible than rules-based systems. Instead of breaking when faced with a novel situation, machine learning simply makes a decision with a lower level of confidence.

Let's look at the example of a new product coming into Karen's catalog. The product is a voice-controlled device like Amazon Echo or Google Home. The device looks somewhat like an IT product, which means the purchase requires IT approval. But, because it's also a way to get information into a computer, it kind of looks like an accessory such as a stylus or a mouse, which means the purchase doesn't require IT approval.

In a rules-based system, this product would be unknown, and when asked to determine which approver to send the product to, the system could break. In a machine learning system, a new product won't break the system. Instead, the system provides an answer with a lower level of confidence than it does for products it has seen before. And just like Karen could get it wrong, the machine learning application could get it wrong too. Accepting this level of uncertainty might be challenging for your company's management and risk teams, but it's no different than having Karen make those same decisions when a new product comes across her desk.

In fact, a machine learning system for business automation workflow can be designed to perform better than a human acting on their own. The optimal workflow often involves both systems and people. The system can be configured to cater to the vast majority of cases but have a mechanism where, when it has a low confidence level, it passes the case to a human operator for a decision. Ideally, this decision is fed back into the machine learning application so that, in the future, the application has a higher level of confidence in its decision.

It's all well and good for you to say you're comfortable with the result. In many instances, in order to make pattern-based decisions in your company, you'll need the approval of your risk and management teams. In a subsequent section, once we take a look at the output of a pattern-based decision, you'll see some potential ways of getting this approval.

1.3.3   How can machine learning improve your business systems?

So far in this chapter, we have been referring to the system that can perform multiple functions in your company as an end-to-end system. Commonly, these systems are referred to as ERP (Enterprise Resource Planning) systems.

ERP systems rose to prominence in the 1980s and 1990s. An *ERP system* is used by many medium and large enterprises to manage most of their business functions like payroll, purchasing, inventory management, capital depreciation, and others. SAP and Oracle dominate the ERP market, but there are several smaller players as well.

In a perfect world, all of your business processes would be incorporated into your ERP system. But we don't live in a perfect world. Your company likely does things slightly differently than your ERP's default configuration, which creates a problem. You have to get someone to program your ERP to work the way your business does. This is expensive and time consuming, and can make your company less able to adjust to new opportunities as they arise. And, if ERP systems were the answer to all enterprise problems, then we should have seen productivity improvements during the uptake of ERP systems in the 1980s and 1990s. But there was little uptake in productivity during this period.

When you implement machine learning to support Karen's decisions, there's little change in the management process involved for your internal customers. They continue to place orders in the same ways they always have. The machine learning algorithms simply make some of the decisions automatically, and the orders get sent to approvers and suppliers appropriately and automatically. In our view, unless the process can be cleanly separated from the other processes in your company, the optimal approach is to first implement a machine learning automation solution and then, over time, migrate these processes to your ERP systems.

> **TIP** Automation is not the only way to become more productive. Before automating, you should ask whether you need to do the process at all. Can you create the required business value without automating?

1.4   Can a machine help Karen make decisions?

Machine learning concepts are difficult to get one's head around. This is, in part, due to the breadth of topics encompassed by the term *machine learning*. For the purposes of this book, think of machine learning as a tool that identifies patterns in data and, when you provide it with new data, it tells you which pattern the new data most closely fits.

As you read through other resources on machine learning, you will see that machine learning can cover many other things. But most of these things can be broken down into a series of decisions. Take machine learning systems for autonomous cars, for example. On the face of it, this sounds very different from the machine learning we are looking at. But it is really just a series of decisions. One machine learning algorithm looks at a scene and decides how to draw boxes around each of the objects in the scene. Another machine learning algorithm decides whether these boxes are things that need to be driven around. And, if so, a third algorithm decides the best way to drive around them.

To determine whether you can use machine learning to help out Karen, let's look at the decisions made in Karen's process. When an order comes in, Karen needs to decide whether to send it straight to the requester's financial approver or whether she should send it to a technical approver first. She needs to send an order to a technical approver if the order is for a technical product like a computer or a laptop. She does not need to send it to a technical approver if it is not a technical product. And she does not need to send the order for technical approval if the requester is from the IT department. Let's assess whether Karen's example is suitable for machine learning.

In Karen's case, the question she asks for every order is, "Should I send this for technical approval?" Her decision will either be yes or no. The things she needs to consider when making her decision are

- Is the product a technical product?
- Is the requester from the IT department?

In machine learning lingo, Karen's decision is called the *target variable*, and the types of things she considers when making the decision are called *features*. When you have a target variable and features, you can use machine learning to make a decision.

1.4.1 Target variables

Target variables come in two flavors:

- Categorical
- Continuous

Categorical variables include things like yes or no; and north, south, east, or west. An important distinction in our machine learning work in this book is whether the categorical variable has only two categories or has more than two categories. If it has only two categories, it is called a *binary target variable*. If it has more than two categories, it is called a *multiclass target variable*. You will set different parameters in your machine learning applications, depending on whether the variable is binary or multiclass. This will be covered in more detail later in the book.

Continuous variables are numbers. For example, if your machine learning application predicts house prices based on features such as neighborhood, number of rooms, distance from schools, and so on, your target variable (the predicted price of the house) is a continuous variable. The price of a house could be any value from tens of thousands of dollars to tens of millions of dollars.

1.4.2 Features

In this book, features are perhaps the most important machine learning concept to understand. We use features all the time in our own decision making. In fact, the things you'll learn in this book about features can help you better understand your own decision-making process.

As an example, let's return to Karen as she makes a decision about whether to send a purchase order to IT for approval. The things that Karen considers when making this decision are its *features*. One thing Karen can consider when she comes across a product she hasn't seen before is who manufactured the product. If a product is from a manufacturer that only produces IT products, then, even though she has never seen that product before, she considers it likely to be an IT product.

Other types of features might be harder for a human to consider but are easier for a machine learning application to incorporate into its decision making. For example, you might want to find out which customers are likely to be more receptive to receiving a sales call from your sales team. One feature that can be important for your repeat customers is whether the sales call would fit in with their regular buying schedule. For example, if the customer normally makes a purchase every two months, is it approximately two months since their last purchase? Using machine learning to assist your decision making allows these kinds of patterns to be incorporated into the decision to call or not call; whereas, it would be difficult for a human to identify such patterns.

Note that there can be several levels to the things (features) Karen considers when making her decision. For example, if she doesn't know whether a product is a technical product or not, then she might consider other information such as who the manufacturer is and what other products are included on the requisition. One of the great things about machine learning is that you don't need to know all the features; you'll see which features are the most important as you put together the machine learning system. If you think it might be relevant, include it in your dataset.

1.5   *How does a machine learn?*

A machine learns the same way you do. It is trained. But how? Machine learning is a process of rewarding a mathematical function for getting answers right and punishing the function for getting answers wrong. But what does it mean to reward or punish a function?

You can think of a *function* as a set of directions on how to get from one place to another. In figure 1.4, to get from point A to point B, the directions might read thus:

1   Go right.
2   Go a bit up.
3   Go a bit down.
4   Go down sharply.
5   Go up!
6   Go right.

A machine learning application is a tool that can determine when the function gets it right (and tells the function to do more of that) or gets it wrong (and tells the function to do less of that). The function knows it got it right because it becomes more successful at predicting the target variable based on the features.

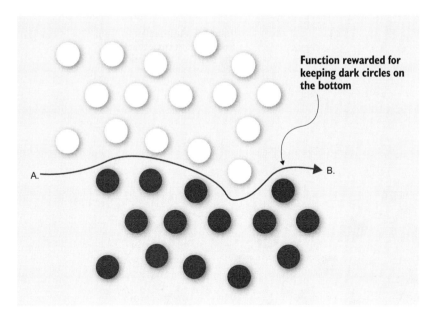

Figure 1.4　Machine learning function to identify a pattern in the data

Let's pull a dataset out of figure 1.4 to look at a bigger sample in figure 1.5. You can see that the dataset comprises two types of circles: dark circles and light circles. In figure 1.5, there is a pattern that we can see in the data. There are lots of light circles at the edges of the dataset and lots of dark circles near the middle. This means that our function, which provides the directions on how to separate the dark circles from light circles, will start at the left of the diagram and do a big loop around the dark circles before returning to its starting point.

When we are training the process to reward the function for getting it right, we could think of this as a process that rewards a function for having a dark circle on the right and punishes it for having a dark circle on the left. You could train it even faster if you also reward the function for having a light circle on the left and punish it for having a light circle on the right.

So, with this as a background, when you're training a machine learning application, what you're doing is showing a bunch of examples to a system that builds a mathematical function to separate certain things in the data. The thing it is separating in the data is the *target variable*. When the function separates more of the target variables, it gets a reward, and when it separates fewer target variables, it gets punished.

Machine learning problems can be broken down into two types:

- Supervised machine learning
- Unsupervised machine learning

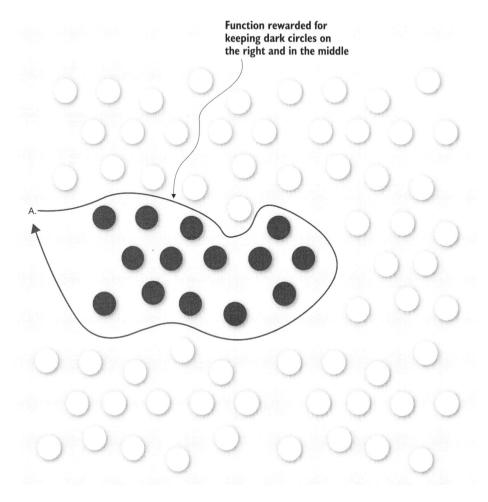

Figure 1.5   Machine learning functions to identify a group of similar items in a dataset

In addition to features, the other important concept in machine learning as far as this book is concerned is the distinction between supervised and unsupervised machine learning.

Like its name suggests, *unsupervised* machine learning is where we point a machine learning application at a bunch of data and tell it to do its thing. Clustering is an example of unsupervised machine learning. We provide the machine learning application with some customer data, for example, and it determines how to group that customer data into clusters of similar customers. In contrast, classification is an example of *supervised* machine learning. For example, you could use your sales team's historical success rate for calling customers as a way of training a machine learning application how to recognize customers who are most likely to be receptive to receiving a sales call.

NOTE In most of the chapters in this book, you'll focus on supervised machine learning where, instead of letting the machine learning application pick out the patterns, you provide the application with a historical dataset containing samples that show the right decision.

One of the big advantages of tackling business automation projects using machine learning is that you can usually get your hands on a good dataset fairly easy. In Karen's case, she has thousands of previous orders to draw from, and for each order, she knows whether it was sent to a technical approver or not. In machine learning lingo, you say that the dataset is *labeled*, which means that each sample shows what the target variable should be for that sample. In Karen's case, the historical dataset she needs is a dataset that shows what product was purchased, whether it was purchased by someone from the IT department or not, and whether Karen sent it to a technical approver or not.

1.6 Getting approval in your company to use machine learning to make decisions

Earlier in the chapter, we described how you could learn enough about decision making using machine learning to help your company. But what does your company need in order to take full advantage of your good work? In theory, it's not that hard. Your company just needs four things:

- It needs a person who can identify opportunities to automate and use machine learning, and someone who can put together a proof of concept that shows the opportunity is worth pursuing. That's you, by the way.
- You need to be able to access the data required to feed your machine learning applications. Your company will likely require you to complete a number of internal forms describing why you want access to that data.
- Your risk and management teams need to be comfortable with using pattern-based approaches to making decisions.
- Your company needs a way to turn your work into an operational system.

In many organizations, the third of these four points is the most difficult. One way to tackle this is to involve your risk team in the process and provide them with the ability to set a threshold on when a decision needs to be reviewed by Karen.

For example, some orders that cross Karen's desk very clearly need to be sent to a technical approver, and the machine learning application must be 100% confident that it should go to a technical approver. Other orders are less clear cut, and instead of returning a 1 (100% confidence), the application might return a 0.72 (a lower level of confidence). You could implement a rule that if the application has less than 75% confidence that the decision is correct, then route the request to Karen for a decision.

If your risk team is involved in setting the confidence level whereby orders must be reviewed by a human, this provides them with a way to establish clear guidelines for which pattern-based decisions can be managed in your company. In chapter 2, you'll read more about Karen and will help her with her work.

1.7   The tools

In the old days (a.k.a. 2017), setting up a scalable machine learning system was very challenging. In addition to identifying features and creating a labeled dataset, you needed to have a wide range of skills, encompassing those of an IT infrastructure administrator, a data scientist, and a back-end web developer. Here are the steps that *used* to be involved in setting up your machine learning system. (In this book, you'll see how to set up your machine learning systems without doing all these steps.)

1 Set up your development environment to build and run a machine learning application (IT infrastructure administrator)
2 Train the machine learning application on your data (data scientist)
3 Validate the machine learning application (data scientist)
4 Host the machine learning application (IT infrastructure administrator)
5 Set up an endpoint that takes your new data and returns a prediction (back-end web developer)

It's little wonder that machine learning is not yet in common use in most companies! Fortunately, nowadays some of these steps can be carried out using cloud-based servers. So although you need to understand how it all fits together, you don't need to know how to set up a development environment, build a server, or create secure endpoints.

In each of the following seven chapters, you'll set up (from scratch) a machine learning system that solves a common business problem. This might sound daunting, but it's not because you'll use a service from Amazon called AWS SageMaker.

1.7.1   What are AWS and SageMaker, and how can they help you?

AWS is Amazon's cloud service. It lets companies of all sizes set up servers and interact with services in the cloud rather than building their own data centers. AWS has dozens of services available to you. These range from compute services such as cloud-based servers (EC2), to messaging and integration services such as SNS (Simple Notification Service) messaging, to domain-specific machine learning services such as Amazon Transcribe (for converting voice to text) and AWS DeepLens (for machine learning from video feeds).

SageMaker is Amazon's environment for building and deploying machine learning applications. Let's look at the functionality it provides using the same five steps discussed earlier (section 1.7). SageMaker is revolutionary because it

- Serves as your development environment in the cloud so you don't have to set up a development environment on your computer
- Uses a preconfigured machine learning application on your data
- Uses inbuilt tools to validate the results from your machine learning application

- Hosts your machine learning application
- Automatically sets up an endpoint that takes in new data and returns predictions

One of the best aspects of SageMaker, aside from the fact that it handles all of the infrastructure for you, is that the development environment it uses is a tool called the Jupyter Notebook, which uses Python as one of its programming languages. But the things you'll learn in this book working with SageMaker will serve you well in whatever machine learning environment you work in. Jupyter notebooks are the de facto standard for data scientists when interacting with machine learning applications, and Python is the fastest growing programming language for data scientists.

Amazon's decision to use Jupyter notebooks and Python to interact with machine learning applications benefits both experienced practitioners as well as people new to data science and machine learning. It's good for experienced machine learning practitioners because it enables them to be immediately productive in SageMaker, and it's good for new practitioners because the skills you learn using SageMaker are applicable everywhere in the fields of machine learning and data science.

1.7.2 What is a Jupyter notebook?

Jupyter notebooks are one of the most popular tools for data science. These combine text, code, and charts in a single document that allows a user to consistently repeat data analysis, from loading and preparing the data to analyzing and displaying the results.

The Jupyter Project started in 2014. In 2017, the Jupyter Project steering committee members were awarded the prestigious ACM Software System award "for developing a software system that has had a lasting influence, reflected in contributions to concepts, in commercial acceptance, or both." This award is a big deal because previous awards were for things like the internet.

In our view, Jupyter notebooks will become nearly as ubiquitous as Excel for business analysis. In fact, one of the main reasons we selected SageMaker as our tool of choice for this book is because when you're learning SageMaker, you're learning Jupyter.

1.8 Setting up SageMaker in preparation for tackling the scenarios in chapters 2 through 7

The workflow that you'll follow in each chapter is as follows:

1 Download the prepared Jupyter notebook and dataset from the links listed in the chapter. Each chapter has one Jupyter notebook and one or more datasets.
2 Upload the dataset to S3, your AWS file storage bucket.
3 Upload the Jupyter notebook to SageMaker.

At this point, you can run the entire notebook, and your machine learning model will be built. The remainder of each chapter takes you through each cell in the notebook and explains how it works.

If you already have an AWS account, you are ready to go. Setting up SageMaker for each chapter should only take a few minutes. Appendixes B and C show you how to do the setup for chapter 2.

If you don't have an AWS account, start with appendix A and progress through to appendix C. These appendixes will step you through signing up for AWS, setting up and uploading your data to the S3 bucket, and creating your notebook in SageMaker. The topics are as follows:

- Appendix A: How to sign up for AWS
- Appendix B: How to set up S3 to store files
- Appendix C: How to set up and run SageMaker

After working your way through these appendixes (to the end of appendix C), you'll have your dataset stored in S3 and a Jupyter notebook set up and running on Sage-Maker. Now you're ready to tackle the scenarios in chapter 2 and beyond.

1.9   *The time to act is now*

You saw earlier in this chapter that there is a group of frontier firms that are rapidly increasing their productivity. Right now these firms are few and far between, and your company might not be competing with any of them. However, it's inevitable that other firms will learn to use techniques like machine learning for business automation to dramatically improve their productivity, and it's inevitable that your company will eventually compete with them. We believe it is a case of eat or be eaten.

The next section of the book consists of six chapters that take you through six scenarios that will equip you for tackling many of the scenarios you might face in your own company, including the following:

- Should you send a purchase order to a technical approver?
- Should you call a customer because they are at risk of churning?
- Should a customer support ticket be handled by a senior support person?
- Should you query an invoice sent to you by a supplier?
- How much power will your company use next month based on historical trends?
- Should you add additional data such as planned holidays and weather forecasts to your power consumption prediction to improve your company's monthly power usage forecast?

After working your way through these chapters, you should be equipped to tackle many of the machine learning decision-making scenarios you'll face in your work and in your company. This book takes you on the journey from being a technically minded non-developer to someone who can set up a machine learning application within your own company.

Summary

- Companies that don't become more productive will be left behind by those that do.
- Machine learning is the key to your company becoming more productive because it automates all of the little decisions that hold your company back.
- Machine learning is simply a way of creating a mathematical function that best fits previous decisions and that can be used to guide current decisions.
- Amazon SageMaker is a service that lets you set up a machine learning application that you can use in your business.
- Jupyter Notebook is one of the most popular tools for data science and machine learning.

## Part 2

Six scenarios: Machine learning for business

Each chapter in this part covers the use of machine learning to enhance the productivity of a single operational area. The areas covered are

- Approving purchase orders
- Evaluating which customers are at risk of churning
- Identifying support requests that should be escalated immediately
- Auditing invoices from suppliers
- Forecasting operational trends, such as power consumption, using time-series data
- Incorporating additional features into time-series forecasting

In each chapter, you download a Jupyter notebook and a dataset and upload it to your AWS SageMaker account. You can then run the notebook to create and test the model. The text in the chapter takes you through the notebook in detail so you understand how it works. You can then use the notebook with datasets from your company to accomplish the same task.

Should you send a purchase order to a technical approver?

This chapter covers
- Identifying a machine learning opportunity
- Identifying what and how much data is required
- Building a machine learning system
- Using machine learning to make decisions

In this chapter, you'll work end to end through a machine learning scenario that makes a decision about whether to send an order to a technical approver or not. And you'll do it without writing any rules! All you'll feed into the machine learning system is a dataset consisting of 1,000 historical orders and a flag that indicates whether that order was sent to a technical approver or not. The machine learning system figures out the patterns from those 1,000 examples and, when given a new order, will be able to correctly determine whether to send the order to a technical approver.

In the first chapter, you'll read about Karen, the person who works in the purchasing department. Her job is to receive requisitions from staff to buy a product or service. For each request, Karen decides which approver needs to review and approve the order; then, after getting approval, she sends the request to the supplier. Karen might not think of herself this way, but she's a *decision maker*. As requests to buy products and services come in, Karen decides who needs to approve each request. For some products, such as computers, Karen needs to send the request to a technical advisor, who determines if the specification is suitable for the person buying the computer. Does Karen need to send this order to a technical approver, or not? This is the decision you'll work on in this chapter.

By the end of this chapter, you'll be able to help Karen out. You'll be able to put together a solution that will look at the requests before they get to Karen and then recommend whether she should send the request to a technical approver. As you work through the examples, you'll become familiar with how to use machine learning to make a decision.

2.1   *The decision*

Figure 2.1 shows Karen's process from a requester placing an order to the supplier receiving the order. Each person icon in the workflow represents a person taking some action. If they have more than one arrow pointing away from them, they need to make a decision.

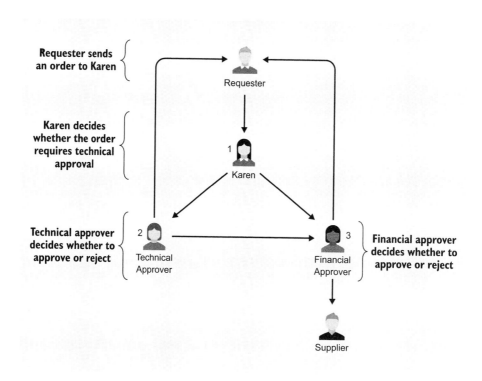

Figure 2.1   Approval workflow for purchasing technical equipment in Karen's company

In Karen's process, there are three decisions (numbered 1, 2, and 3):

1 The first decision is the one we are going to look at in this chapter: should Karen send this order to a technical approver?

2 The second decision is made by the technical approver after Karen routes an order to them: should the technical approver accept the order and send it to finance, or should it be rejected and sent back to the requester?

3 The third decision is made by the financial approver: should they approve the order and send it to the supplier, or should it be rejected and sent back to the requester?

Each of these decisions may be well suited for machine learning—and, in fact, they are. Let's look at the first decision (Karen's decision) in more detail to understand why it's suitable for machine learning.

2.2 The data

In discussions with Karen, you've learned that the approach she generally takes is that if a product looks like an IT product, she'll send it to a technical approver. The exception to her rule is that if it's something that can be plugged in and used, such as a mouse or a keyboard, she doesn't send it for technical approval. Nor does she send it for technical approval if the requester is from the IT department.

Table 2.1 shows the dataset you will work with in this scenario. This dataset contains the past 1,000 orders that Karen has processed.

It's good practice when preparing a labeled dataset for supervised machine learning to put the target variable in the first column. In this scenario, your target variable is this: *should Karen send the order to a technical approver?* In your dataset, if Karen sent the order for technical approval, you put a 1 in the tech_approval_required column. If she did not send the order for technical approval, you put a 0 in that column. The rest of the columns are *features*. These are things that you think are going to be useful in determining whether an item should be sent to an approver. Just like target variables come in two types, categorical and continuous, features also come in two types: categorical and continuous.

Categorical features in table 2.1 are those in the requester_id, role, and product columns. A *categorical feature* is something that can be divided into a number of distinct groups. These are often text rather than numbers, as you can see in the following columns:

- *requester_id*—ID of the requester.
- *role*—If the requester is from the IT department, these are labeled tech.
- *product*—The type of product.

Continuous features are those in the last three columns in table 2.1. *Continuous features* are always numbers. The continuous features in this dataset are quantity, price, and total.

Table 2.1   **Technical Approval Required dataset contains information from prior orders received by Karen.**

tech_approval_required	requester_id	role	product	quantity	price	total
0	E2300	tech	Desk	1	664	664
0	E2300	tech	Keyboard	9	649	5841
0	E2374	non-tech	Keyboard	1	821	821
1	E2374	non-tech	Desktop Computer	24	655	15720
0	E2327	non-tech	Desk	1	758	758
0	E2354	non-tech	Desk	1	576	576
1	E2348	non-tech	Desktop Computer	21	1006	21126
0	E2304	tech	Chair	3	155	465
0	E2363	non-tech	Keyboard	1	1028	1028
0	E2343	non-tech	Desk	3	487	1461

The fields selected for this dataset are those that will allow you to replicate Karen's decision-making process. There are many other fields that you could have selected, and there are some very sophisticated tools being released that help in selecting those features. But for the purposes of this scenario, you'll use your intuition about the problem you're solving to select your features. As you'll see, this approach can quickly lead to some excellent results. Now you're ready to do some machine learning:

- Your end goal is to be able to submit an order to the machine learning model and have it return a result that recommends sending the order to a technical approver or not.
- You have identified the features you'll use to make the decision (the type of product and whether the requester is from the IT department).
- You have created your labeled historical dataset (the dataset shown in table 2.1).

2.3   *Putting on your training wheels*

Now that you have your labeled dataset, you can train a machine learning model to make decisions. But what is a model and how do you train it?

You'll learn more about how machine learning works in the following chapters. For now, all you need to know is that a *machine learning model* is a mathematical function that is rewarded for guessing right and punished for guessing wrong. In order to get more guesses right, the function associates certain values in each feature with right guesses or wrong guesses. As it works through more and more samples, it gets better at guessing. When it's run through all the samples, you say that the model is *trained*.

The mathematical function that underlies a machine learning model is called the *machine learning algorithm*. Each machine learning algorithm has a number of parameters you can set to get a better-performing model. In this chapter, you are going to accept all of the default settings for the algorithm you'll use. In subsequent chapters, we'll discuss how to fine tune the algorithm to get better results.

One of the most confusing aspects for machine learning beginners is deciding which machine learning algorithm to use. In the supervised machine learning exercises in this book, we focus on just one algorithm: XGBoost. XGBoost is a good choice because

- It is fairly forgiving; it works well across a wide range of problems without significant tuning.
- It doesn't require a lot of data to provide good results.
- It is easy to explain why it returns a particular prediction in a certain scenario.
- It is a high-performing algorithm and the go-to algorithm for many participants in machine learning competitions with small datasets.

In a later chapter, you'll learn how XGBoost works under the hood, but for now, let's discuss how to use it. If you want to read more about it on the AWS site, you can do so here: https://docs.aws.amazon.com/sagemaker/latest/dg/xgboost.html.

> **NOTE** If you haven't already installed and configured all the tools you'll need as you work through this chapter and the book, visit appendixes A, B, and C, and follow the instructions you find there. After working your way through the appendixes (to the end of appendix C), you'll have your dataset stored in S3 (AWS's file storage service) and a Jupyter notebook set up and running in SageMaker.

2.4 Running the Jupyter notebook and making predictions

Let's step through the Jupyter notebook and make predictions about whether to send an order to a technical approver or not. In this chapter, we will look at the notebook in six parts:

- Load and examine the data.
- Get the data into the right shape.
- Create training, validation, and test datasets.
- Train the machine learning model.
- Host the machine learning model.
- Test the model and use it to make decisions.

To follow along, you should have completed two things:

- Load the dataset orders_with_predicted_value.csv into S3.
- Upload the Jupyter notebook tech_approval_required.ipynb to SageMaker.

Appendixes B and C take you through how to do each of these steps in detail for the dataset you'll use in this chapter. In summary:

- Download the dataset at https://s3.amazonaws.com/mlforbusiness/ch02/orders _with_predicted_value.csv.
- Upload the dataset to your S3 bucket that you have set up to hold the datasets for this book.
- Download the Jupyter notebook at https://s3.amazonaws.com/mlforbusiness/ ch02/tech_approval_required.ipynb.
- Upload the Jupyter notebook to your SageMaker notebook instance.

Don't be frightened by the code in the Jupyter notebook. As you work through this book, you'll become familiar with each aspect of it. In this chapter, you'll run the code rather than edit it. In fact, in this chapter, you do not need to modify any of the code with the exception of the first two lines, where you tell the code which S3 bucket to use and which folder in that bucket contains your dataset.

Figure 2.2   Selecting a notebook instance from the Amazon SageMaker menu

To start, open the SageMaker service from the AWS console in your browser by logging into the AWS console at http:// console.aws.amazon.com. Click Notebook Instances in the left-hand menu on Sage-Maker (figure 2.2). This takes you to a screen that shows your notebook instances.

If the notebook you uploaded in appendix C is not running, you will see a screen like the one shown in figure 2.3. Click the Start link to start the notebook instance.

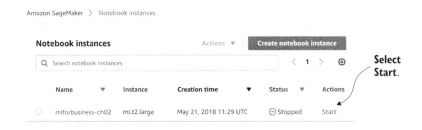

Figure 2.3   Notebook instance with a Stopped status

Once you have started your notebook instance, or if your notebook was already started, you'll see a screen like that shown in figure 2.4. Click the Open link.

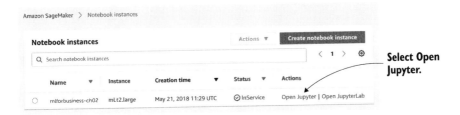

Figure 2.4   Opening Jupyter from a notebook instance

When you click the Open link, a new tab opens in your browser, and you'll see the ch02 folder you created in appendix C (figure 2.5).

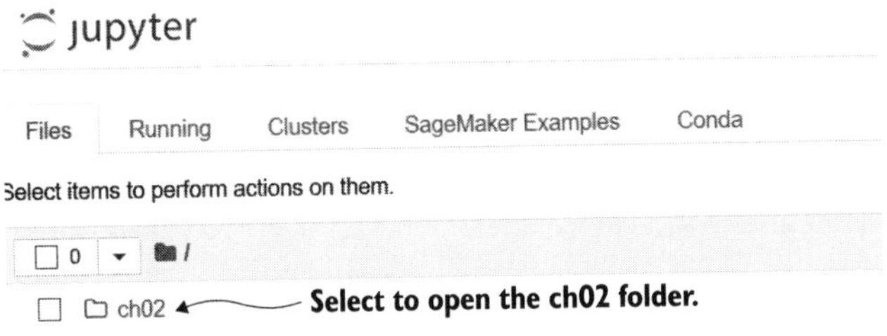

Figure 2.5   Selecting the ch02 folder

Finally, when you click ch02, you'll see the notebook you uploaded in appendix C: tech-approval-required.ipynb. Click this notebook to open it in a new browser tab (figure 2.6).

Figure 2.6   Opening the tech-approval-required notebook

Figure 2.7 shows a Jupyter notebook. Jupyter notebooks are an amazing coding environment that combines text with code in sections. An example of the text cell is the text for heading 2.4.1, *Part 1: Load and examine the data.* An example of a code cell are the following lines:

```
data_bucket = 'mlforbusiness'
subfolder = 'ch02'
dataset = 'orders_with_predicted_value.csv'
```

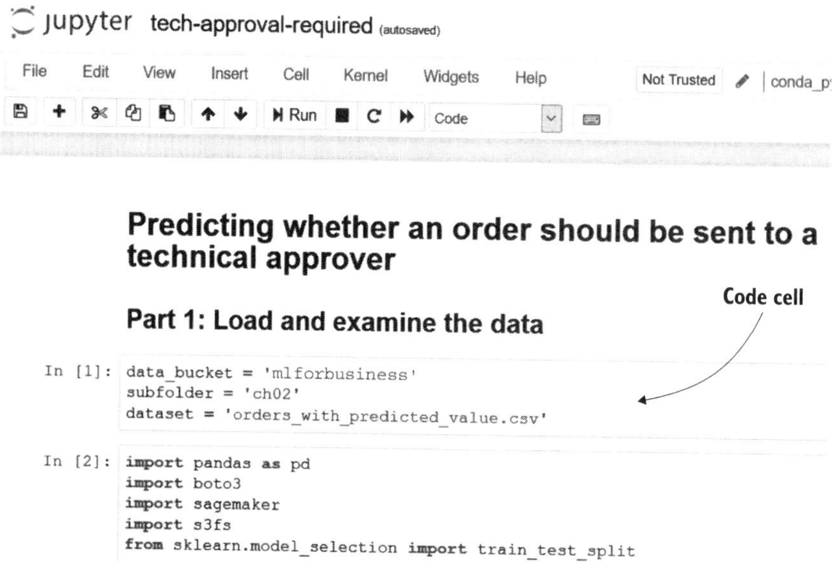

Figure 2.7   Inside the Jupyter notebook

To run the code in a Jupyter notebook, press Ctrl + Enter ↵ when your cursor is in a code cell.

2.4.1   Part 1: Loading and examining the data

The code in listings 2.1 through 2.4 loads the data so you can look at it. The only two values in this entire notebook that you need to modify are the `data_bucket` and the `subfolder`. You should use the bucket and subfolder names you set up as per the instructions in appendix B.

> **NOTE**   This walkthrough will just familiarize you with the code so that, when you see it again in subsequent chapters, you'll know how it fits into the Sage-Maker workflow.

The following listing shows how to identify the bucket and subfolder where the data is stored.

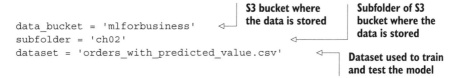

Listing 2.1 Setting up the S3 bucket and subfolder

```
data_bucket = 'mlforbusiness'
subfolder = 'ch02'
dataset = 'orders_with_predicted_value.csv'
```

S3 bucket where the data is stored

Subfolder of S3 bucket where the data is stored

Dataset used to train and test the model

As you'll recall, a Jupyter notebook is where you can write and run code. There are two ways you can run code in a Jupyter notebook. You can run the code in one of the cells, or you can run the code in more than one of the cells.

To run the code in one cell, click the cell to select it, and then press Ctrl+Enter↵. When you do so, you'll see an asterisk (*) appear to left of the cell. This means that the code in the cell is running. When the asterisk is replaced by a number, the code has finished running. The number shows how many cells have been run since you opened the notebook.

If you want, after you have updated the name of the data bucket and the subfolder (listing 2.1), you can run the notebook. This loads the data, builds and trains the machine learning model, sets up the endpoint, and generates predictions from the test data. SageMaker takes about 10 min to complete these actions for the datasets you'll use in this book. It may take longer if you load large datasets from your company.

To run the entire notebook, click Cell in the toolbar at the top of the Jupyter notebook, then click Run All (figure 2.8).

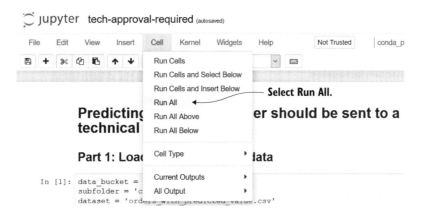

Figure 2.8   Running the Jupyter notebook

SETTING UP THE NOTEBOOK

Next, you'll set up the Python libraries required by the notebook (listing 2.2). To run the notebook, you don't need to change any of these values:

- *pandas*—A Python library commonly used in data science projects. In this book, we'll touch only the surface of what pandas can do. You'll load pandas as pd. As you'll see later in this chapter, this means that we will preface any use of any module in the pandas library with pd.
- *boto3* and *sagemaker*—The libraries created by Amazon to help Python users interact with AWS resources: boto3 is used to interact with S3, and sagemaker, unsurprisingly, is used to interact with SageMaker. You will also use a module called *s3fs*, which makes it easier to use boto3 with S3.
- *sklearn*—The final library you'll import. It is short for *scikit-learn*, which is a comprehensive library of machine learning algorithms that is used widely in both the commercial and scientific communities. Here we only import the train_test_split function that we'll use later.

You'll also need to create a role on SageMaker that allows the sagemaker library to use the resources it needs to build and serve the machine learning application. You do this by calling the sagemaker function get_execution_role.

Listing 2.2   Importing modules

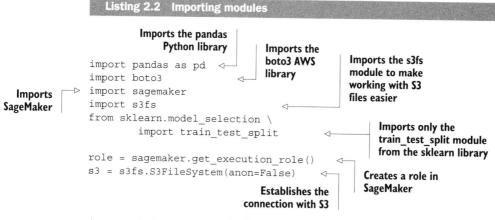

As a reminder, as you walk through each of the cells in the Jupyter notebook, to run the code in a cell, click the cell and press Ctrl + Enter ↵.

LOADING AND VIEWING THE DATA

Now that you've identified the bucket and subfolder and set up the notebook, you can take a look at the data. The best way to view the data is to use the pandas library you imported in listing 2.2.

The code in listing 2.3 creates a pandas data structure called a *DataFrame*. You can think of a DataFrame as a table like a spreadsheet. The first line assigns the name *df* to the DataFrame. The data in the DataFrame is the orders data from S3. It is read into the DataFrame by using the pandas function `read_csv`. The line `df.head()` displays the first five rows of the df DataFrame.

Listing 2.3   Viewing the dataset

```
df = pd.read_csv(
    f's3://{data_bucket}/{subfolder}/{dataset}')       ◁   Reads the S3
df.head()                                                   orders_with_predicted_value
                                                            .csv dataset in listing 2.1
                                          ◁
                                              Displays the top five rows of the
                                              DataFrame loaded in the line above
```

Running the code displays the top five rows in the dataset. (To run the code, insert your cursor in the cell and press ⌈Ctrl⌋+⌈Enter ↵⌋.) The dataset will look similar to the dataset in table 2.2.

Table 2.2   Technical Approval Required dataset displayed in Excel

tech_approval_required	requester_id	role	product	quantity	price	total
0	E2300	tech	Desk	1	664	664
0	E2300	tech	Keyboard	9	649	5841
0	E2374	non-tech	Keyboard	1	821	821
1	E2374	non-tech	Desktop Computer	24	655	15720
0	E2327	non-tech	Desk	1	758	758

To recap, the dataset you uploaded to S3 and are now displaying in the df DataFrame lists the last 1,000 orders that Karen processed. She sent some of those orders to a technical approver, and some she did not.

The code in listing 2.4 displays how many rows are in the dataset and how many of the rows were sent for technical approval. Running this code shows that out of 1,000 rows in the dataset, 807 were not sent to a technical approver, and 193 were sent.

Listing 2.4   Determining how many rows were sent for technical approval

```
                                                        Displays the
                                                        number of rows
print(f'Number of rows in dataset: {df.shape[0]}')   ◁
print(df[df.columns[0]].value_counts())          ◁

You don't need to understand this line of code. The output displays the number of
    rows that went to a technical approver and the number of rows that did not.
```

In listing 2.4, the shape property of a DataFrame provides information about the number of rows and the number of columns. Here `df.shape[0]` shows the number of rows, and `df.shape[1]` shows the number of columns. The `value_counts` property of the df DataFrame shows the number of rows in the dataset where the order was sent to a technical approver. It contains a `1` if it was sent for technical approval and a `0` if it was not.

2.4.2   Part 2: Getting the data into the right shape

For this part of the notebook, you'll prepare the data for use in the machine learning model. You'll learn more about this topic in later chapters but, for now, it is enough to know that there are standard approaches to preparing data, and we are using one we'll apply to each of our machine learning exercises.

One important point to understand about most machine learning models is that they typically work with numbers rather than text-based data. We'll discuss why this is so in a subsequent chapter when we go into the details of the XGBoost algorithm. For now, it is enough to know that you need to convert the text-based data to numerical data before you can use it to train your machine learning model. Fortunately, there are easy-to-use tools that will help with this.

First, we'll use the pandas get_dummies function to convert all of the text data into numbers. It does this by creating a separate column for every unique text value. For example, the product column contains text values such as Desk, Keyboard, and Mouse. When you use the get_dummies function, it turns every value into a column and places a 0 or 1 in the row, depending on whether the row contains a value or not.

Table 2.3 shows a simple table with three rows. The table shows the price for a desk, a keyboard, and a mouse.

Table 2.3   Simple three-row dataset with prices for a desk, a keyboard, and a mouse

product	price
Desk	664
Keyboard	69
Mouse	89

When you use the get_dummies function, it takes each of the unique values in the non-numeric columns and creates new columns from those. In our example, this looks like the values in table 2.4. Notice that the get_dummies function removes the product column and creates three columns from the three unique values in the dataset. It also places a 1 in the new column that contains the value from that row and zeros in every other column.

Table 2.4   The three-row dataset after applying the get_dummies function

price	product_Desk	product_Keyboard	product_Mouse
664	1	0	0
69	0	1	0
89	0	0	1

Listing 2.5 shows the code that creates table 2.4. To run the code, insert your cursor in the cell, and press $\boxed{\text{Ctrl}}$+$\boxed{\text{Enter} \hookleftarrow}$. You can see that this dataset is very wide (111 columns in our example).

Listing 2.5 Converting text values to columns

```
encoded_data = pd.get_dummies(df)     ◁──  Creates a new pandas DataFrame to store
encoded_data.head()     ◁──┐                the table with columns for each unique
                           │                text value in the original table
                           └── The pandas function to display
                               the first five rows of the table
```

A machine learning algorithm can now work with this data because it is all numbers. But there is a problem. Your dataset is now probably very wide. In our sample dataset in figures 2.3 and 2.4, the dataset went from 2 columns wide to 4 columns wide. In a real dataset, it can go to thousands of columns wide. Even our sample dataset in the SageMaker Jupyter notebook goes to 111 columns when you run the code in the cells.

This is not a problem for the machine learning algorithm. It can easily handle datasets with thousands of columns. It's a problem for you because it becomes more difficult to reason about the data. For this reason, and for the types of machine learning decision-making problems we look at in this book, you can often get results that are just as accurate by reducing the number of columns to only the most relevant ones. This is important for your ability to explain to others what is happening in the algorithm in a way that is convincing. For example, in the dataset you work with in this chapter, the most highly correlated columns are the ones relating to technical product types and the ones relating to whether the requester has a tech role or not. This makes sense, and it can be explained concisely to others.

A *relevant* column for this machine learning problem is a column that contains values that are correlated to the value you are trying to predict. You say that two values are correlated when a change in one value is accompanied by a change in another value. If these both increase or decrease together, you say that they are *positively correlated*—they both move in the same direction. And when one goes up and the other goes down (or vice versa), you say that they are *negatively correlated*—they move in opposite directions. For our purposes, the machine learning algorithm doesn't really care whether a column is positively or negatively correlated, just that it is correlated.

Correlation is important because the machine learning algorithm is trying to predict a value based on the values in other columns in the dataset. The values in the dataset that contribute most to the prediction are those that are correlated to the predicted value.

You'll find the most correlated columns by applying another pandas function called corr. You apply the corr function by appending .corr() to the pandas Data-Frame you named encoded_data in listing 2.5. After the function, you need to provide the name of the column you are attempting to predict. In this case, the column you are attempting to predict is the tech_approval_required column. Listing 2.6 shows the code that does this. Note that the .abs() function at the end of the listing is simply turning all of the correlations positive.

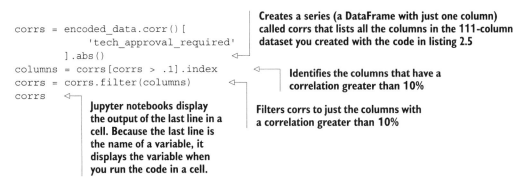

Listing 2.6   Identifying correlated columns

```
corrs = encoded_data.corr()[
        'tech_approval_required'
    ].abs()
columns = corrs[corrs > .1].index
corrs = corrs.filter(columns)
corrs
```

Creates a series (a DataFrame with just one column) called corrs that lists all the columns in the 111-column dataset you created with the code in listing 2.5

Identifies the columns that have a correlation greater than 10%

Filters corrs to just the columns with a correlation greater than 10%

Jupyter notebooks display the output of the last line in a cell. Because the last line is the name of a variable, it displays the variable when you run the code in a cell.

The code in listing 2.6 identifies the columns that have a correlation greater than 10%. You don't need to know exactly how this code works. You are simply finding all of the columns that have a correlation greater than 10% with the tech_approval_required column. Why 10%? It removes the irrelevant noise from the dataset which, while this step does not help the machine learning algorithm, improves your ability to talk about the data in a meaningful way. With fewer columns to consider, you can more easily prepare an explanation of what the algorithm is doing.

Table 2.5 shows the columns with a correlation greater than 10%.

Table 2.5   Correlation with predicted value

Column name	Correlation with predicted value
tech_approval_required	1.000000
role_non-tech	0.122454
role_tech	0.122454
product_Chair	0.134168
product_Cleaning	0.191539
product_Desk	0.292137
product_Desktop Computer	0.752144
product_Keyboard	0.242224
product_Laptop Computer	0.516693
product_Mouse	0.190708

Now that you have identified the most highly correlated columns, you need to filter the encoded_data table to contain just those columns. You do so with the code in listing 2.7. The first line filters the columns to just the correlated columns, and the second line displays the table when you run the code. (Remember, to run the code, insert your cursor in the cell and press ⌈Ctrl⌉+⌈Enter ⏎⌋.)

Listing 2.7 Showing only correlated columns

```
encoded_data = encoded_data[columns]        ◁──┐  Filters columns to only those that
encoded_data.head()        ◁──┐                    are correlated with the
                                                   tech_approval_required column
            Displays the table when you
            run the code in the cell
```

2.4.3 *Part 3: Creating training, validation, and test datasets*

The next step in the machine learning process is to create a dataset that you'll use to train the algorithm. While you're at it, you'll also create the dataset you'll use to validate the results of the training and the dataset you'll use to test the results. To do this, you'll split the dataset into three parts:

- Train
- Validate
- Test

The machine learning algorithm uses the training data to train the model. You should put the largest chunk of data into the training dataset. The validation data is used by the algorithm to determine whether the algorithm is improving. This should be the next-largest chunk of data. Finally, the test data, the smallest chunk, is used by you to determine how well the algorithm performs. Once you have the three datasets, you will convert them to CSV format and then save them to S3.

In listing 2.8, you create two datasets: a dataset with 70% of the data for training and a dataset with 30% of the data for validation and testing. Then you split the validation and test data into two separate datasets: a validation dataset and a test dataset. The validation dataset will contain 20% of the total rows, which equals 66.7% of the validation and test dataset. The test dataset will contain 10% of the total rows, which equals 33.3% of the validation and test dataset. To run the code, insert your cursor in the cell and press ⌈Ctrl⌉+⌈Enter ⏎⌋.

Listing 2.8 Splitting data into train, validate, and test datasets

```
train_df, val_and_test_data = train_test_split(
        encoded_data,
        test_size=0.3,              │  Puts 70% of the data
        random_state=0)        ◁──┘  into the train dataset
val_df, test_df = train_test_split(
        val_and_test_data,
        test_size=0.333,            │  Puts 20% of the data in to the
        random_state=0)        ◁──┤  validation data and 10% of the
                                       data into the test dataset
```

> **NOTE** The `random_state` argument ensures that repeating the command splits the data in the same way.

In listing 2.8, you split the data into three DataFrames. In listing 2.9, you'll convert the datasets to CSV format.

Input and CSV formats

CSV is one of the two formats you can use as input to the XGBoost machine learning model. The code in this book uses CSV format. That's because if you want to view the data in a spreadsheet, it's easy to import into spreadsheet applications like Microsoft Excel. The drawback of using CSV format is that it takes up a lot of space if you have a dataset with lots of columns (like our encoded_data dataset after using the `get_dummies` function in listing 2.5).

The other format that XBGoost can use is libsvm. Unlike a CSV file, where even the columns containing zeros need to be filled out, the libsvm format only includes the columns that do not contain zeros. It does this by concatenating the column number and the value together. So the data you looked at in table 2.2 would look like this:

```
1:664 2:1
1:69 3:1
1:89 4:1
```

The first entry in each row shows the price (664, 69, or 89). The number in front of the price indicates that this is in the first column of the dataset. The second entry in each row contains the column number (2, 3, or 4) and the non-zero value of the entry (which in our case is always 1). So `1:89 4:1` means that the first column in the row contains the number 89, and the fourth column contains the number 1. All the other values are zero.

You can see that using libsvm over CSV has changed the width of our dataset from four columns to two columns. But don't get too hung up on this. SageMaker and XGBoost work just fine with CSV files with thousands of columns; but if your dataset is very wide (tens of thousands of columns), you might want to use libsvm instead of CSV. Otherwise, use CSV because it's easier to work with.

Listing 2.9 shows how to use the pandas function `to_csv` to create a CSV dataset from the pandas DataFrames you created in listing 2.8. To run the code, insert your cursor in the cell and press ⌈Ctrl⌉+⌈Enter ↵⌉.

Listing 2.9 Converting the data to CSV

```
train_data = train_df.to_csv(None, header=False, index=False).encode()
val_data = val_df.to_csv(None, header=False, index=False).encode()
test_data = test_df.to_csv(None, header=True, index=False).encode()
```

The `None` argument in the `to_csv` function indicates that you do not want to save to a file. The `header` argument indicates whether the column names will be included in the CSV file or not. For the train_data and val_data datasets, you don't include the column headers (header=False) because the machine learning algorithm is expecting each column to contain only numbers. For the test_data dataset, it is best to include headers because you'll be running the trained algorithm against the test data, and it is helpful to have column names in the data when you do so. The index=False argument tells the function to not include a column with the row numbers. The encode() function ensures that the text in the CSV file is in the right format.

> **NOTE** Encoding text in the right format can be one of the most frustrating parts of machine learning. Fortunately, a lot of the complexity of this is handled by the pandas library, so you generally won't have to worry about that. Just remember to always use the encode() function if you save the file to CSV.

In listing 2.9, you created CSV files from the train, val, and test DataFrames. However, the CSV files are not stored anywhere yet other than in the memory of the Jupyter notebook. In listing 2.10, you will save the CSV files to S3.

In listing 2.2 in the fourth line, you imported a Python module called s3fs. This module makes it easy to work with S3. In the last line of the same listing, you assigned the variable s3 to the S3 filesystem. You will now use this variable to work with S3. To do this, you'll use Python's with...open syntax to indicate the filename and location, and the write function to write the contents of a variable to that location (listing 2.10).

Remember to use 'wb' when creating the file to indicate that you are writing the contents of the file in binary mode rather than text mode. (You don't need to know how this works, just that it allows the file to be read back exactly as it was saved.) To run the code, insert your cursor in the cell and press Ctrl + Enter ↵ .

Listing 2.10 Saving the CSV file to S3

```
with s3.open(f'{data_bucket}/{subfolder}/processed/train.csv', 'wb') as f:
    f.write(train_data)          ◁―┐ Writes train.csv to S3

with s3.open(f'{data_bucket}/{subfolder}/processed/val.csv', 'wb') as f:
    f.write(val_data)            ◁―┐ Writes val.csv to S3

with s3.open(f'{data_bucket}/{subfolder}/processed/test.csv', 'wb') as f:
    f.write(test_data)           ◁―┐ Writes test.csv to S3
```

2.4.4 Part 4: Training the model

Now you can start training the model. You don't need to understand in detail how this works at this point, just what it is doing, so the code in this part will not be annotated to the same extent as the code in the earlier listings.

First, you need to load your CSV data into SageMaker. This is done using a Sage-Maker function called s3_input. In listing 2.11, the s3_input files are called train_input and test_input. Note that you don't need to load the test.csv file into SageMaker because it is not used to train or validate the model. Instead, you will use it at the end to test the results. To run the code, insert your cursor in the cell and press [Ctrl]+[Enter↵].

Listing 2.11   Preparing the CSV data for SageMaker

```
train_input = sagemaker.s3_input(
    s3_data=f's3://{data_bucket}/{subfolder}/processed/train.csv',
    content_type='csv')
val_input = sagemaker.s3_input(
    s3_data=f's3://{data_bucket}/{subfolder}/processed/val.csv',
    content_type='csv')
```

The next listing (listing 2.12) is truly magical. It is what allows a person with no systems engineering experience to do machine learning. In this listing, you train the machine learning model. This sounds simple, but the ease with which you can do this using SageMaker is a massive step forward from having to set up your own infrastructure to train a machine learning model. In listing 2.12, you

1 Set up a variable called sess to store the SageMaker session.
2 Define in which container AWS will store the model (use the containers given in listing 2.12).
3 Create the model (which is stored in the variable estimator in listing 2.12).
4 Set hyperparameters for the estimator.

You will learn more about each of these steps in subsequent chapters, so you don't need to understand this deeply at this point in the book. You just need to know that this code will create your model, start a server to run your model, and then train the model on the data. If you click [Ctrl]+[Enter↵] in this notebook cell, the model runs.

Listing 2.12   Training the model

```
sess = sagemaker.Session()

container = sagemaker.amazon.amazon_estimator.get_image_uri(
    boto3.Session().region_name,
    'xgboost',
    'latest')

estimator = sagemaker.estimator.Estimator(
    container,
    role,
    train_instance_count=1,
    train_instance_type='ml.m5.large',
    output_path= \
        f's3://{data_bucket}/{subfolder}/output',
    sagemaker_session=sess)

estimator.set_hyperparameters(
    max_depth=5,
    subsample=0.7,
    objective='binary:logistic',
```

Sets the type of server that SageMaker uses to run your model

Stores the output of the model at this location in S3

SageMaker has some very sophisticated hyperparameter tuning capability. To use the tuning function, you just need to make sure you set the objective correctly. For the current dataset, where you are trying to predict a 1 or 0, you should set this as binary:logistic. We'll cover this in more detail in later chapters.

The maximum number of rounds of training that will occur. This is covered in more detail in chapter 3.

```
        eval_metric = 'auc',
        num_round=100,
        early_stopping_rounds=10)

  estimator.fit({'train': train_input, 'validation': val_input})
```

Tells SageMaker to tune the hyperparameters to achieve the best area under curve result. Again, we'll cover this in more detail in later chapters.

The number of rounds that will occur where there is no improvement in the model before training is terminated

It takes about 5 minutes to train the model, so you can sit back and reflect on how happy you are to not be manually configuring a server and installing the software to train your model. The server only runs for about a minute, so you will only be charged for about a minute of compute time. At the time of writing of this book, the m5-large server was priced at under US$0.10 per hour. Once you have stored the model on S3, you can use it again whenever you like without retraining the model. More on this in later chapters.

2.4.5　*Part 5: Hosting the model*

The next section of the code is also magical. In this section, you will launch another server to host the model. This is the server that you will use to make predictions from the trained model.

Again, at this point in the book, you don't need to understand how the code in the listing in this section works—just that it's creating a server that you'll use to make predictions. The code in listing 2.13 calls this endpoint order-approval and uses Python's try-except block to create it.

A try-except block tries to run some code, and if there is an error, it runs the code after the except line. You do this because you only want to set up the endpoint if you haven't already set one up with that name. The listing tries to set up an endpoint called order-approval. If there is no endpoint named order-approval, then it sets one up. If there is an order-approval endpoint, the try code generates an error, and the except code runs. The except code in this case simply says to use the endpoint named order-approval.

Listing 2.13　Hosting the model

```
endpoint_name = 'order-approval'
try:
    sess.delete_endpoint(
        sagemaker.predictor.RealTimePredictor(
            endpoint=endpoint_name).endpoint)
    print('Warning: Existing endpoint deleted\
to make way for your new endpoint.')
except:
    pass
```

```
predictor = estimator.deploy(initial_instance_count=1,
            instance_type='ml.t2.medium',
            endpoint_name=endpoint_name)
```
The type of server you
are using, in this case,
an ml.t2.medium server.

```
from sagemaker.predictor import csv_serializer, json_serializer
predictor.content_type = 'text/csv'
predictor.serializer = csv_serializer
predictor.deserializer = None
```

The code in listing 2.13 sets up a server sized as a t2.medium server. This is a smaller server than the m5.large server we used to train the model because making predictions from a model is less computationally intensive than creating the model. Both the try block and the except block create a variable called predictor that you'll draw on to test and use the model. The final four lines in the code set up the predictor to work with the CSV file input so you can work with it more easily.

Note that when you click ⌈Ctrl⌉+⌈Enter↵⌉ in the notebook cell, the code will take another 5 minutes or so to run the first time. It takes time because it is setting up a server to host the model and to create an endpoint so you can use the model.

2.4.6   *Part 6: Testing the model*

Now that you have the model trained and hosted on a server (the endpoint named predictor), you can start using it to make predictions. The first three lines of the next listing create a function that you'll apply to each row of the test data.

Listing 2.14   Getting the predictions

```
def get_prediction(row):
    prediction = round(float(predictor.predict(row[1:]).decode('utf-8')))
    return prediction

with s3.open(f'{data_bucket}/{subfolder}/processed/test.csv') as f:
    test_data = pd.read_csv(f)

test_data['prediction'] = test_data.apply(get_prediction, axis=1)
test_data.set_index('prediction', inplace=True)
test_data
```

The function get_prediction in listing 2.14 takes every column in the test data (except for the first column, because that is the value you are trying to predict), sends it to the predictor, and returns the prediction. In this case, the prediction is 1 if the order should be sent to an approver, and 0 if it should *not* be sent to an approver.

The next two lines open the test.csv file and read the contents into a pandas DataFrame called test_data. You can now work with this DataFrame in the same way you worked with the original dataset in listing 2.7. The final three lines apply the function created in the first three lines of the listing.

When you click Ctrl+Enter← in the cell containing the code in listing 2.14, you see the results of each row in the test file. Table 2.6 shows the top two rows of the test data. Each row represents a single order. For example, if an order for a desk was placed by a person in a technical role, the role_tech and the product_desk columns would have a 1. All other columns would be 0.

Table 2.6 Test results from the predictor

prediction	tech_ approval_ required	role_ non-tech	role_ tech	product_ Chair	product_ Cleaning	product_ Desk	product_ Desktop Computer	product_ Keyboard	product_ Laptop Computer	product_ Mouse
1	1	1	0	0	0	0	1	0	0	0
0	0	1	0	0	1	0	0	0	0	0

The 1 in the prediction column in first row says that the model predicts that this order should be sent to a technical approver. The 1 in the tech_approval_required column says that in your test data, this order was labeled as requiring technical approval. This means that the machine learning model predicted this order correctly.

To see why, look at the values in the columns to the right of the tech_approval_ required column. You can see that this order was placed by someone who is not in a technical role because there is a 1 in the role_non-tech column and a 0 in the role_tech column. And you can see that the product ordered was a desktop computer because the product_Desktop Computer column has a 1.

The 0 in the prediction column in the second row says that the model predicts this order does *not* require technical approval. The 0 in the tech_approval_required column, because it is the same value as that in the prediction column, says that the model predicted this correctly.

The 1 in the role_non-tech column says this order was also placed by a non-technical person. However, the 1 in the product_Cleaning column indicates that the order was for cleaning products; therefore, it does not require technical approval.

As you look through the results, you can see that your machine learning model got almost every test result correct! You have just created a machine learning model that can correctly decide whether to send orders to a technical approver, all without writing any rules. To determine how accurate the results are, you can test how many of the predictions match the test data, as shown in the following listing.

Listing 2.15 Testing the model

```
(test_data['prediction'] == \
    test_data['tech_approval_required']).mean()
```
◁—— **Displays the percentage of predictions that match the test dataset**

2.5   Deleting the endpoint and shutting down your notebook instance

It is *important* that you shut down your notebook instance and delete your endpoints when you are not using them. If you leave them running, you will be charged for each second they are up. The charges for the machines we use in this book are not large (if you were to leave a notebook instance or endpoint on for a month, it would cost about US$20). But, there is no point in paying for something you are not using.

2.5.1   Deleting the endpoint

To delete the endpoint, click Endpoints on the left-hand menu you see when you are looking at the SageMaker tab (figure 2.9).

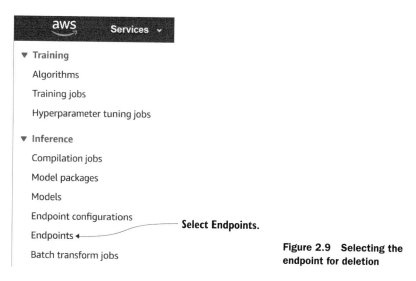

Figure 2.9   Selecting the endpoint for deletion

You will see a list of all of your running endpoints (figure 2.10). To ensure you are not charged for endpoints you are not using, you should delete all of the endpoints you

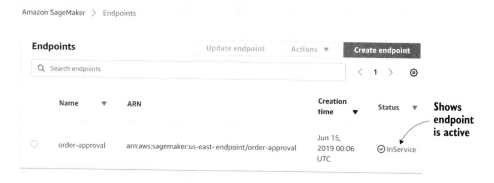

Figure 2.10   Viewing the active endpoint(s)

are not using (remember that endpoints are easy to create, so even if you will not use the endpoint for only a few hours, you might want to delete it).

To delete the endpoint, click the radio button to the left of order-approval, click the Actions menu item, then click the Delete menu item that appears (figure 2.11).

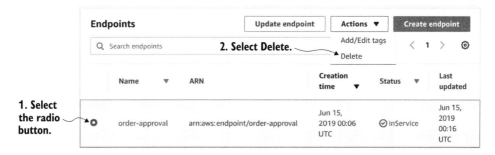

Figure 2.11   Deleting the endpoint

You have now deleted the endpoint, so you'll no longer incur AWS charges for it. You can confirm that all of your endpoints have been deleted when you see the text "There are currently no resources" displayed on the Endpoints page (figure 2.12).

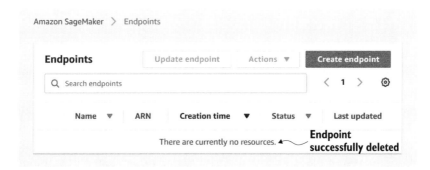

Figure 2.12   Endpoint deleted

2.5.2 *Shutting down the notebook instance*

The final step is to shut down the notebook instance. Unlike endpoints, you do not delete the notebook. You just shut it down so you can start it again, and it will have all of the code in your Jupyter notebook ready to go. To shut down the notebook instance, click Notebook instances in the left-hand menu on SageMaker (figure 2.13).

To shut down the notebook, select the radio button next to the notebook instance name and click Stop on the Actions menu (figure 2.14). After your notebook instance has shut down, you can confirm that it is no longer running by checking the Status to ensure it says Stopped.

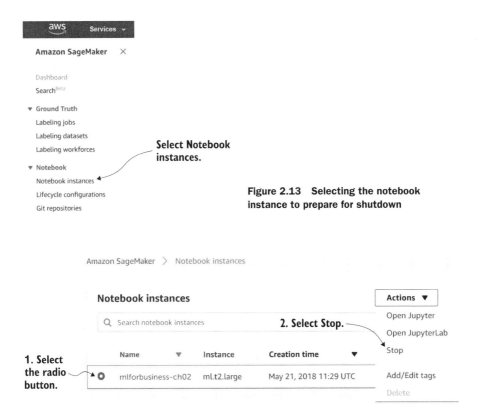

Figure 2.13   Selecting the notebook instance to prepare for shutdown

Figure 2.14   Shutting down the notebook

This chapter was all about helping Karen decide whether to send an order to a technical approver. In this chapter, you worked end to end through a machine learning scenario. The scenario you worked through involved how to decide whether to send an order to a technical approver. The skills you learned in this chapter will be used throughout the rest of the book as you work through other examples of using machine learning to make decisions in business automation.

Summary

- You can uncover machine learning opportunities by identifying decision points.
- It's simple to set up SageMaker and build a machine learning system using AWS SageMaker and Jupyter notebooks.
- You send data to the machine learning endpoints to make predictions.
- You can test the predictions by sending the data to a CSV file for viewing.
- To ensure you are not charged for endpoints you are not using, you should delete all unused endpoints.

Should you call a customer because they are at risk of churning?

Carlos takes it personally when a customer stops ordering from his company. He's the Head of Operations for a commercial bakery that sells high-quality bread and other baked goods to restaurants and hotels. Most of his customers have used his bakery for a long time, but he still regularly loses customers to his competitors. To help retain customers, Carlos calls those who have stopped using his bakery. He hears a similar story from each of these customers: they like his bread, but it's expensive and cuts into their desired profit margins, so they try bread from another, less expensive bakery. After this trial, his customers conclude that the quality of their meals would still be acceptable even if they served a lower quality bread.

Churn is the term used when you lose a customer. It's a good word for Carlos's situation because it indicates that a customer probably hasn't stopped ordering bread; they're just ordering it from someone else.

Carlos comes to you for help in identifying those customers who are in the process of trying another bakery. Once he's identified the customer, he can call them to determine if there's something he can do to keep them. In Carlos's conversations with his lost customers, he sees a common pattern:

- Customers place orders in a regular pattern, typically daily.
- A customer tries another bakery, thus reducing the number of orders from Carlos's bakery.
- The customer negotiates an agreement with the other bakery, which may or may not result in a temporary resurgence in orders placed with Carlos's bakery.
- Customers stop ordering from his bakery altogether.

In this chapter, you are going to help Carlos understand which customers are at risk of churning so he can call them to determine whether there is some way to address their move to another supplier. To help Carlos, you'll look at the business process in a similar way that you looked at Karen's process in chapter 2.

For Karen's process, you looked at how orders moved from requester to approver, and the features that Karen used to make a decision about whether to send the order to a technical approver or not. You then built a SageMaker XGBoost application that automated the decision. Similarly, with Carlos's decision about whether to call a customer because they are at risk of churning, you'll build a SageMaker XGBoost application that looks at Carlos's customers each week and makes a decision about whether Carlos should call them.

3.1   What are you making decisions about?

At first glance, it looks like you are working with ordering data like you did in chapter 2, where Karen looks at an order and decides whether to send it to a technical approver or not. In this chapter, Carlos reviews a customer's orders and decides whether to call that customer. The difference between Karen's process flow in chapter 2 and Carlos's process flow in this chapter is that, in chapter 2, you made decisions about orders: should Karen send this order to an approver. In this chapter, you make decisions about customers: should Carlos call a customer.

This means that instead of just taking the order data and using that as your dataset, you need to first transform the order data into customer data. In later chapters, you'll learn how to use some automated tools to do this, but in this chapter, you'll learn about the process conceptually, and you'll be provided with the transformed dataset. But before we look at the data, let's look at the process we want to automate.

3.2   The process flow

Figure 3.1 shows the process flow. You start with the Orders database, which contains records of which customers have bought which products and when.

Carlos believes that there is a pattern to customers' orders before they decide to move to a competitor. This means that you need to turn order data into customer

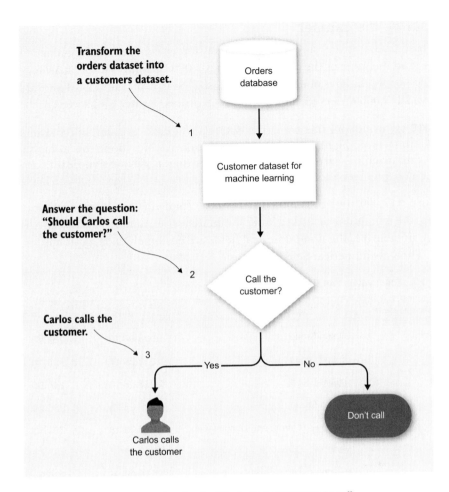

Transform the orders dataset into a customers dataset.

Orders database

1

Customer dataset for machine learning

Answer the question: "Should Carlos call the customer?"

2

Call the customer?

Carlos calls the customer.

3

Yes — No

Carlos calls the customer

Don't call

Figure 3.1   Carlos's process flow for deciding which customers to call

data. One of the easiest ways to think about this is to picture the data as a table like it might be displayed in Excel. Your order data has a single row for each of the orders. If there are 1,000 orders, there will be 1,000 rows in your table. If these 1,000 orders were from 100 customers, when you turn your order data into customer data, your table with 1,000 rows will become a table with 100 rows.

This is shown in step 1 in figure 3.1: transform the orders dataset into a customer dataset. You'll see how to do this in the next section. Let's move on to step 2 now, which is the primary focus of this chapter. In step 2, you answer the question, should Carlos call a customer?

After you've prepared the customer database, you'll use that data to prepare a SageMaker notebook. When the notebook is complete, you'll send data about a customer to the SageMaker endpoint and return a decision about whether Carlos should call that customer.

3.3   *Preparing the dataset*

The base dataset is very simple. It has the customer code, customer name, date of the order, and the value of the order. Carlos has 3,000 customers who, on average, place 3 orders per week. This means that, over the course of the past 3 months, Carlos received 117,000 orders (3,000 customer × 3 orders per week × 13 weeks).

> **NOTE**   Throughout this book, the datasets you'll use are simplified examples of datasets you might encounter in your work. We have done this to highlight certain machine learning techniques rather than to devote significant parts of each chapter to understanding the data.

To turn 117,000 rows into a 3,000-row table (one row per customer), you need to group the non-numerical data and summarize the numerical data. In the dataset shown in table 3.1, the non-numerical fields are customer_code, customer_name, and date. The only numerical field is amount.

Table 3.1   Order dataset for Carlos's customers

customer_code	customer_name	date	amount
393	Gibson Group	2018-08-18	264.18
393	Gibson Group	2018-08-17	320.14
393	Gibson Group	2018-08-16	145.95
393	Gibson Group	2018-08-15	280.59
840	Meadows, Carroll, and Cunningham	2018-08-18	284.12
840	Meadows, Carroll, and Cunningham	2018-08-17	232.41
840	Meadows, Carroll, and Cunningham	2018-08-16	235.95
840	Meadows, Carroll, and Cunningham	2018-08-15	184.59

Grouping customer_code and customer_name is easy. You want a single row per customer_code. And you can simply use the customer name associated with each customer code. In table 3.1, there are two different customer_codes in the rows 393 and 840, and each has a company associated with it: Gibson Group and Meadows, Carroll, and Cunningham.

Grouping the dates is the interesting part of the dataset preparation in this chapter. In discussions with Carlos, you learned that he believes there is a pattern to the customers that stop using his bakery. The pattern looks like this:

1 A customer believes they can use a lower quality product without impacting their business.
2 They try another bakery's products.
3 They set up a contract with the other bakery.
4 They stop using Carlos's bakery.

Carlos's ordering pattern will be stable over time, then drop while his customers try a competitor's products, and then return to normal while a contract with his competitor is negotiated. Carlos believes that this pattern should be reflected in the customers' ordering behavior.

In this chapter, you'll use XGBoost to see if you can identify which customers will stop using Carlos's bakery. Although several tools exist to help you prepare the data, in this chapter, you won't use those tools because the focus of this chapter is on machine learning rather than data preparation. In a subsequent chapter, however, we'll show you how to use these tools with great effect. In this chapter, you'll take Carlos's advice that most of his customers follow a weekly ordering pattern, so you'll summarize the data by week.

You'll apply two transformations to the data:

- Normalize the data
- Calculate the change from week to week

The first transformation is to calculate the percentage spend, relative to the average week. This normalizes all of the data so that instead of dollars, you are looking at a weekly change relative to the *average* sales. The second transformation is to show the change from week to week. You do this because you want the machine learning algorithm to see the patterns in the weekly changes as well as the relative figures for the same time period.

Note that for this chapter, we'll apply these transformations for you, but later chapters will go more into how to transform data. Because the purpose of this chapter is to learn more about XGBoost and machine learning, we'll tell you what the data looks like so you won't have to do the transformations yourself.

3.3.1 Transformation 1: Normalizing the data

For our dataset, we'll do the following:

1 Take the sum of the total spent over the year for each of Carlos's customers and call that total_spend.
2 Find the average spent per week by dividing total_spend by 52.
3 For each week, calculate the total spent per week divided by the average spent per week to get a weekly spend as a percentage of an average spend.
4 Create a column for each week.

Table 3.2 shows the results of this transformation.

Table 3.2 Customer dataset grouped by week after normalizing the data

customer_code	customer_name	total_sales	week_minus_4	week_minus_3	week_minus_2	last_week
393	Gibson Group	6013.96	1.13	1.18	0.43	2.09
840	Meadows, Carroll, and Cunningham	5762.40	0.52	1.43	0.87	1.84

3.3.2   *Transformation 2: Calculating the change from week to week*

As table 3.3 shows, for each week from the column named week_minus_3 to last_week, you subtract the value from the preceding week and call it the delta between the weeks. For example, in week_minus_3, the Gibson Group has sales that are 1.18 times their average week. In week_minus_4, their sales are 1.13 times their average sales. This means that their weekly sales rose by 0.05 of their normal sales from week_minus_4 to week_minus_3. This is the delta between week_minus_3 and week_minus_4 and is recorded as 0.05 in the 4-3_delta column.

Table 3.3   Customer dataset grouped by week, showing changes per week

customer_code	customer_name	total_sales	week_minus_4	week_minus_3	week_minus_2	last_week	4-3_delta	3-2_delta	2-1_delta
393	Gibson Group	6013.96	1.13	1.18	0.43	2.09	0.05	-0.75	1.66
840	Meadows, Carroll, and Cunningham	5762.40	0.52	1.43	0.87	1.84	0.91	-0.56	0.97

The following week was a disaster in sales for the Gibson Group: sales decreased by 0.75 times their average weekly sales. This is shown by a –0.75 in the 3-2_delta column. Their sales rebounded in the last week though, as they went to 2.09 times their average weekly sales. This is shown by the 1.66 in the 2-1_delta column.

Now that you've prepared the data, let's move on to setting up the machine learning application by first looking at how XGBoost works.

3.4   *XGBoost primer*

In chapter 2, you used XGBoost to help Karen decide which approver to send an order to, but we didn't go into much detail on how it works. We'll cover this now.

3.4.1   *How XGBoost works*

XGBoost can be understood at a number of levels. How deep you go in your understanding depends on your needs. A high-level person will be satisfied with a high-level answer. A more detailed person will require a more detailed understanding. Carlos and Karen will both need to understand the model enough to show their managers they know what's going on. How deep they have to go really depends on their managers.

At the highest level, in the circle example from chapter 1 (reproduced in figure 3.2), we separated the dark circles from the light circles using two approaches:

- Rewarding the function for getting a dark circle on the right and punishing it for getting a dark circle on the left.
- Rewarding the function for getting a light circle on the left and punishing it for getting a light circle on the right.

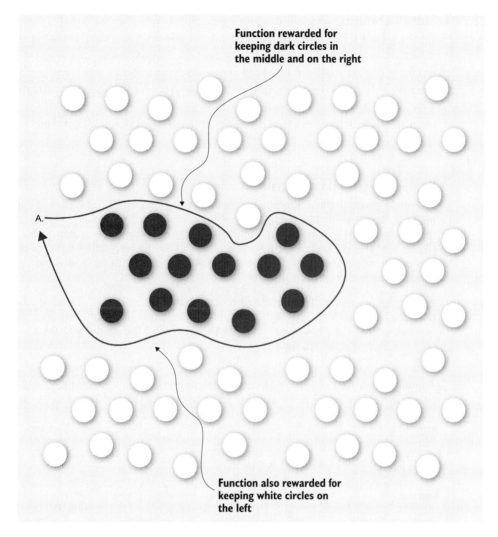

Figure 3.2 Machine learning function to identify a group of similar items (reprinted from chapter 1)

This could be considered an *ensemble* machine learning model, which is a model that uses multiple approaches when it learns. In a way, XGBoost is also an ensemble machine learning model, which means it uses a number of different approaches to improve the effectiveness of its learning. Let's go another level deeper into the explanation.

XGBoost stands for Extreme Gradient Boosting. Consider the name in two parts:

- Gradient boosting
- Extreme

Gradient boosting is a technique where different learners are used to improve a function. You can think of this like ice hockey players' sticks handling the puck down the ice. Instead of trying to push the puck straight ahead, they use small corrections to guide the puck in the right direction. Gradient boosting follows a similar approach.

The *Extreme* part of the name is in recognition that XGBoost has a number of other characteristics that makes the model particularly accurate. For example, the model automatically handles regularization of the data so you're not inadvertently thrown off by a dataset with big differences in the values you look at.

And finally, for the next level of depth, the sidebar gives Richard's more detailed explanation.

Richie's explanation of XGBoost

XGBoost is an incredibly powerful machine learning model. To begin with, it supports multiple forms of regularization. This is important because gradient boosting algorithms are known to have potential problems with overfitting. An *overfit model* is one that is very strongly tied to the unique features of the training data and does not generalize well to unseen data. As we add more rounds to XGBoost, we can see this when our validation accuracy starts deteriorating.

Apart from restricting the number of rounds with early stopping, XGBoost also controls overfitting with column and row subsampling and the parameters eta, gamma, lambda, and alpha. This penalizes specific aspects of the model that tend to make it fit the training data too tightly.

Another feature is that XGBoost builds each tree in parallel on all available cores. Although each step of gradient boosting needs to be carried out serially, XGBoost's use of all available cores for building each tree gives it a big advantage over other algorithms, particularly when solving more complex problems.

XGBoost also supports *out-of-core computation*. When data does not fit into memory, it divides that data into blocks and stores those on disk in a compressed form. It even supports sharding of these blocks across multiple disks. These blocks are then decompressed on the fly by an independent thread while loading into memory.

XGBoost has been extended to support massively parallel processing big data frameworks such as Spark, Flink, and Hadoop. This means it can be used for building extremely large and complex models with potentially billions of rows and millions of features that run at high speed.

XGBoost is *sparsity aware*, meaning that it handles missing values without any requirement for imputation. We have taken this for granted, but many machine learning algorithms require values for all attributes of all samples; in which case, we would have had to impute an appropriate value. This is not always easy to do without skewing the results of the model in some way. Furthermore, XGBoost handles missing values in a very efficient way: its performance is proportional to the number of present values and is independent of the number of missing values.

Finally, XGBoost implements a highly efficient algorithm for optimizing the objective known as *Newton boosting*. Unfortunately, an explanation of this algorithm is beyond the scope of this book.

You can read more about XGBoost on Amazon's site: https://docs.aws.amazon.com/sagemaker/latest/dg/xgboost.html.

3.4.2 How the machine learning model determines whether the function is getting better or getting worse AUC

XGBoost is good at learning. But what does it mean to learn? It simply means that the model gets punished less and rewarded more. And how does the machine learning model know whether it should be punished or rewarded? The area under the curve (AUC) is a metric that is commonly used in machine learning as the basis for rewarding or punishing the function. The curve is the "When the function gets a greater area under the curve, it is rewarded" guideline. When the function gets a reduced AUC, it is punished.

To get a feel for how AUC works, imagine you are a celebrity in a fancy resort. You are used to being pampered, and you expect that to happen. One of the staff attending to your every whim is the shade umbrella adjuster. Let's call him *Function*. When Function fails to adjust the umbrella so that you are covered by its shade, you berate him. When he consistently keeps you in the shade, you give him a tip. That is how a machine learning model works: it rewards Function when he increases the AUC and punishes him when he reduces the AUC. Now over to Richie for a more technical explanation.

> ### Richie's explanation of the area under the curve (AUC)
>
> When we tell XGBoost that our objective is *binary:logistic*, what we are asking it for is actually not a prediction of a positive or negative label. We are instead asking for the probability of a positive label. As a result, we get a continuous value between 0 and 1. It is then up to us to decide what probability will produce a positive prediction.
>
> It might make sense to choose 0.5 (50%) as our cutoff, but at other times, we might want to be really certain of our prediction before predicting a positive. Typically, we would do this when the cost of the decision associated with a positive label is quite high. In other cases, the cost of missing a positive can be more important and justify choosing a cutoff much less than 0.5.
>
> The plot in this sidebar's figure shows true positives on the y-axis as a fraction between 0 and 1, and false positives on the x-axis as a fraction between 0 and 1:
>
> - The *true positive rate* is the portion of all positives that are actually identified as positive by our model.
> - The *false positive rate* is the portion of incorrect positive predictions as a percentage of all negative numbers.
>
> This plot is known as an *ROC curve*.[a] When we use AUC as our evaluation metric, we are telling XGBoost to optimize our model by maximizing the area under the ROC curve to give us the best possible results when averaged across all cutoff probabilities between 0 and 1.

(continued)

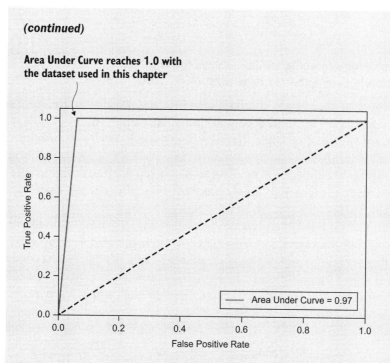

Area Under Curve reaches 1.0 with the dataset used in this chapter

The area under the curve (AUC) showing true and false positive values

Whichever value you choose for your cutoff produces both TP (true positive) and corresponding FP (false positive) values. If you choose a probability that allows you to capture most or all of the true positives by picking a low cutoff (such as 0.1), you will also accidentally predict more negatives as positives. Whichever value you pick will be a trade-off between these two competing measures of model accuracy.

When the curve is well above the diagonal (as in this figure), you get an AUC value close to 1. A model that simply matches the TP and FP rates for each cutoff will have an AUC of 0.5 and will directly match the diagonal dotted line in the figure.

a   ROC stands for Receiver Operator Characteristic. It was first developed by engineers during World War II for detecting enemy objects in battle, and the name has stuck.

3.5   *Getting ready to build the model*

Now that you have a deeper understanding of how XGBoost works, you can set up another notebook on SageMaker and make some decisions. As you did in chapter 2, you are going to do the following:

- Upload a dataset to S3.
- Set up a notebook on SageMaker.
- Upload the starting notebook.
- Run it against the data.

Along the way, we'll go into some details we glossed over in chapter 2.

> **TIP** If you're jumping into the book at this chapter, you might want to visit the appendixes, which show you how to do the following:

- Appendix A: sign up for AWS, Amazon's web service
- Appendix B: set up S3, AWS's file storage service
- Appendix C: set up SageMaker

3.5.1 Uploading a dataset to S3

To set up the dataset for this chapter, you'll follow the same steps as you did in appendix B. You don't need to set up another bucket though. You can just go to the same bucket you created earlier. In our example, we called the bucket *mlforbusiness*, but your bucket will be called something different. When you go to your S3 account, you will see something like that shown in figure 3.3.

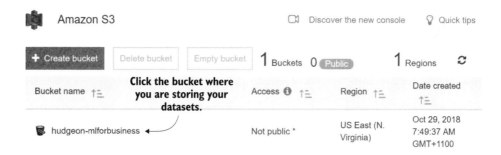

Figure 3.3   Viewing the list of buckets in S3

Click this bucket to see the ch02 folder you created in the previous chapter. For this chapter, you'll create a new folder called *ch03*. You do this by clicking Create Folder and following the prompts to create a new folder.

Once you've created the folder, you are returned to the folder list inside your bucket. There you will see you now have a folder called ch03.

Now that you have the ch03 folder set up in your bucket, you can upload your data file and start setting up the decision-making model in SageMaker. To do so, click the folder and download the data file at this link:

https://s3.amazonaws.com/mlforbusiness/ch03/churn_data.csv.

Then upload the CSV file into your ch03 folder by clicking the Upload button. Now you're ready to set up the notebook instance.

3.5.2   *Setting up a notebook on SageMaker*

Like you did in chapter 2, you'll set up a notebook on SageMaker. This process is much faster for this chapter because, unlike in chapter 2, you now have a notebook instance set up and ready to run. You just need to run it and upload the Jupyter notebook we prepared for this chapter. (If you skipped chapter 2, follow the instructions in appendix C on how to set up SageMaker.)

When you go to SageMaker, you'll see your notebook instances. The notebook instance you created for chapter 2 (or that you've just created by following the instructions in appendix C) will either say Open or Start. If it says Start, click the Start link and wait a couple of minutes for SageMaker to start. Once the screen displays Open Jupyter, select that link to open your notebook list.

Once it opens, create a new folder for chapter 3 by clicking New and selecting Folder at the bottom of the dropdown list (figure 3.4). This creates a new folder called Untitled Folder.

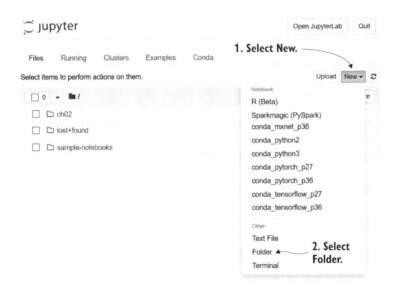

Figure 3.4   Creating a new folder in SageMaker

When you tick the checkbox next to Untitled Folder, you will see the Rename button appear. Click it, and change the folder name to ch03 (figure 3.5).

Click the ch03 folder, and you will see an empty notebook list. Just as we already prepared the CSV data you uploaded to S3 (churn_data.csv), we've already prepared the Jupyter Notebook you'll now use. You can download it to your computer by navigating to this URL:

https://s3.amazonaws.com/mlforbusiness/ch03/customer_churn.ipynb.

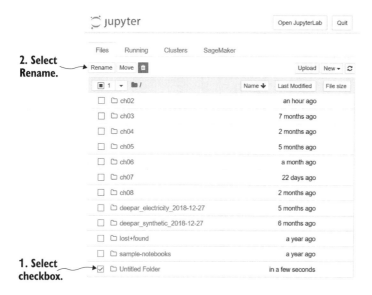

Figure 3.5 Renaming a folder in SageMaker

Click Upload to upload the customer-churn.ipynb notebook to the ch03 folder (figure 3.6).

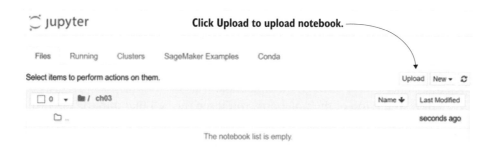

Figure 3.6 Uploading a notebook to SageMaker

After uploading the file, you'll see the notebook in your list. Click it to open it. Now, just like in chapter 2, you are a few keystrokes away from being able to run your machine learning model.

3.6   *Building the model*

As in chapter 2, you will go through the code in six parts:

- Load and examine the data.
- Get the data into the right shape.

- Create training, validation, and test datasets.
- Train the machine learning model.
- Host the machine learning model.
- Test the model and use it to make decisions.

3.6.1   Part 1: Loading and examining the data

First, you need to tell SageMaker where your data is. Update the code in the first cell of the notebook to point to your S3 bucket and folders (listing 3.1). If you called your S3 folder ch03 and did not rename the churn_data.csv file, then you just need to update the name of the data bucket to the name of the S3 bucket you uploaded the data to. Once you have done that, you can actually run the entire notebook. As you did in chapter 2, to run the notebook, click Cell in the toolbar at the top of the Jupyter Notebook, then click Run All.

Listing 3.1   Setting up the notebook and storing the data

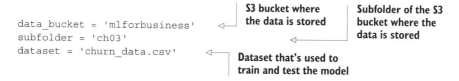

When you run the notebook, SageMaker loads the data, trains the model, sets up the endpoint, and generates decisions from the test data. SageMaker takes about 10 minutes to complete these actions, so you have time to get yourself a cup of coffee or tea while this is happening.

When you return with your hot beverage, if you scroll to the bottom of your notebook, you should see the decisions that were made on the test data. But before we get into that, let's work through the notebook.

Back at the top of the notebook, you'll see the cell that imports the Python libraries and modules you'll use in this notebook. You'll hear more about these in a subsequent chapter. For now, let's move to the next cell. If you didn't click Run All in the notebook, click the cell and press [Ctrl]+[Enter↵] to run the code in this cell, as shown in listing 3.1.

Moving on to the next cell, you will now import all of the Python libraries and modules that SageMaker uses to prepare the data, train the machine learning model, and set up the endpoint.

As you learned in chapter 2, pandas is one of the most commonly used Python libraries in data science. In the code cell shown in listing 3.2, you'll import pandas as pd. When you see pd in the cell, it means you are using a pandas function. Other items that you import include these:

- *boto3*—Amazon's Python library that helps you work with AWS services in Python.
- *sagemaker*—Amazon's Python module to work with SageMaker.

- *s3fs*—A module that makes it easier to use boto3 to manage files on S3.
- *sklearn.metrics*—A new import (it wasn't used in chapter 2). This module lets you generate summary reports on the output of the machine learning model.

Listing 3.2 Importing the modules

Imports the pandas Python library

Imports the boto3 AWS library

Imports the s3fs module to make working with S3 files easier

Imports SageMaker

```
import pandas as pd
import boto3
import sagemaker
import s3fs
from sklearn.model_selection \
    import train_test_split
import sklearn.metrics as metrics

role = sagemaker.get_execution_role()
s3 = s3fs.S3FileSystem(anon=False)
```

Imports only the train_test_split module from the sklearn library

Imports the metrics module from the sklearn library

Creates a role in SageMaker

Establishes the connection with S3

In the cell in listing 3.3, we are using the pandas read_csv function to read our data and the head function to display the top five rows. This is one of the first things you'll do in each of the chapters so you can see the data and understand its shape. To load and view the data, click the cell with your mouse to select it, and then press Ctrl+Enter⏎ to run the code.

Listing 3.3 Loading and viewing the data

```
df = pd.read_csv(
    f's3://{data_bucket}/{subfolder}/{dataset}')
df.head()
```

Reads the S3 churn_data.csv dataset in listing 3.1

Displays the top five rows of the DataFrame

You can see that the data has a single customer per row and that it reflects the format of the data in table 3.3. The first column in table 3.4 indicates whether the customer churned or did not churn. If the customer churned, the first column contains a 1. If they remain a customer, it should show a 0. Note that these data rows are provided by way of example, and the rows of data you see might be different.

You can see from the first five customers that none of them have churned. This is what you would expect because Carlos doesn't lose that many customers.

To see how many rows are in the dataset, you run the pandas shape function as shown in listing 3.4. To see how many customers in the dataset have churned, you run the pandas value_counts function.

Table 3.4   Dataset for Carlos's customers displayed in Excel

churned	id	customer_ code	co_name	total_ spend	week_ minus_4	week_ minus_3	week_ minus_2	last_ week	4-3_ delta	3-2_ delta	2-1_ delta
0	1	1826	Hoffman, Martinez, and Chandler	68567.34	0.81	0.02	0.74	1.45	0.79	-0.72	-0.71
0	2	772	Lee Martin and Escobar	74335.27	1.87	1.02	1.29	1.19	0.85	-0.27	0.10

Listing 3.4   Number of churned customers in the dataset

```
print(f'Number of rows in dataset: {df.shape[0]}')
print(df['churned'].value_counts())
```

Displays the total number of rows

Displays the number of rows where a customer churned and the number of rows where the customer did not

You can see from this data that out of 2,999 rows of data, 166 customers have churned. This represents a churn rate of about 5% per week, which is higher than the rate that Carlos experiences. Carlos's true churn rate is about 0.5% per week (or about 15 customers per week).

We did something a little sneaky with the data in this instance to bring the churn rate up to this level. The dataset actually contains the churned customers from the past three months and a random selection of non-churned customers over that same period to bring the total number of customers up to 2,999 (the actual number of customers that Carlos has). We did this because we are going to cover how to handle extremely rare events in a subsequent chapter and, for this chapter, we wanted to use a similar toolset to that which we used in chapter 2.

There are risks in the approach we took with the data in this chapter. If there are differences in the ordering patterns of churned customers over the past three months, then our results might be invalid. In discussions with Carlos, he believes that the pattern of churning and normal customers remains steady over time, so we felt confident we can use this approach.

The other point to note is that this approach might not be well received if we were writing an academic paper. One of the lessons you'll learn as you work with your own company's data is that you rarely get everything you want. You have to constantly assess whether you can make good decisions based on the data you have.

3.6.2 Part 2: Getting the data into the right shape

Now that you can see your dataset in the notebook, you can start working with it. XGBoost can only work with numbers, so we need to either remove our categorical data or encode it.

Encoding data means that you set each distinct value in the dataset as a column and then put a 1 in the rows that contain the value of the column and a zero in the other rows in that column. This worked well for your products in Karen's dataset, but it will not help you out with Carlos's dataset. That's because the categorical data (customer_name, customer_code, and id) are unique—these occur only once in the dataset. Turning these into columns would not improve the model either.

Your best approach in this case is also the simplest approach: just remove the categorical data. To remove the data, use the pandas drop function, and display the first five rows of the dataset again by using the head function. You use axis=1 to indicate that you want to remove columns rather than rows in the pandas DataFrame.

Listing 3.5 Removing the categorical data

```
encoded_data = df.drop(                          Removes categorical columns
    ['id', 'customer_code', 'co_name'],          by calling the drop function
    axis=1)                                       on the df DataFrame
encoded_data.head()        Displays the first five
                           rows of the DataFrame
```

Removing the columns shows the dataset without the categorical information (table 3.5).

Table 3.5 The transformed dataset without categorical information

churned	total_ spend	week_ minus_4	week_ minus_3	week_ minus_2	last_ week	4-3_delta	3-2_delta	2-1_delta
0	68567.34	0.81	0.02	0.74	1.45	0.79	-0.72	-0.71
0	74335.27	1.87	1.02	1.29	1.19	0.85	-0.27	0.10

3.6.3 Part 3: Creating training, validation, and test datasets

Now that you have your data in a format that XGBoost can work with, you can split the data into test, validation, and training datasets as you did in chapter 2. One important difference with the approach we are taking going forward is that we are using the stratify parameter during the split.

The stratify parameter is particularly useful for datasets where the target variable you are predicting is relatively rare. The parameter works by shuffling the deck as it's building the machine learning model and making sure that the train, validate, and test datasets contain similar ratios of target variables. This ensures that the model does not get thrown off course by an unrepresentative selection of customers in any of the datasets.

We glossed over this code in chapter 2. We'll go into more depth here and show you how to use `stratify` (listing 3.6). You create training and testing samples from a dataset, with 70% allocated to the training data and 30% allocated to the testing and validation samples. The `stratify` argument tells the function to use `y` to stratify the data so that a *random* sample is balanced proportionally according to the distinct values in `y`.

You might notice that the code to split the dataset is slightly different than the code used in chapter 2. Because you are using `stratify`, you have to explicitly declare your target column (`churned` in this example). The `stratify` function returns a couple of additional values that you don't care about. The underscores in the `y =` `test_and_val_data` line (those beginning with `val_df`) are simply placeholders for variables. Don't worry if this seems a bit arcane. You don't need to understand this part of the code in order to train, validate, and test the model.

You then split the testing and validation data, with two thirds allocated to validation and one third to testing (listing 3.6). Over the entire dataset, 70% of the data is allocated to training, 20% to validation, and 10% to testing.

Listing 3.6   Creating the training, validation, and test datasets

```
y = encoded_data['churned']
train_df, test_and_val_data, _, _ = train_test_split(      ⊲┐ Sets the target
    encoded_data,                                             │ variable for use in
    y,                                                        │ splitting the data
    test_size=0.3,
    stratify=y,
    random_state=0)    ⊲─

y = test_and_val_data['churned']
val_df, test_df, _, _ = train_test_split(
    testing_data,
    y,
    test_size=0.333,
    stratify=y,
    random_state=0)    ⊲─

print(train_df.shape, val_df.shape, test_df.shape)
print()
print('Train')
print(train_df['churned'].value_counts())    ⊲─
print()
print('Validate')
print(val_df['churned'].value_counts())
print()
print('Test')
print(test_df['churned'].value_counts())
```

Creates training and testing samples from dataset df. random_state and ensures that repeating the command splits the data in the same way

Splits testing and validation data into a validation dataset and a testing dataset

The value_counts function shows the number of customers who did not churn (denoted by a 0) and the number of churned customers (denoted by a 1) in the train, validate, and test datasets.

Just as you did in chapter 2, you convert the three datasets to CSV and save the data to S3. The following listing creates the datasets that you'll save to the same S3 folder as your original churn_data.csv file.

Listing 3.7 Converting the datasets to CSV and saving to S3

```
train_data = train_df.to_csv(None, header=False, index=False).encode()
val_data = val_df.to_csv(None, header=False, index=False).encode()
test_data = test_df.to_csv(None, header=True, index=False).encode()

with s3.open(f'{data_bucket}/{subfolder}/processed/train.csv', 'wb') as f:
    f.write(train_data)          ⟵  Writes the train.csv file to S3

with s3.open(f'{data_bucket}/{subfolder}/processed/val.csv', 'wb') as f:
    f.write(val_data)            ⟵  Writes the val.csv file to S3

with s3.open(f'{data_bucket}/{subfolder}/processed/test.csv', 'wb') as f:
    f.write(test_data)           ⟵  Writes the test.csv file to S3

train_input = sagemaker.s3_input(
    s3_data=f's3://{data_bucket}/{subfolder}/processed/train.csv',
    content_type='csv')
val_input = sagemaker.s3_input(
    s3_data=f's3://{data_bucket}/{subfolder}/processed/val.csv',
    content_type='csv')
```

Figure 3.7 shows the datasets you now have in S3.

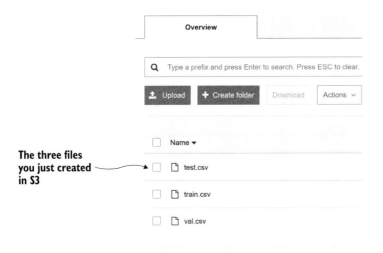

Figure 3.7 CSV file listing for the S3 folder

3.6.4 *Part 4: Training the model*

Now you train the model. In chapter 2, we didn't go into much detail about what is happening with the training. Now that you have a better understanding of XGBoost, we'll explain the process a bit more.

The interesting parts of the following listing (listing 3.8) are the `estimator` hyper-parameters. We'll discuss `max_depth` and `subsample` in a later chapter. For now, the hyperparameters of interest to us are

- *objective*—As in chapter 2, you set this hyperparameter to `binary:logistic`. You use this setting when your target variable is 1 or 0. If your target variable is a multiclass variable or a continuous variable, then you use other settings, as we'll discuss in later chapters.

- *eval_metric*—The evaluation metric you are optimizing for. The metric argument `auc` stands for area under the curve, as discussed by Richie earlier in the chapter.

- *num_round*—How many times you want to let the machine learning model run through the training data (the number of rounds). With each loop through the data, the function gets better at separating the dark circles from the light circles, for example (to refer back to the explanation of machine learning in chapter 1). After a while though, the model gets too good; it begins to find patterns in the test data that are not reflected in the real world. This is called *overfitting*. The larger the number of rounds, the more likely you are to be overfitting. To avoid this, you set early stopping rounds.

- *early_stopping_rounds*—The number of rounds where the algorithm fails to improve.

- *scale_pos_weight*—The scale positive weight is used with imbalanced datasets to make sure the model puts enough emphasis on correctly predicting rare classes during training. In the current dataset, about 1 in 17 customers will churn. So we set `scale_pos_weight` to 17 to accommodate for this imbalance. This tells XGBoost to focus more on customers who actually churn rather than on happy customers who are still happy.

NOTE   If you have the time and interest, try retraining your model without setting `scale_pos_weight` and see what effect this has on your results.

Listing 3.8   Training the model

```
sess = sagemaker.Session()

container = sagemaker.amazon.amazon_estimator.get_image_uri(
        boto3.Session().region_name,
        'xgboost',
        'latest')

estimator = sagemaker.estimator.Estimator(
    container,
    role,
    train_instance_count=1,
    train_instance_type='ml.m5.large',      ⟵  Sets the type of server
    output_path= \                               that SageMaker uses
                                                 to run your model
```

```
            f's3://{data_bucket}/{subfolder}/output',        ◁──┐  Stores the output of the
        sagemaker_session=sess)                                 │  model at this location in S3

        estimator.set_hyperparameters(                   ┌── Binary logistic objective
            max_depth=3,                                 │   hyperparameter
            subsample=0.7,
            objective='binary:logistic',    ◁────┐
            eval_metric='auc',              ◁──── ├── Area under the curve (AUC)
            num_round=100,                        │   evaluation metric hyperparameter
            early_stopping_rounds=10,       ◁──┐
            scale_pos_weight=17)               │  Early stopping rounds
                                               │  hyperparameter
        estimator.fit({'train': train_input, 'validation': val_input})
```

Number of rounds hyperparameter

Scale positive weight hyperparameter

When you ran this cell in the current chapter (and in chapter 2), you saw a number of rows of red notifications pop up in the notebook. We passed over this without comment, but these actually contain some interesting information. In particular, you can see if the model is overfitting by looking at this data.

> ### Richie's explanation of overfitting
> We touched on overfitting earlier in the XGBoost explanation. *Overfitting* is the process of building a model that maps too closely or exactly to the provided training data and fails to predict unseen data as accurately or reliably. This is also sometimes known as *a model that does not generalize well*. Unseen data includes test data, validation data, and data that can be provided to our endpoint in production.

When you run the training, the model does a couple of things in each round of training. First, it trains, and second, it validates. The red notifications that you see are the result of that validation process. As you read through the notifications, you can see that the validation score improves for the first 48 rounds and then starts getting worse.

What you are seeing is *overfitting*. The algorithm is improving at building a function that separates the dark circles from the light circles in the training set (as in chapter 1), but it is getting worse at doing it in the validation dataset. This means the model is starting to pick up patterns in the test data that do not exist in the real world (or at least in our validation dataset).

One of the great features in XGBoost is that it deftly handles overfitting for you. The `early_stopping_rounds` hyperparameter in listing 3.8 stops the training when there's no improvement in the past 10 rounds.

The output shown in listing 3.9 is taken from the output of the Train the Model cell in the notebook. You can see that round 15 had an AUC of 0.976057 and that round 16 had an AUC of 0.975683, and that neither of these is better than the previous best of 0.980493 from round 6. Because we set `early_stopping_rounds=10`, the training stops at round 16, which is 10 rounds past the best result in round 6.

Listing 3.9   Training rounds output

```
[15]#011train-auc:0.98571#011validation-auc:0.976057
[16]#011train-auc:0.986562#011validation-auc:0.975683
Stopping. Best iteration:
[6]#011train-auc:0.97752#011validation-auc:0.980493
```

3.6.5   *Part 5: Hosting the model*

Now that you have a trained model, you can host it on SageMaker so it is ready to make decisions (listing 3.10). We've covered a lot of ground in this chapter, so we'll delve into how the hosting works in a subsequent chapter. For now, just know that it is setting up a server that receives data and returns decisions.

Listing 3.10   Hosting the model

```
endpoint_name = 'customer-churn'

try:
    sess.delete_endpoint(
        sagemaker.predictor.RealTimePredictor(
            endpoint=endpoint_name).endpoint)
    print(
        'Warning: Existing endpoint deleted to make way for new endpoint.')
except:
    pass

predictor = estimator.deploy(initial_instance_count=1,     ⟵  Indicates the server
                instance_type='ml.t2.medium',                  type (in this case, an
                endpoint_name=endpoint_name)                    ml.t2.medium server)

from sagemaker.predictor import csv_serializer, json_serializer
predictor.content_type = 'text/csv'
predictor.serializer = csv_serializer
predictor.deserializer = None
```

3.6.6   *Part 6: Testing the model*

Now that the endpoint is set up and hosted, you can start making decisions. Start by running your test data through the system to see how the model works on data it hasn't seen before.

The first three lines in listing 3.11 create a function that returns 1 if the customer is more likely to churn and 0 if they are less likely to churn. The next two lines open the test CSV file you created in listing 3.7. And the last two lines apply the get_prediction function to every row in the test dataset to display the data.

Listing 3.11   Making predictions using the test data

```
def get_prediction(row):
    prob = float(predictor.predict(row[1:]).decode('utf-8'))
    return 1 if prob > 0.5 else 0     ⟵  Returns a value between 0 and 1
```

```
with s3.open(f'{data_bucket}/{subfolder}/processed/test.csv') as f:
    test_data = pd.read_csv(f)

test_data['decison'] = test_data.apply(get_prediction, axis=1)
test_data.set_index('decision', inplace=True)
test_data[:10]
```

In your results, you want to only show a 1 or 0. If the prediction is greater than 0.5 (if prob > 0.5), get_prediction sets the prediction as 1. Otherwise, it sets the prediction as 0.

The results look pretty good (table 3.6). Every row that has a 1 in the churn column also has a 1 in the decision column. There are some rows with a 1 in the decision column and a 0 in the churn column, which means Carlos is going to call them even though they are not at risk of churning. But this is acceptable to Carlos. Far better to call a customer that's not going to churn than to not call a customer that will churn.

Table 3.6 Results of the test

decision	churned	total_ spend	week_ minus_4	week_ minus_3	week_ minus_2	last_ week	4-3_ delta	3-2_ delta	2-1_ delta
0	0	17175.67	1.47	0.61	1.86	1.53	0.86	−1.25	0.33
0	0	68881.33	0.82	2.26	1.59	1.72	−1.44	0.67	-0.13
...	...	...	...	...	...	...	...	...	...
1	1	71528.99	2.48	1.36	0.09	1.24	1.12	1.27	−1.15

To see how the model performs overall, you can look at how many customers churned in the test dataset compared to how many Carlos would have called. To do this, you use the value_counts function as shown in the next listing.

Listing 3.12 Checking the predictions made using the test data

```
print(test_data['churned'].value_counts())          ◁── Counts the number of
                                                          customers who churned
print(test_data['prediction'].value_counts())       ◁── Counts the number of
                                                          customers who did not churn
print(
    metrics.accuracy_score(
        test_data['churned'],
        test_data['prediction']))    ◁── Calculates the accuracy of
                                          the prediction
```

The value_counts function shows that Carlos would have called 33 customers and that, if he did nothing, 17 would have churned. But this isn't very helpful for two reasons:

- What this tells us is that 94.67% of our predictions are correct, but that's not as good as it sounds because only about 6% of Carlos's customers churned. If we were to guess that none of our customers churned, we would be 94% accurate.
- It doesn't tell us how many of those he called would have churned.

For this, you need to create a confusion matrix:

```
0    283
1     17
Name: churned, dtype: int64
0    267
1     33
Name: prediction, dtype: int64
0.94.67
```

A confusion matrix is one of the most confusingly named terms in machine learning. But, because it is also one of the most helpful tools in understanding the performance of a model, we'll cover it here.

Although the term is confusing, creating a confusion matrix is easy. You use an sklearn function as shown in the next listing.

Listing 3.13 Creating the confusion matrix

```
print(
    metrics.confusion_matrix(          ◁─┐  Creates the
        test_data['churned'],             │  confusion matrix
        test_data['prediction']))
```

A *confusion matrix* is a table containing an equal number of rows and columns. The number of rows and columns corresponds to the number of possible values (classes) for the target variable. In Carlos's dataset, the target variable could be a 0 or a 1, so the confusion matrix has two rows and two columns. In a more general sense though, the rows of the matrix represent the actual class, and the columns represent the predicted class. (Note: Wikipedia currently has rows and columns reversed to this explanation; however, our description is the way the `sklearn.confusion_matrix` function works.)

In the following output, the first row represents happy customers (0) and the second row represents churns (1). The left column shows predicted happy customers, and the right column displays predicted churns. For Carlos, the right column also shows how many customers he called. You can see that Carlos called 16 customers who did not churn and 17 customers who did churn.

```
[[267   16]
 [  0   17]]
```

Importantly, the 0 at the bottom left shows how many customers who churned were predicted not to churn and that he did not call. To Carlos's great satisfaction, that number is 0.

> ## Richie's note on interpretable machine learning
>
> Throughout this book, we focus on providing examples of business problems that can be solved by machine learning using one of several algorithms. We also attempt to explain in high-level terms how these algorithms work. Generally, we use fairly simple metrics, such as accuracy, to indicate whether a model is working or not. But what if you were asked to explain why your model worked?
>
> Which of your features really matter most in determining whether the model works, and why? For example, is the model biased in ways that can harm minority groups in your customer base or workforce? Questions like this are becoming increasingly prevalent, particularly due to the widespread use of neural networks, which are particularly opaque.
>
> One advantage of XGBoost over neural networks (that we have not previously touched on) is that XGBoost supports the examination of feature importances to help address the explainability issue. At the time of writing, Amazon does not support this directly in the SageMaker XGBoost API; however, the model is stored on S3 as an archive named model.tar.gz. By accessing this file, we can view feature importances. The following listing provides sample code on how to do this.

Listing 3.14 Sample code used to access SageMaker's XGBoost model.tar.gz

```
model_path = f'{estimator.output_path}/\
{estimator._current_job_name}/output/model.tar.gz'
s3.get(model_path, 'xgb_tar.gz')
with tarfile.open('xgb_tar.gz') as tar:
    with tar.extractfile('xgboost-model') as m:S
        xgb_model = pickle.load(m)

xgb_scores = xgb_model.get_score()
print(xgb_scores)
```

Note that we do not include this code in the notebook as it is beyond the scope of what we want to cover here. But for those of you who want to dive deeper, you can do so using this code, or for more details, see the XGBoost documentation at

https://xgboost.readthedocs.io/en/latest/python/python_api.html.

3.7 Deleting the endpoint and shutting down your notebook instance

It is important that you shut down your notebook instance and delete your endpoint. We don't want you to get charged for SageMaker services that you're not using.

3.7.1 Deleting the endpoint

Appendix D describes how to shut down your notebook instance and delete your endpoint using the SageMaker console, or you can do that with the code in the next listing.

> **Listing 3.15   Deleting the notebook**

```
# Remove the endpoint (optional)
# Comment out this cell if you want the endpoint to persist after Run All
sess.delete_endpoint(text_classifier.endpoint)
```

To delete the endpoint, uncomment the code in the listing, then click Ctrl+Enter↵ to run the code in the cell.

3.7.2 *Shutting down the notebook instance*

To shut down the notebook, go back to your browser tab where you have SageMaker open. Click the Notebook Instances menu item to view all of your notebook instances. Select the radio button next to the notebook instance name, as shown in figure 3.8, then click Stop on the Actions menu. It will take a couple of minutes to shut down.

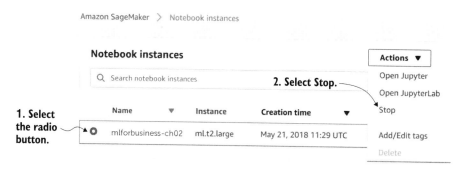

Figure 3.8   Shutting down the notebook

3.8   *Checking to make sure the endpoint is deleted*

If you didn't delete the endpoint using the notebook (or if you just want to make sure it's deleted), you can do this from the SageMaker console. To delete the endpoint, click the radio button to the left of the endpoint name, then click the Actions menu item and click Delete in the menu that appears.

   When you have successfully deleted the endpoint, you will no longer incur AWS charges for it. You can confirm that all of your endpoints have been deleted when you see the text "There are currently no resources" displayed at the bottom of the End-points page (figure 3.9).

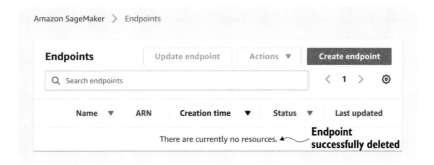

Figure 3.9   Verifying that you have successfully deleted the endpoint

Summary

- You created a machine learning model to determine which customers to call because they are at risk of taking their business to a competitor.
- XGBoost is a gradient-boosting, machine learning model that uses an ensemble of different approaches to improve the effectiveness of its learning.
- Stratify is one technique to help you handle imbalanced datasets. It shuffles the deck as it builds the machine learning model, making sure that the train, validate, and test datasets contain similar ratios of target variables.
- A confusion matrix is one of the most confusingly named terms in machine learning, but it is also one of the most helpful tools in understanding the performance of a model.

Should an incident be escalated to your support team?

This chapter covers

- An overview of natural language processing (NLP)
- How to approach an NLP machine learning scenario
- How to prepare data for an NLP scenario
- SageMaker's text analytics engine, BlazingText
- How to interpret BlazingText results

Naomi heads up an IT team that handles customer support tickets for a number of companies. A customer sends a tweet to a Twitter account, and Naomi's team replies with a resolution or a request for further information. A large percentage of the tweets can be handled by sending links to information that helps customers resolve their issues. But about a quarter of the responses are to people who need more help than that. They need to feel they've been heard and tend to get very cranky if they don't. These are the customers that, with the right intervention, become the strongest advocates; with the wrong intervention, they become the loudest detractors. Naomi wants to know who these customers are as early as possible so that her support team can intervene in the right way.

She and her team have spent the past few years automating responses to the most common queries and manually escalating the queries that must be handled by a person. Naomi wants to build a triage system that reviews each request as it comes in to determine whether the response should be automatic or should be handed off to a person.

Fortunately for Naomi, she has a couple of years of historical tweets that her team has reviewed and decided whether they can be handled automatically or should be handled by a person. In this chapter, you'll take Naomi's historical data and use it to decide whether new tweets should be handled automatically or escalated to one of Naomi's team members.

4.1 What are you making decisions about?

As always, the first thing you want to look at is what you're making decisions about. In this chapter, the decision Naomi is making is, *should this tweet be escalated to a person?*

The approach that Naomi's team has taken over the past few years is to escalate tweets in which the customer appears frustrated. Her team did not apply any hard and fast rules when making this decision. They just had a feeling that the customer was frustrated so they escalated the tweet. In this chapter, you are going to build a machine learning model that learns how to identify frustration based on the tweets that Naomi's team has previously escalated.

4.2 The process flow

The process flow for this decision is shown in figure 4.1. It starts when a customer sends a tweet to the company's support account. Naomi's team reviews the tweet to

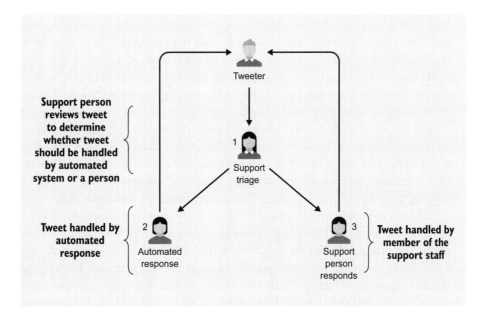

Figure 4.1 Tweet response workflow for Naomi's customer support tickets

determine whether they need to respond personally or whether it can be handled by their bot. The final step is a tweet response from either the bot or Naomi's team.

Naomi wants to replace the determination at step 1 of figure 4.1 with a machine learning application that can make a decision based on how frustrated the incoming tweet seems. This chapter shows you how to prepare this application.

4.3   *Preparing the dataset*

In the previous two chapters, you prepared a synthetic dataset from scratch. For this chapter, you are going to take a dataset of tweets sent to tech companies in 2017. The dataset is published by a company called Kaggle, which runs machine learning competitions.

Kaggle, competition, and public datasets

Kaggle is a fascinating company. Founded in 2010, Kaggle gamifies machine learning by pitting teams of data scientists against each other to solve machine learning problems for prize money. In mid-2017, shortly before being acquired by Google, Kaggle announced it had reached a milestone of one million registered competitors.

Even if you have no intention of competing in data science competitions, Kaggle is a good resource to become familiar with because it has public datasets that you can use in your machine learning training and work.

To determine what data is required to solve a particular problem, you need to focus on the objective you are pursuing and, in this case, think about the minimum data Naomi needs to achieve her objective. Once you have that, you can decide whether you can achieve her objective using only that data supplied, or you need to expand the data to allow Naomi to better achieve her objective.

As a reminder, Naomi's objective is to identify the tweets that should be handled by a person, based on her team's past history of escalating tweets. So Naomi's dataset should contain an incoming tweet and a flag indicating whether it was escalated or not.

The dataset we use in this chapter is based on a dataset uploaded to Kaggle by Stuart Axelbrooke from Thought Vector. (The original dataset can be viewed at https://www.kaggle.com/thoughtvector/customer-support-on-twitter/.) This dataset contains over 3 million tweets sent to customer support departments for several companies ranging from Apple and Amazon to British Airways and Southwest Air.

Like every dataset you'll find in your company, you can't just use this data as is. It needs to be formatted in a way that allows your machine learning algorithm do its thing. The original dataset on Kaggle contains both the original tweet and the response. In the scenario in this chapter, only the original tweet is relevant. To prepare the data for this chapter, we removed all the tweets except the original tweet and used the responses to label the original tweet as escalated or not escalated. The resulting dataset contains a tweet with that label and these columns:

- *tweet_id*—Uniquely identifies the tweet
- *author_id*—Uniquely identifies the author
- *created_at*—Shows the time of the tweet
- *in_reply_to*—Shows which company is being contacted
- *text*—Contains the text in the tweet
- *escalate*—Indicates whether the tweet was escalated or not

Table 4.1 shows the first three tweets in the dataset. Each of the tweets is to Sprint Care, the support team for the US phone company, Sprint. You can see that the first tweet ("and how do you propose we do that") was not escalated by Naomi's team. But the second tweet ("I have sent several private messages and no one is responding as usual") was escalated. Naomi's team let their automated response system handle the first tweet but escalated the second tweet to a member of her team for a personal response.

Table 4.1 Tweet dataset

tweet_id	author_id	created_at	in_reply_to	text	escalate
2	115712	Tue Oct 31 22:11 2017	sprintcare	@sprintcare and how do you propose we do that	False
3	115712	Tue Oct 31 22:08 2017	sprintcare	@sprintcare I have sent several private messages and no one is responding as usual	True
5	115712	Tue Oct 31 21:49 2017	sprintcare	@sprintcare I did.	False

In this chapter, you'll build a machine learning application to handle the task of whether to escalate the tweet. But this application will be a little different than the machine learning applications you built in previous chapters. In order to decide which tweets should be escalated, the machine learning application needs to know something about language and meaning, which you might think is pretty difficult to do. Fortunately, some very smart people have been working on this problem for a while. They call it *natural language processing*, or NLP.

4.4 NLP (natural language processing)

The goal of NLP is to be able to use computers to work with language as effectively as computers can work with numbers or variables. This is a hard problem because of the richness of language. (The previous sentence is a good example of the difficulty of this problem.) The term *rich* means something slightly different when referring to language than it does when referring to a person. And the sentence "Well, that's rich!" can mean the opposite of how rich is used in other contexts.

Scientists have worked on NLP since the advent of computing, but it has only been recently that they have made significant strides in this area. NLP originally focused on getting computers to understand the structure of each language. In English, a typical sentence has a subject, verb, and an object, such as this sentence: "Sam throws the ball"; whereas in Japanese, a sentence typically follows a subject, object, verb pattern. But the success of this approach was hampered by the mind-boggling number and variety of exceptions and slowed by the necessity to individually describe each different language. The same code you use for English NLP won't work for Japanese NLP.

The big breakthrough in NLP occurred in 2013 when NIPS published a paper on word vectors.[1] With this approach, you don't look at parts of the language at all! You just apply a mathematical algorithm to a bunch of text and work with the output of the algorithm. This has two advantages:

- It naturally handles exceptions and inconsistencies in a language.
- It is language-agnostic and can work with Japanese text as easily as it can work with English text.

In SageMaker, working with word vectors is as easy as working with the data you worked with in chapters 2 and 3. But there are a few decisions you need to make when configuring SageMaker that require you to have some appreciation of what is happening under the hood.

4.4.1   *Creating word vectors*

Just as you used the pandas function `get_dummies` in chapter 2 to convert categorical data (such as desk, keyboard, and mouse) to a wide dataset, the first step in creating a word vector is to convert all the words in your text into wide datasets. As an example, the word *queen* is represented by the dataset 0,1,0,0,0, as shown in figure 4.2. The word *queen* has 1 under it, while every other word in the row has a 0. This can be described as a *single dimensional vector.*

Using a single dimensional vector, you test for equality and nothing else. That is, you can determine whether the vector is equal to the word *queen*, and in figure 4.2, you can see that it is.

| King | Queen | Man | Woman | Princess |
| 0 | 1 | 0 | 0 | 0 |

Figure 4.2   Single dimensional vector testing for equality

---

[1] See "Distributed Representations of Words and Phrases and their Compositionality" by Tomas Mikolov et al. at https://papers.nips.cc/paper/5021-distributed-representations-of-words-and-phrases-and-their-compositionality.pdf.

Mikolov's breakthrough was the realization that *meaning* can be captured by a *multidimensional* vector with the representation of each word distributed across each dimension. Figure 4.3 shows conceptually how dimensions look in a vector. Each dimension can be thought of as a group of related words. In Mikolov's algorithm, these groups of related words don't have labels, but to show how meaning can emerge from multidimensional vectors, we have provided four labels on the left side of the figure: Royalty, Masculinity, Femininity, and Elderliness.

	King	Queen	Man	Woman	Princess
Royalty	0.99	0.99	0.02	0.02	0.98
Masculinity	0.99	0.05	0.99	0.01	0.02
Femininity	0.05	0.99	0.02	0.99	0.94
Elderliness	0.7	0.6	0.5	0.5	0.1

Figure 4.3 Multidimensional vectors capture meaning in languages.

Looking at the first dimension in figure 4.3, Royalty, you can see that the values in the King, Queen, and Princess columns are higher than the values in the Man and Woman columns; whereas, for Masculinity, the values in the King and Man columns are higher than in the others. From this you start to get the picture that a King is Masculine Royalty whereas a Queen is non-masculine Royalty. If you can imagine working your way through hundreds of vectors, you can see how meaning emerges.

Back to Naomi's problem, as each tweet comes in, the application breaks the tweet down into multidimensional vectors and compares it to the tweets labeled by Naomi's team. The application identifies which tweets in the training dataset have similar vectors. It then looks at the label of the trained tweets and assigns that label to the incoming tweet. For example, if an incoming tweet has the phrase "no one is responding as usual," the tweets in the training data with similar vectors would likely have been escalated, and so the incoming tweet would be escalated as well.

The magic of the mathematics behind word vectors is that it groups the words being defined. Each of these groups is a dimension in the vector. For example, in the tweet where the tweeter says "no one is responding as usual," the words *as usual* might be grouped into a dimension with other pairs of words such as *of course, yeah obviously,* and *a doy,* which indicate frustration.

The King/Queen, Man/Woman example is used regularly in the explanation of word vectors. Adrian Colyer's excellent blog, "the morning paper," discusses word vectors in more detail at https://blog.acolyer.org/?s=the+amazing+power+of+word+vectors. Figures 4.2 and 4.3 are based on figures from the first part of this article. If you are interested in exploring this topic further, the rest of Adrian's article is a good place to start.

4.4.2   *Deciding how many words to include in each group*

In order to work with vectors in SageMaker, the only decision you need to make is whether SageMaker should use single words, pairs of words, or word triplets when creating the groups. For example, if SageMaker uses the word pair *as usual,* it can get better results than if it uses the single word *as* and the single word *usual,* because the word pair expresses a different concept than do the individual words.

In our work, we normally use word pairs but have occasionally gotten better results from triplets. In one project where we were extracting and categorizing marketing terms, using triplets resulted in much higher accuracy, probably because marketing fluff is often expressed in word triplets such as *world class results, high powered engine,* and *fat burning machine.*

NLP uses the terms unigram, bigram, and trigram for single-, double-, and triple-word groups. Figures 4.4, 4.5, and 4.6 show examples of single-word (unigram), double-word (bigram), and triple-word (trigram) word groups, respectively.

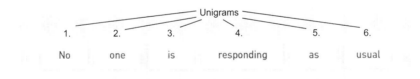

Figure 4.4   NLP defines single words as unigrams.

As figure 4.4 shows, *unigrams* are single words. Unigrams work well when word order is not important. For example, if you were creating word vectors for medical research, unigrams do a good job of identifying similar concepts.

As figure 4.5 shows, *bigrams* are pairs of words. Bigrams work well when word order is important, such as in sentiment analysis. The bigram *as usual* conveys frustration, but the unigrams *as* and *usual* do not.

As figure 4.6 shows, *trigrams* are groups of three words. In practice, we don't see much improvement in moving from bigrams to trigrams, but on occasion there can be. One project we worked on to identify marketing terms delivered significantly better results using trigrams, probably because the trigrams better captured the common

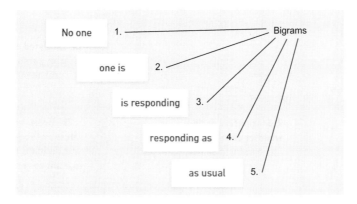

Figure 4.5   Pairs of words are known as bigrams.

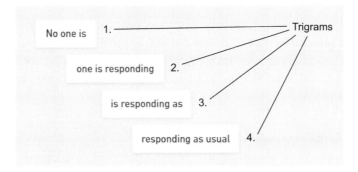

Figure 4.6   Words grouped into threes are trigrams.

pattern *hyperbole noun noun* (as in *greatest coffee maker*) and the pattern *hyperbole adjective noun* (as in *fastest diesel car*).

In our case study, the machine learning application will use an algorithm called *BlazingText*. This predicts whether a tweet should be escalated.

4.5   *What is BlazingText and how does it work?*

BlazingText is a version of an algorithm, called fastText, developed by researchers at Facebook in 2017. And fastText is a version of the algorithm developed by Google's own Mikolov and others. Figure 4.7 shows the workflow after BlazingText is put into use. In step 1, a tweet is sent by a person requiring support. In step 2, BlazingText decides whether the tweet should be escalated to a person for a response. In step 3, the tweet is escalated to a person (step 3a) or handled by a bot (step 3b).

In order for BlazingText to decide whether a tweet should be escalated, it needs to determine whether the person sending the tweet is feeling frustrated or not. To do this, BlazingText doesn't actually need to know whether the person is feeling frustrated

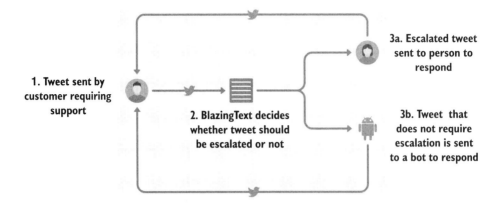

1. Tweet sent by customer requiring support

2. BlazingText decides whether tweet should be escalated or not

3a. Escalated tweet sent to person to respond

3b. Tweet that does not require escalation is sent to a bot to respond

Figure 4.7   The BlazingText workflow to determine whether a tweet should be escalated

or even understand what the tweet was about. It just needs to determine how similar the tweet is to other tweets that have been labeled as frustrated or not frustrated. With that as background, you are ready to start building the model. If you like, you can read more about BlazingText on Amazon's site at https://docs.aws.amazon.com/sagemaker/latest/dg/blazingtext.html.

Refresher on how SageMaker is structured

Now that you're getting comfortable with using Jupyter Notebook, it is a good time to review how SageMaker is structured. When you first set up SageMaker, you created a notebook instance, which is a server that AWS configures to run your notebooks. In appendix C, we instructed you to select a medium-sized server instance because it has enough grunt to do anything we cover in this book. As you work with larger datasets in your own work, you might need to use a larger server.

When you run your notebook for the case studies in this book, AWS creates two additional servers. The first is a temporary server that is used to train the machine learning model. The second server AWS creates is the endpoint server. This server stays up until you remove the endpoint. To delete the endpoint in SageMaker, click the radio button to the left of the endpoint name, then click the Actions menu item, and click Delete in the menu that appears.

4.6   *Getting ready to build the model*

Now that you have a deeper understanding of how BlazingText works, you'll set up another notebook in SageMaker and make some decisions. You are going to do the following (as you did in chapters 2 and 3):

1 Upload a dataset to S3
2 Set up a notebook on SageMaker

3 Upload the starting notebook

4 Run it against the data

TIP If you're jumping into the book at this chapter, you might want to visit the appendixes, which show you how to do the following:

- Appendix A: sign up for AWS, Amazon's web service
- Appendix B: set up S3, AWS's file storage service
- Appendix C: set up SageMaker

4.6.1 Uploading a dataset to S3

To set up your dataset for this chapter, you'll follow the same steps as you did in appendix B. You don't need to set up another bucket though. You can just go to the same bucket you created earlier. In our example, we called the bucket *mlforbusiness*, but your bucket will be called something different. When you go to your S3 account, you will see something like that shown in figure 4.8.

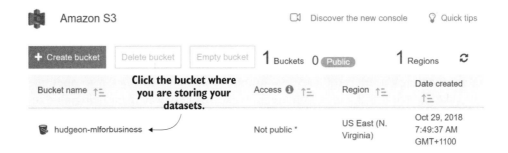

Figure 4.8 Viewing the list of buckets

Click this bucket to see the ch02 and ch03 folders you created in the previous chapters. For this chapter, you'll create a new folder called *ch04*. You do this by clicking Create Folder and following the prompts to create a new folder.

Once you've created the folder, you are returned to the folder list inside your bucket. There you'll see you now have a folder called ch04.

Now that you have the ch04 folder set up in your bucket, you can upload your data file and start setting up the decision-making model in SageMaker. To do so, click the folder and download the data file at this link:

https://s3.amazonaws.com/mlforbusiness/ch04/inbound.csv.

Then upload the CSV file into the ch04 folder by clicking Upload. Now you're ready to set up the notebook instance.

4.6.2   *Setting up a notebook on SageMaker*

Like you did for chapters 2 and 3, you'll set up a notebook on SageMaker. If you skipped chapters 2 and 3, follow the instructions in appendix C on how to set up SageMaker.

When you go to SageMaker, you'll see your notebook instances. The notebook instance you created for chapters 2 and 3 (or that you've just created by following the instructions in appendix C) will either say Open or Start. If it says Start, click the Start link and wait a couple of minutes for SageMaker to start. Once it displays Open Jupyter, select that link to open your notebook list.

Once it opens, create a new folder for chapter 4 by clicking New and selecting Folder at the bottom of the dropdown list. This creates a new folder called Untitled Folder. To rename the folder, tick the checkbox next to Untitled Folder, and you will see the Rename button appear. Click Rename and change the name to ch04. Click the ch04 folder, and you will see an empty notebook list.

Just as we already prepared the CSV data you uploaded to S3, we've already prepared the Jupyter notebook you'll now use. You can download it to your computer by navigating to this URL:

https://s3.amazonaws.com/mlforbusiness/ch04/customer_support.ipynb.

Click Upload to upload the customer_support.ipynb notebook to the folder. After uploading the file, you'll see the notebook in your list. Click it to open it. Now, just like in chapters 2 and 3, you are a few keystrokes away from being able to run your machine learning model.

4.7   *Building the model*

As in chapters 2 and 3, you will go through the code in six parts:

- Load and examine the data.
- Get the data into the right shape.
- Create training and validation datasets (there's no need for a test dataset in this example).
- Train the machine learning model.
- Host the machine learning model.
- Test the model and use it to make decisions

Refresher on running code in Jupyter notebooks

SageMaker uses Jupyter Notebook as its interface. Jupyter Notebook is an open-source data science application that allows you to mix code with text. As shown in the figure, the code sections of a Jupyter notebook have a grey background, and the text sections have a white background.

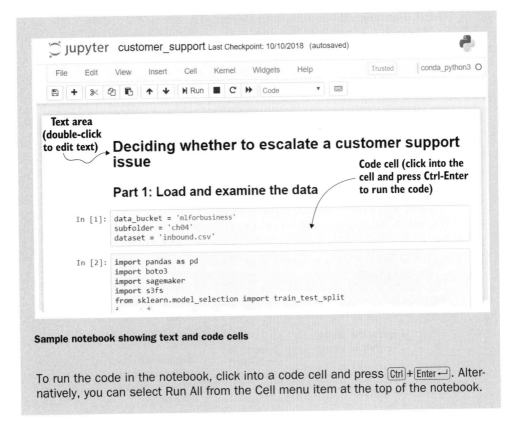

Sample notebook showing text and code cells

To run the code in the notebook, click into a code cell and press Ctrl+Enter⏎. Alternatively, you can select Run All from the Cell menu item at the top of the notebook.

4.7.1 Part 1: Loading and examining the data

As in the previous two chapters, the first step is to say where you are storing the data. To do that, you need to change 'mlforbusiness' to the name of the bucket you created when you uploaded the data and rename its subfolder to the name of the subfolder on S3 where you store the data (listing 4.1).

If you named the S3 folder ch04, then you don't need to change the name of the folder. If you kept the name of the CSV file that you uploaded earlier in the chapter, then you don't need to change the inbound.csv line of code. If you changed the name of the CSV file, then update inbound.csv to the name you changed it to. And, as always, to run the code in the notebook cell, click the cell and press Ctrl+Enter⏎.

Listing 4.1 Say where you are storing the data

```
data_bucket = 'mlforbusiness'
subfolder = 'ch04'
dataset = 'inbound.csv'
```

S3 bucket where the data is stored

Subfolder of the S3 bucket where the data is stored

Dataset that's used to train and test the model

The Python modules and libraries imported in listing 4.2 are the same as the import code in chapters 2 and 3, with the exception of lines 6, 7, and 8. These lines import Python's json module. This module is used to work with data structured in *JSON* format (a structured mark-up language for describing data). Lines 6 and 7 import Python's json and csv modules. These two formats define the data.

The next new library you import is NLTK (https://www.nltk.org/). This is a commonly used library for getting text ready to use in a machine learning model. In this chapter, you will use NLTK to *tokenize* words. Tokenizing text involves splitting the text and stripping out those things that make it harder for the machine learning model to do what it needs to do.

In this chapter, you use the standard word_tokenize function that splits text into words in a way that consistently handles abbreviations and other anomalies. Blazing-Text often works better when you don't spend a lot of time preprocessing the text, so this is all you'll do to prepare each tweet (in addition to applying the labeling, of course, which you'll do in listing 4.8). To run the code, click in the notebook cell and press Ctrl+Enter↵.

Listing 4.2   Importing the modules

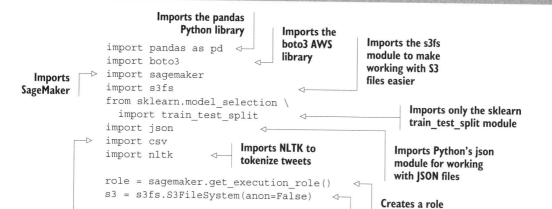

You've worked with CSV files throughout the book. JSON is a type of structured markup language similar to XML but simpler to work with. The following listing shows an example of an invoice described in JSON format.

Listing 4.3   Sample JSON format

```
{
  "Invoice": {
    "Header": {
      "Invoice Number": "INV1234833",
      "Invoice Date": "2018-11-01"
    },
```

```
   "Lines": [
     {
       "Description": "Punnet of strawberries",
       "Qty": 6,
       "Unit Price": 3
     },
     {
       "Description": "Punnet of blueberries",
       "Qty": 6,
       "Unit Price": 4
     }
   ]
 }
}
```

Next, you'll load and view the data. The dataset you are loading has a half-million rows but loads in only a few seconds, even on the medium-sized server we are using in our SageMaker instance. To time and display how long the code in a cell takes to run, you can include the line %%time in the cell, as shown in the following listing.

Listing 4.4 Loading and viewing the data

```
%%time          ◁──┐ Displays how long it takes
                      to run the code in the cell
df = pd.read_csv(
    f's3://{data_bucket}/{subfolder}/{dataset}')   ◁──┐ Reads the S3 inbound.csv
display(df.head())        ◁──┐ Displays the top five    dataset in listing 4.1
                              rows of the DataFrame
```

Table 4.2 shows the output of running display(df.head()). Note that using the .head() function on your DataFrame displays only the top five rows.

Table 4.2 The top five rows in the tweet dataset

row_id	tweet_id	author_id	created_at	in_reply_to	text	escalate
0	2	115712	Tue Oct 31 22:11 2017	sprintcare	@sprintcare and how do you propose we do that	False
1	3	115712	Tue Oct 31 22:08 2017	sprintcare	@sprintcare I have sent several private messag...	True
2	5	115712	Tue Oct 31 21:49 2017	sprintcare	@sprintcare I did.	False
3	16	115713	Tue Oct 31 20:00:43 +0000 2017	sprintcare	@sprintcare Since I signed up with you....Sinc...	False
4	22	115716	Tue Oct 31 22:16:48 +0000 2017	Ask_Spectrum	@Ask_Spectrum Would you like me to email you a...	False

You can see from the first five tweets that only one was escalated. At this point, we don't know if that is expected or unexpected. Listing 4.5 shows how many rows are in the dataset and how many were escalated or not. To get this information, you run the pandas `shape` and `value_counts` functions.

Listing 4.5 Showing the number of escalated tweets in the dataset

```
print(f'Number of rows in dataset: {df.shape[0]}')      ◁── Displays the number of
print(df['escalated'].value_counts())    ◁──             rows in the dataset

        Displays the number of rows where a tweet was escalated
        and the number of rows where the tweet was not escalated
```

The next listing shows the output from the code in listing 4.5.

Listing 4.6 Total number of tweets and the number of escalated tweets

```
Number of rows in dataset: 520793
False    417800
True     102993
Name: escalate, dtype: int64
```

Out of the dataset of more than 500,000 tweets, just over 100,000 were manually escalated. If Naomi can have a machine learning algorithm read and escalate tweets, then her team will only have to read 20% of the tweets they currently review.

4.7.2 *Part 2: Getting the data into the right shape*

Now that you can see your dataset in the notebook, you can start working with it. First, you create train and validation data for the machine learning model. As in the previous two chapters, you use sklearn's `train_test_split` function to create the datasets. With BlazingText, you can see the accuracy of the model in the logs as it is validating the model, so there is no need to create a test dataset.

Listing 4.7 Creating train and validate datasets

```
train_df, val_df, _, _ = train_test_split(
    df,
    df['escalate'],          Creates the train and
    test_size=0.2,           validation datasets
    random_state=0)    ◁──
print(f'{train_df.shape[0]} rows in training data')    ◁──   Displays the
print(f'{val_df.shape[0]} rows in validation data')    ◁──   number of rows in
                                                              the training data
        Displays the number of rows in the validation data
```

Unlike the XGBoost algorithm that we worked with in previous chapters, BlazingText *cannot* work directly with CSV data. It needs the data in a different format, which you will do in listings 4.8 through 4.10.

Formatting data for BlazingText

BlazingText requires a label in the format __label__0 for a tweet that was not esca-lated and __label__1 for a tweet that was escalated. The label is then followed by the tokenized text of the tweet. *Tokenizing* is the process of taking text and breaking it into parts that are linguistically meaningful. This is a difficult task to perform but, fortunately for you, the hard work is handled by the NLTK library.

Listing 4.8 defines two functions. The first function, preprocess, takes a DataFrame containing either the validation or training datasets you created in listing 4.7, turns it into a list, and then for each row in the list, calls the second function transform_instance to convert the row to the format __label__0 or __label__1, followed by the text of the tweet. To run the preprocess function on the validation data, you call the function on the val_df DataFrame you created in listing 4.8.

You'll run this code first on the validation dataset and then on the training dataset. The validation dataset has 100,000 rows, and this cell will take about 30 seconds to run on that data. The training dataset has 400,000 rows and will take about 2 minutes to run. Most of the time is spent converting the dataset to a DataFrame and back again. This is fine for a dataset of a half-million rows. If you are working with a dataset with millions of rows, you'll need to start working directly with the csv module rather than using pandas. To learn more about the cvs module, visit https://docs.python.org/3/library/csv.html.

Listing 4.8 Transforming each row to the format used by BlazingText

```
def preprocess(df):                            ← Turns the DataFrame into a list
    all_rows = df.values.tolist()
    transformed_rows = list(                    ← Applies transform_instance
      map(transform_instance, all_rows))           to every row in the list
    transformed_df = pd.DataFrame(transformed_rows)   ← Turns it back into
    return transformed_df                              a DataFrame
```
Returns the DataFrame

```
def transform_instance(row):                    ← Creates an empty list that holds
    cur_row = []                                   the label followed by each of
    label = '__label__1' if row[5] == True \       the words in the tweet
        else '__label__0'                       ← Creates a label with the
    cur_row.append(label)                          value of 1 if escalated
    cur_row.extend(                                or 0 if not
        nltk.word_tokenize(row[4].lower()))     ← Sets the first element
    return cur_row                                 of the cur_row list as
                                                   the label
```
Returns the row

```
transformed_validation_rows = preprocess(val_df)
display(transformed_validation_rows.head())     ← Sets each of the
```
Runs the preprocess function   *Displays the first five rows of data*   Sets each of the words as a separate element in the list

The data shown in table 4.3 shows the first few rows of data in the format BlazingText requires. You can see that the first two tweets were labeled 1 (escalate), and the third row is labeled 0 (don't escalate).

Table 4.3   Validation data for Naomi's tweets

Labeled preprocessed data
__label__1 @ 115990 no joke … this is one of the worst customer experiences i have had verizon . maybe time for @ 115714 @ 115911 @ att ? https://t.co/vqmlkvvwxe
__label__1 @ amazonhelp neither man seems to know how to deliver a package . that is their entire job ! both should lose their jobs immediately.
__label__0 @ xboxsupport yes i see nothing about resolutions or what size videos is exported only quality i have a 34 '' ultrawide monitor 21:9 2560x1080 what i need https://t.co/apvwd1dlq8

Now that you have the text in the format BlazingText can work with, and that text is sitting in a DataFrame, you can use the pandas `to_csv` to store the data on S3 so you can load it into the BlazingText algorithm. The code in the following listing writes out the validation data to S3.

Listing 4.9   Transforming the data for BlazingText

```
s3_validation_data = f's3://{data_bucket}/\
{subfolder}/processed/validation.csv'

data = transformed_validation_rows.to_csv(
        header=False,
        index=False,
        quoting=csv.QUOTE_NONE,
        sep='|',
        escapechar='^').encode()
with s3.open(s3_validation_data, 'wb') as f:
    f.write(data)
```

Next, you'll preprocess the training data by calling the `preprocess` function on the train_df DataFrame you created in listing 4.7.

Listing 4.10   Preprocessing and writing training data

```
%%time
transformed_train_rows = preprocess(train_df)
display(transformed_train_rows.head())

s3_train_data = f's3://{data_bucket}/{subfolder}/processed/train.csv'

data = transformed_train_rows.to_csv(
        header=False,
        index=False,
        quoting=csv.QUOTE_NONE,
        sep='|',
```

```
        escapechar='^').encode()
with s3.open(s3_train_data, 'wb') as f:
    f.write(data)
```

With that, the train and test datasets are saved to S3 in a format ready for use in the model. The next section takes you though the process of getting the data into Sage-Maker so it's ready to kick off the training process.

4.7.3 Part 3: Creating training and validation datasets

Now that you have your data in a format that BlazingText can work with, you can create the training and validation datasets.

Listing 4.11 Creating the training, validation, and test datasets

```
%%time

train_data = sagemaker.session.s3_input(
    s3_train_data,
    distribution='FullyReplicated',              Creates the
    content_type='text/plain',                   train_data dataset
    s3_data_type='S3Prefix')          ◁─┘
validation_data = sagemaker.session.s3_input(
    s3_validation_data,
    distribution='FullyReplicated',
    content_type='text/plain',            Creates the
    s3_data_type='S3Prefix')          ◁─┘ validation_data dataset
```

With that, the data is in a SageMaker session, and you are ready to start training the model.

4.7.4 Part 4: Training the model

Now that you have prepared the data, you can start training the model. This involves three steps:

- Setting up a container
- Setting the hyperparameters for the model
- Fitting the model

The hyperparameters are the interesting part of this code:

- *epochs*—Similar to the num_round parameter for XGBoost in chapters 2 and 3, it specifies how many passes BlazingText performs over the training data. We chose the value of 10 after trying lower values and seeing that more epochs were required. Depending on how the results converge or begin overfitting, you might need to shift this value up or down.
- *vector_dim*—Specifies the dimension of the word vectors that the algorithm learns; default is 100. We set this to 10 because experience has shown that a value as low as 10 is usually still effective and consumes less server time.

- *early_stopping*—Similar to early stopping in XGBoost. The number of epochs can be set to a high value, and early stopping ensures that the training finishes when it stops, improving against the validation dataset.
- *patience*—Sets how many epochs should pass without improvement before early stopping kicks in.
- *min_epochs*—Sets a minimum number of epochs that will be performed even if there is no improvement and the patience threshold is reached.
- *word_ngrams*—N-grams were discussed in figures 4.4, 4.5, and 4.6 earlier in this chapter. Briefly, unigrams are single words, bigrams are pairs of words, and trigrams are groups of three words.

In listing 4.12, the first line sets up a container to run the model. A *container* is just the server that runs the model. The next group of lines configures the server. The set_hyperparameters function sets the hyperparameters for the model. The final line in the next listing kicks off the training of the model.

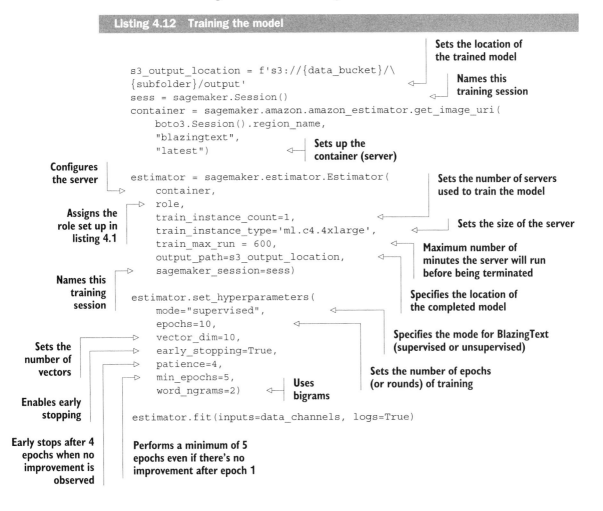

Listing 4.12   Training the model

```
s3_output_location = f's3://{data_bucket}/\
{subfolder}/output'
sess = sagemaker.Session()
container = sagemaker.amazon.amazon_estimator.get_image_uri(
    boto3.Session().region_name,
    "blazingtext",
    "latest")

estimator = sagemaker.estimator.Estimator(
    container,
    role,
    train_instance_count=1,
    train_instance_type='ml.c4.4xlarge',
    train_max_run = 600,
    output_path=s3_output_location,
    sagemaker_session=sess)

estimator.set_hyperparameters(
    mode="supervised",
    epochs=10,
    vector_dim=10,
    early_stopping=True,
    patience=4,
    min_epochs=5,
    word_ngrams=2)

estimator.fit(inputs=data_channels, logs=True)
```

Sets the location of the trained model

Names this training session

Sets up the container (server)

Configures the server

Sets the number of servers used to train the model

Assigns the role set up in listing 4.1

Sets the size of the server

Maximum number of minutes the server will run before being terminated

Names this training session

Specifies the location of the completed model

Sets the number of vectors

Specifies the mode for BlazingText (supervised or unsupervised)

Enables early stopping

Sets the number of epochs (or rounds) of training

Early stops after 4 epochs when no improvement is observed

Uses bigrams

Performs a minimum of 5 epochs even if there's no improvement after epoch 1

NOTE BlazingText can run in supervised or unsupervised mode. Because this chapter uses labeled text, we operate in supervised mode.

When you ran this cell in the current chapter (and in chapters 2 and 3), you saw a number of rows with red notifications pop up in the notebook. The red notifications that appear when you run this cell look very different from the XGBoost notifications.

Each type of machine learning model provides information that is relevant to understanding how the algorithm is progressing. For the purposes of this book, the most important information comes at the end of the notifications: the training and validation accuracy scores, which display when the training finishes. The model in the following listing shows a training accuracy of over 98.88% and a validation accuracy of 92.28%. Each epoch is described by the validation accuracy.

Listing 4.13 Training rounds output

```
...
-------------- End of epoch: 9
Using 16 threads for prediction!
Validation accuracy: 0.922196
Validation accuracy improved! Storing best weights...
##### Alpha: 0.0005  Progress: 98.95%  Million Words/sec: 26.89 #####
-------------- End of epoch: 10
Using 16 threads for prediction!
Validation accuracy: 0.922455
Validation accuracy improved! Storing best weights...
##### Alpha: 0.0000  Progress: 100.00%  Million Words/sec: 25.78 #####
Training finished.
Average throughput in Million words/sec: 26.64
Total training time in seconds: 3.40
                                              Training
                                              accuracy
#train_accuracy: 0.9888                    ◁─┘
Number of train examples: 416634
                                              Validation
                                              accuracy
#validation_accuracy: 0.9228               ◁─┘
Number of validation examples: 104159

2018-10-07 06:56:20 Uploading - Uploading generated training model
2018-10-07 06:56:35 Completed - Training job completed
Billable seconds: 49
```

4.7.5   *Part 5: Hosting the model*

Now that you have a trained model, you can host it on SageMaker so it is ready to make decisions (listings 4.14 and 4.15). We've covered a lot of ground in this chapter, so we'll delve into how the hosting works in a subsequent chapter. For now, just know that it is setting up a server that receives data and returns decisions.

Listing 4.14   Hosting the model

```
endpoint_name = 'customer-support'          ◄──   In order to not create duplicate
try:                                              endpoints, name your endpoint.
    sess.delete_endpoint(
        sagemaker.predictor.RealTimePredictor(          Deletes existing endpoint
            endpoint=endpoint_name).endpoint)   ◄──┤   of that name
    print(
        'Warning: Existing endpoint deleted to make way for new endpoint.')
except:
    pass
```

Next, in listing 4.15, you create and deploy the endpoint. SageMaker is highly scalable and can handle very large datasets. For the datasets we use in this book, you only need a t2.medium machine to host your endpoint.

Listing 4.15   Creating a new endpoint to host the model

```
print('Deploying new endpoint...')
text_classifier = estimator.deploy(
    initial_instance_count = 1,
    instance_type = 'ml.t2.medium',            Creates a new
    endpoint_name=endpoint_name)       ◄──┘    endpoint
```

4.7.6   *Part 6: Testing the model*

Now that the endpoint is set up and hosted, you can start making decisions. In listing 4.16, you set a sample tweet, tokenize it, and then make a prediction.

Try changing the text in the first line and clicking Ctrl+Enter⏎ to test different tweets. For example, changing the text *disappointed* to *happy* or *ambivalent* changes the label from 1 to 0. This means that the tweet "Help me I'm very disappointed" will be escalated, but the tweets "Help me I'm very happy" and "Help me I'm very ambivalent" will not be escalated.

Listing 4.16   Making predictions using the test data

```
                  tweet = "Help me I'm very disappointed!"
Sample   ┌─▷                                                  Creates a payload in a format that
tweet    │                                                    the text_classifier you created in
         │        tokenized_tweet = \                         listing 4.15 can interpret
Tokenizes│            [' '.join(nltk.word_tokenize(tweet))]
the   ┌─▷         payload = {"instances" : tokenized_tweet}   ◄──
tweets│           response = \                                         Gets the
                      text_classifier.predict(json.dumps(payload))  ◄── response
                  escalate = pd.read_json(response)      ◄──
                  escalate        ◄──                    Converts the response to
                          └──  Displays the decision     a pandas DataFrame
```

4.8 Deleting the endpoint and shutting down your notebook instance

It is important that you shut down your notebook instance and delete your endpoint. We don't want you to get charged for SageMaker services that you're not using.

4.8.1 Deleting the endpoint

Appendix D describes how to shut down your notebook instance and delete your endpoint using the SageMaker console, or you can do that with the code in the next listing.

Listing 4.17 Deleting the notebook

```
# Remove the endpoint (optional)
# Comment out this cell if you want the endpoint to persist after Run All
sess.delete_endpoint(text_classifier.endpoint)
```

To delete the endpoint, uncomment the code in the listing, then click Ctrl+Enter⏎ to run the code in the cell.

4.8.2 Shutting down the notebook instance

To shut down the notebook, go back to your browser tab where you have SageMaker open. Click the Notebook Instances menu item to view all of your notebook instances. Select the radio button next to the notebook instance name as shown in figure 4.9, then click Stop on the Actions menu. It takes a couple of minutes to shut down.

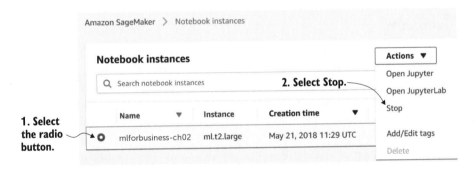

Figure 4.9   Shutting down the notebook

4.9 Checking to make sure the endpoint is deleted

If you didn't delete the endpoint using the notebook (or if you just want to make sure it is deleted), you can do this from the SageMaker console. To delete the endpoint, click the radio button to the left of the endpoint name, then click the Actions menu item and click Delete in the menu that appears.

When you have successfully deleted the endpoint, you will no longer incur AWS charges for it. You can confirm that all of your endpoints have been deleted when you

see the text "There are currently no resources" displayed at the bottom of the Endpoints page (figure 4.10).

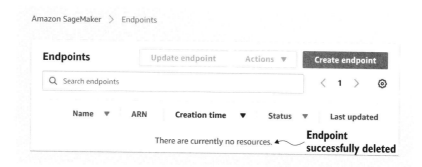

Figure 4.10   Verifying that you have successfully deleted the endpoint

Naomi is very pleased with your results. She can now run all the tweets received by her
team through your machine learning application to determine whether they should
be escalated. And it identifies frustration in about the same way her team members
used to identify discontented tweets (because the machine learning algorithm was
trained using her team's past decisions about whether to escalate a tweet). It's pretty
amazing. Imagine how hard it would have been to try to establish rules to identify frustrated tweeters.

Summary

- You determine which tweets to escalate using natural language processing (NLP)
  that captures meaning by a multidimensional word vector.
- In order to work with vectors in SageMaker, the only decision you need to make
  is whether SageMaker should use single words, pairs of words, or word triplets
  when creating the groups. To indicate this, NLP uses the terms unigram, bigram,
  and trigram, respectively.
- BlazingText is an algorithm that allows you to classify labeled text to set up your
  data for an NLP scenario.
- NLTK is a commonly used library for getting text ready to use in a machine
  learning model by tokenizing text.
- Tokenizing text involves splitting the text and stripping out those things that
  make it harder for the machine learning model to do what it needs to do.

Should you question an invoice sent by a supplier?

Brett works as a lawyer for a large bank. He is responsible for checking that the law firms hired by the bank bill the bank correctly. How tough can this be, you ask? Pretty tough is the answer. Last year, Brett's bank used hundreds of different firms across thousands of different legal matters, and each invoice submitted by a firm contains dozens or hundreds of lines. Tracking this using spreadsheets is a nightmare.

In this chapter, you'll use SageMaker and the Random Cut Forest algorithm to create a model that highlights the invoice lines that Brett should query with a law firm. Brett can then apply this process to every invoice to keep the lawyers working for his bank on their toes, saving the bank hundreds of thousands of dollars per year. Off we go!

5.1   *What are you making decisions about?*

As always, the first thing we want to look at is what we're making decisions about. In this chapter, at first glance, it appears the question Brett must decide is, should this invoice line be looked at more closely to determine if the law firm is billing us correctly? But, if you build a machine learning algorithm to definitively answer that question correctly 100% of the time, you'll almost certainly fail. Fortunately for you and Brett, that is not the real question you are trying to answer.

To understand the true value that Brett brings to the bank, let's look at his process. Prior to Brett and his team performing their functions, the bank found that law firm costs were spiraling out of control. The approach that Brett's team has taken over the past few years is to manually review each invoice and use gut instinct to determine whether they should query costs with the law firm. When Brett reads an invoice, he usually gets a pretty good feel for whether the costs are in line with the type of case the law firm is working on. He can tell pretty accurately whether the firm has billed an unusually high number of hours from partners rather than junior lawyers on the case, or whether a firm seems to be padding the number of hours their paralegals are spending on a matter.

When Brett comes across an apparent anomaly, an invoice that he feels has incorrect charges, he contacts the law firm and requests that they provide further information on their fees. The law firm responds in one of two ways:

- They provide additional information to justify their fees.
- They reduce their fees to an amount that is more in line with a typical matter of this type.

It is important to note that Brett really doesn't have a lot of clout in this relationship. If his bank instructs a law firm to work on a case, and they say that a particular piece of research took 5 hours of paralegal time, there is little Brett can do to dispute that. Brett can say that it seems like a lot of time. But the law firm can respond with, "Well, that's how long it took," and Brett has to accept that.

But this way of looking at Brett's job is too restrictive. The interesting thing about Brett's job is that Brett is effective not because he can identify 100% of the invoice lines that should be queried, but because the law firms know that Brett is pretty good at picking up anomalies. So, if the law firms charge more than they would normally charge for a particular type of service, they know they need to be prepared to justify it.

Lawyers really dislike justifying their costs, not because they can't, but because it takes time that they'd rather spend billing other clients. Consequently, when lawyers prepare their timesheets, if they know that there is a good chance that a line has more time on it than can easily be justified, they will weigh whether they should adjust their time downward or not. This decision, multiplied over the thousands of lines billed to the bank each year, results in hundreds of thousands of dollars in savings for the bank.

The real question you are trying to answer in this scenario is, what invoice lines does Brett need to query to encourage the law firms to bill the bank correctly?

And this question is fundamentally different from the original question about how to accurately determine which line is an anomaly. If you are trying to correctly identify anomalies, your success is determined by your accuracy. However, in this case, if you are simply trying to identify enough anomalies to encourage the law firms to bill the bank correctly, then your success is determined by how efficiently you can hit the threshold of *enough anomalies*.

What percentage of anomalies is *enough anomalies*?

A great deal of time and effort can be expended answering this question accurately. If a lawyer knew that one out every thousand anomalous lines would be queried, their behavior might not change at all. But if they knew that 9 out of 10 anomalous lines would be queried, then they would probably prepare their timesheets with a little more consideration.

In an academic paper, you want to clearly identify this threshold. In the business world, you need to weigh the benefits of accuracy against the cost of not being able to work on another project because you are spending time identifying a threshold. In Brett's case, it is probably sufficient to compare the results of the algorithm against how well a member of Brett's team can perform the task. If it comes out about the same, then you've hit the threshold.

5.2   *The process flow*

The process flow for this decision is shown in figure 5.1. It starts when a lawyer creates an invoice and sends it to Brett (1). On receiving the invoice, Brett or a member of his

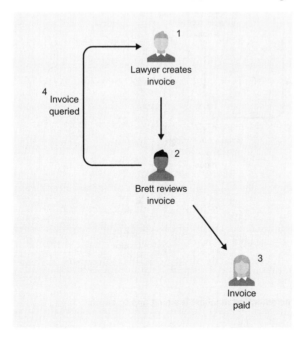

Figure 5.1   Current workflow showing Brett's process for reviewing invoices received from lawyers

team reviews the invoice (2) and then does one of two things, depending on whether the fees listed in the invoice seem reasonable:

- The invoice is passed on to Accounts Payable for payment (3).
- The invoice is sent back to the lawyer with a request for clarification of some of the charges (4).

With thousands of invoices to review annually, this is a full-time job for Brett and his two staff members.

Figure 5.2 shows the new workflow after you implement the machine learning application you'll build in this chapter. When the lawyer sends the invoice (1), instead of Brett or his team reviewing the invoice, it is passed through a machine learning model that determines whether the invoice contains any anomalies (2). If there are no anomalies, the invoice is passed through to Accounts Payable without further review by Brett's team (3). If an anomaly is detected, the application sends the invoice back to the lawyer and requests further information on the fees charged (4). The role Brett plays in this process is to review a certain number of these transactions to ensure the system is functioning as designed (5).

Now that Brett is not required to review invoices he is able to spend more time on other aspects of his role such as maintaining and improving relationships with suppliers.

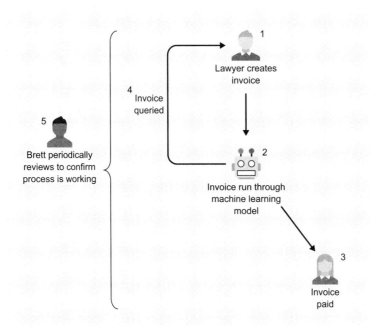

Figure 5.2   New workflow after implementing machine learning app to catch anomalies in invoices

5.3   *Preparing the dataset*

The dataset you are using in this chapter is a synthetic dataset created by Richie. It contains 100,000 rows of invoice line data from law firms retained by Brett's bank.

> **Synthetic data vs. real data**
>
> Synthetic data is data created by you, the analyst, as opposed to data found in the real world. When you are working with data from your own company, your data will be real data rather than synthetic data.
>
> A good set of real data is more fun to work with than synthetic data because it is typically more nuanced than synthetic data. With real data, there are interesting patterns you can find in the data that you weren't expecting to see. Synthetic data, on the other hand, is great in that it shows exactly the concept you want to show, but it lacks the element of surprise and the joy of discovery that working with real data provides.
>
> In chapters 2 and 3, you worked with synthetic data (purchase order data and customer churn data). In chapter 4, you worked with real data (tweets to customer support teams). In chapter 6, you'll be back to working with real data (electricity usage data).

Law firm invoices are usually quite detailed and show how many minutes the firm spent performing each task. Law firms typically have a stratified fee structure, where junior lawyers and paralegals (staff who perform work that doesn't need to be performed by a qualified lawyer) are billed at a lower cost than senior lawyers and law firm partners. The important information on law firm invoices is the type of material worked on (antitrust, for example), the resource that performed the work (paralegal, junior lawyer, partner, and so on), how many minutes were spent on the activity, and how much it cost. The dataset you'll use in this chapter contains the following columns:

- *Matter Number*—An identifier for each invoice. If two lines have the same matter number, it means that they are on the same invoice.
- *Firm Name*—The name of the law firm.
- *Matter Type*—The type of matter the invoice relates to.
- *Resource*—The type of resource that performs the activity.
- *Activity*—The type of activity performed by the resource.
- *Minutes*—How many minutes it took to perform the activity.
- *Fee*—The hourly rate for the resource.
- *Total*—The total fee.
- *Error*—A column indicating whether the invoice line contains an error. Note that this column exists in this dataset to allow you to determine how successful the model was at picking the lines with errors. In a real-life dataset, you wouldn't have this field.

Table 5.1 shows three invoice lines in the dataset.

Table 5.1 Dataset invoice lines for the lawyers submitting invoices to the bank

Matter Number	Firm Name	Matter Type	Resource	Activity	Minutes	Fee	Total	Error
0	Cox Group	Antitrust	Paralegal	Attend Court	110	50	91.67	False
0	Cox Group	Antitrust	Junior	Attend Court	505	150	1262.50	True
0	Cox Group	Antitrust	Paralegal	Attend Meeting	60	50	50.00	False

In this chapter, you'll build a machine learning application to pick the lines that contain errors. In machine learning lingo, you are identifying anomalies in the data.

5.4 *What are anomalies*

Anomalies are the data points that have something unusual about them. Defining *unusual* is not always easy. For example, the image in figure 5.3 contains an anomaly that is pretty easy to spot. All the characters in the image are capital *S*'s with the exception of the single number 5.

Figure 5.3 A simple anomaly. It's easy to spot the anomaly in this dataset.

But what about the image shown in figure 5.4? The anomaly is less easy to spot.

There are actually two anomalies in this dataset. The first anomaly is similar to the anomaly in figure 5.3. The number 5 in the bottom right of the image is the only number. Every other character is a letter. The last anomaly is difficult: the only characters that appear in pairs are vowels. Admittedly, the last anomaly would be almost impossible for a human to identify but, given enough data, a machine learning algorithm could find it.

```
F G R T Z M Q Y I S Z H D V N G J L M C
S Y G D H Y K X A F U I E P W R X D E E
Y X K F S E I P D B P S W M U C Z S F T
G X O H R W L C U J Y D M Q D G J I E C
U D B I W U Z I P F D S W 5 J W Q T Y E
N C F K I Y P R Z U U W B E D I O Y R P
Q U G T W P T O K R W R J D Y F M S G L
```

Figure 5.4   A complex anomaly. It's far more difficult to spot the second anomaly in this dataset.

Just like the images in figures 5.3 and 5.4, Brett's job is to identify anomalies in the invoices sent to his bank by law firms. Some invoices have anomalies that are easy to find. The invoice might contain a high fee for the resource, such as a law firm charging $500 per hour for a paralegal or junior lawyer, or the invoice might contain a high number of hours for a particular activity, such as a meeting being billed for 360 minutes.

But other anomalies are more difficult to find. For example, antitrust matters might typically involve longer court sessions than insolvency matters. If so, a 500-minute court session for an insolvency matter might be an anomaly, but the same court session for an antitrust matter might not.

One of the challenges you might have noticed in identifying anomalies in figures 5.3 and 5.4 is that you did not know what type of anomaly you were looking for. This is not dissimilar to identifying anomalies in real-world data. If you had been told that the anomaly had to do with numbers versus letters, you would have easily identified the 5 in figures 5.3 and 5.4. Brett, who is a trained lawyer and has been reviewing legal invoices for years, can pick out anomalies quickly and easily, but he might not consciously know why he feels that a particular line is an anomaly.

In this chapter, you will not define any rules to help the model determine what lines contain anomalies. In fact, you won't even tell the model which lines contain anomalies. The model will figure it out for itself. This is called *unsupervised* machine learning.

5.5   *Supervised vs. unsupervised machine learning*

In the example you are working through in this chapter, you could have had Brett label the invoice lines he would normally query and use that to train an XGBoost model in a manner similar to the XGBoost models you trained in chapters 2 and 3. But what if you didn't have Brett working for you? Could you still use machine learning to tackle this problem? It turns out you can.

The machine learning application in this chapter uses an unsupervised algorithm called Random Cut Forest to determine whether an invoice should be queried. The difference between a supervised algorithm and an unsupervised algorithm is that with an *unsupervised* algorithm, you don't provide any labeled data. You just provide the data and the algorithm decides how to interpret it.

In chapters 2, 3, and 4, the machine learning algorithms you used were *supervised*. In this chapter, the algorithm you will use is unsupervised. In chapter 2, your dataset had a column called tech_approval_required that the model used to learn whether technical approval was required. In chapter 3, your dataset had a column called churned that the model used to learn whether a customer churned or not. In chapter 4, your dataset had a column called escalate to learn whether a particular tweet should be escalated.

In this chapter, you are not going to tell the model which invoices should be queried. Instead, you are going to let the algorithm figure out which invoices contain anomalies, and you will query the invoices that have anomalies over a certain threshold. This is unsupervised machine learning.

5.6   *What is Random Cut Forest and how does it work?*

The machine learning algorithm you'll use in this chapter, Random Cut Forest, is a wonderfully descriptive name because the algorithm takes random data points (Random), cuts them to the same number of points and creates trees (Cut). It then looks at all of the trees together (Forest) to determine whether a particular data point is an anomaly—hence, *Random Cut Forest*.

A tree is an ordered way of storing numerical data. The simplest type of tree is called a *binary tree*. It's a great way to store data because it's easy and fast for a computer to work with. To create a tree, you randomly subdivide the data points until you have isolated the point you are testing to determine whether it is an anomaly. Each time you subdivide the data points, it creates a new level of the tree. The fewer times you need to subdivide the data points before you isolate the target data point, the more likely the data point is to be an anomaly for that sample of data.

In the two sections that follow, you'll look at two examples of trees with a target data point injected. In the first sample, the target data point will appear to be an anomaly. In the second sample, the target data point will not be an anomaly. When you look at the samples together as a forest, you'll see that the latter point is not likely to be an anomaly.

5.6.1   *Sample 1*

Figure 5.5 shows six dark dots that represent six data points that have been pulled at random from the dataset. The white dot represents the target data point that you are testing to determine whether it is an anomaly. Visually, you can see that this white dot sits somewhat apart from the other values in this sample of data, so it might be an anomaly. But how do you determine this algorithmically? This is where the tree representation comes in.

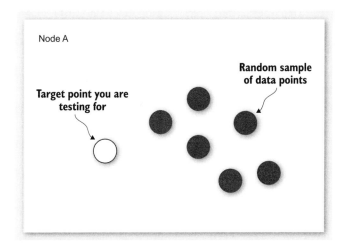

Figure 5.5   Sample 1: The white dot represents an anomaly.

Figure 5.6 shows the top level of the tree. The top level is a single node that represents all of the data points in the sample (including the target data point you are testing). If the node contains any data points other than the target point you are testing for, the color of the node is shown as dark. (The top-level node is always dark because it represents all of the data points in the sample.)

Figure 5.6   Sample 1: Level-1 tree represents a node with all of the data points in one group.

Figure 5.7 shows the data points after the first subdivision. The dividing line is inserted at random through the data points. Each side of the subdivision represents a node in the tree.

Figure 5.8 shows the next level of the tree. The left side of figure 5.7 becomes Node B on the left of the tree. The right side of figure 5.7 becomes Node C on the right of the tree. Both nodes in the tree are shown as dark because both sides of the subdivided diagram in figure 5.7 contain at least one dark dot.

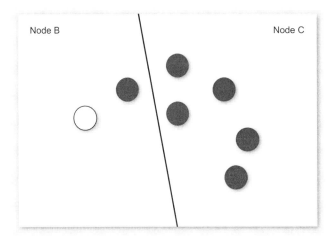

Figure 5.7   Sample 1: Level-2 data points divided between two nodes after the first subdivision.

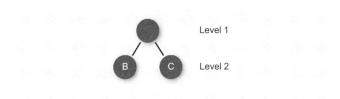

Figure 5.8   Sample 1: Level-2 tree represents the data points split into two groups, where both nodes are shown as dark.

The next step is to further subdivide the part of the diagram that contains the target data point. This is shown in figure 5.9. You can see that Node C on the right is untouched, whereas the left side is subdivided into Nodes D and E. Node E contains only the target data point, so no further subdivision is required.

Figure 5.10 shows the final tree. Node E is shown in white because it contains the target data point. The tree has three levels. The smaller the tree, the greater the likelihood that the point is an anomaly. A three-level tree is a pretty small tree, indicating that the target data point might be an anomaly.

Now, let's take a look at another sample of six data points that are clustered more closely around the target data point.

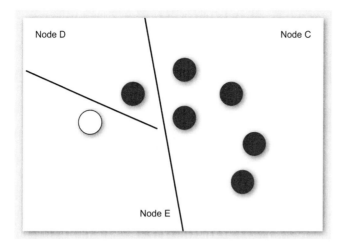

Figure 5.9 Sample 1: Level-3 data points separate the target data point from the values in the dataset.

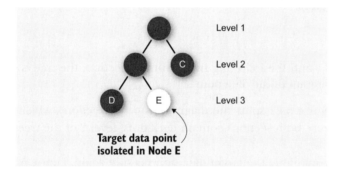

Figure 5.10 Sample 1: Level-3 tree represents one of the level-2 groups split again to isolate the target data point.

5.6.2 *Sample 2*

In the second data sample, the randomly selected data points are clustered more closely around the target data point. It is important to note that our target data point is the same data point that was used in sample 1. The only difference is that a different sample of data points was drawn from the dataset. You can see in figure 5.11 that the data points in the sample (dark dots) are more closely clustered around the target data point than they were in sample 1.

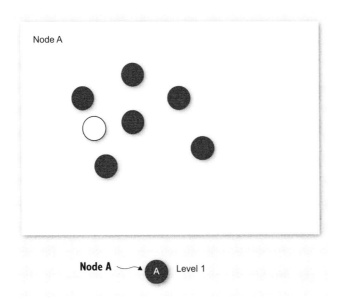

Figure 5.11   Sample 2: Level-1 data points and tree represent all of the data points in a single group.

NOTE   In figure 5.11 and the following figures in this section, the tree is displayed below the diagram of the data points.

Just as in sample 1, figure 5.12 splits the diagram into two sections, which we have labeled B and C. Because both sections contain dark dots, level 2 of the tree diagram is shown as dark.

Next, the section containing the target data point is split again. Figure 5.13 shows that section B has been split into two sections labeled D and E, and a new level has been added to the tree. Both of these sections contain one or more dark dots, so level 3 of the tree diagram is shown as dark.

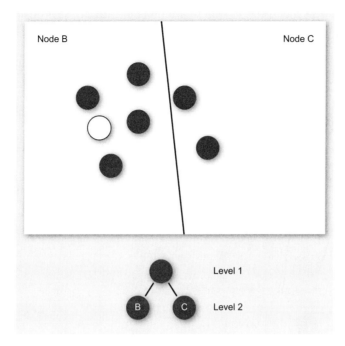

Figure 5.12 Sample 2: Level-2 data points and tree represent the level-1 groups split into two groups.

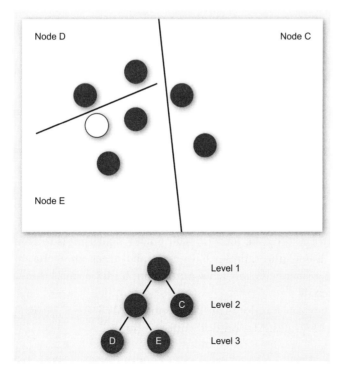

Figure 5.13 Sample 2: Level-3 data points and tree represent one of the level-2 groups split into two groups.

The target data point is in section E, so that section is split into two sections labeled F and G as shown in figure 5.14.

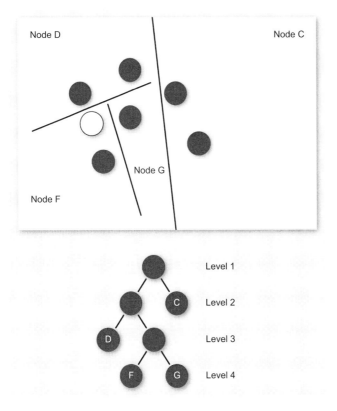

Figure 5.14 Sample 2: Level-4 data points and tree represent one of the level-3 groups split into two groups.

The target data point is in section F, so that section is split into two sections labeled H and J as shown in figure 5.15. Section J contains only the target data point, so it is shown as white. No further splitting is required. The resulting diagram has 5 levels, which indicates that the target data point is not likely to be an anomaly.

The final step performed by the Random Cut Forest algorithm is to combine the trees into a forest. If lots of the samples have very small trees, then the target data point is likely to be an anomaly. If only a few of the samples have small trees, then it is likely to *not* be an anomaly.

You can read more about Random Cut Forest on the AWS site at https://docs.aws .amazon.com/sagemaker/latest/dg/randomcutforest.html.

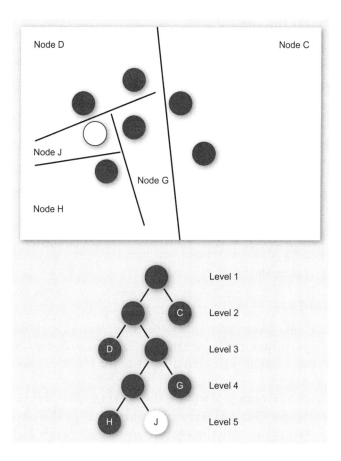

Figure 5.15   Sample 2: Level-5 data points and tree represent one of the level-4 groups split into two groups, isolating the target data point.

Richie's explanation of the forest part of Random Cut Forest

Random Cut Forest partitions the dataset into the number of trees in the forest (specified by the `num_trees` hyperparameter). During training, a total of `num_trees` × `num_samples_per_tree` individual data points get sampled from the full dataset without replacement. For a small dataset, this can be equal to the total number of observations, but for large datasets, it need not be.

During inference, however, a brand new data point gets assigned an anomaly score by cycling through all the trees in the forest and determining what anomaly score to give it from each tree. This score then gets averaged to determine if this point should actually be considered an anomaly or not.

5.7   *Getting ready to build the model*

Now that you have a deeper understanding of how Random Cut Forest works, you can set up another notebook on SageMaker and make some decisions. As you did in chapters 2, 3, and 4, you are going to do the following:

1 Upload a dataset to S3
2 Set up a notebook on SageMaker
3 Upload the starting notebook
4 Run it against the data

TIP   If you're jumping into the book at this chapter, you might want to visit the appendixes, which show you how to do the following:

- Appendix A: sign up for AWS, Amazon's web service
- Appendix B: set up S3, AWS's file storage service
- Appendix C: set up SageMaker

5.7.1   *Uploading a dataset to S3*

To set up the dataset for this chapter, you'll follow the same steps as you did in appendix B. You don't need to set up another bucket though. You can go to the same bucket you created earlier. In our example, we called it *mlforbusiness*, but your bucket will be called something different.

When you go to your S3 account, you will see the bucket you created to hold the data files for previous chapters. Click this bucket to see the ch02, ch03, and ch04 folders you created in previous chapters. For this chapter, you'll create a new folder called *ch05*. You do this by clicking Create Folder and following the prompts to create a new folder.

Once you've created the folder, you are returned to the folder list inside your bucket. There you'll see you now have a folder called ch05. Now that you have the ch05 folder set up in your bucket, you can upload your data file and start setting up the decision-making model in SageMaker. To do so, click the folder and download the data file at this link:

https://s3.amazonaws.com/mlforbusiness/ch05/activities.csv.

Then upload the CSV file into your ch05 folder by clicking Upload. Now you're ready to set up the notebook instance.

5.7.2 *Setting up a notebook on SageMaker*

Like you did in chapters 2, 3, and 4, you'll set up a notebook on SageMaker. If you skipped the earlier chapters, follow the instructions in appendix C on how to set up SageMaker.

When you go to SageMaker, you'll see your notebook instances. The notebook instance you created for earlier chapters (or that you've just created by following the instructions in appendix C) will either say Open or Start. If it says Start, click the Start link and wait a couple of minutes for SageMaker to start. Once the screen displays Open Jupyter, click the Open Jupyter link to open up your notebook list.

Once it opens, create a new folder for chapter 5 by clicking New and selecting Folder at the bottom of the dropdown list. This creates a new folder called Untitled Folder. When you tick the checkbox next to Untitled Folder, you will see the Rename button appear. Click it and change the folder name to ch05. Click the ch05 folder, and you will see an empty notebook list.

Just as we already prepared the CSV data you uploaded to S3 (activities.csv), we've already prepared the Jupyter notebook you'll now use. You can download it to your computer by navigating to this URL:

https://s3.amazonaws.com/mlforbusiness/ch05/detect_suspicious_lines.ipynb.

Click Upload to upload the detect_suspicious_lines.ipynb notebook to the ch05 folder. After uploading the file, you'll see the notebook in your list. Click it to open it. Now, just like in the previous chapters, you are a few keystrokes away from being able to run your machine learning model.

5.8 *Building the model*

As in the previous chapters, you will go through the code in six parts:

1 Load and examine the data.
2 Get the data into the right shape.
3 Create training and validation datasets (there's no need for a test dataset in this example).
4 Train the machine learning model.
5 Host the machine learning model.
6 Test the model and use it to make decisions.

> ### Refresher on running code in Jupyter notebooks
> SageMaker uses Jupyter Notebook as its interface. Jupyter Notebook is an open-source data science application that allows you to mix code with text. As shown in the figure, the code sections of a Jupyter notebook have a gray background, and the text sections have a white background.

(continued)

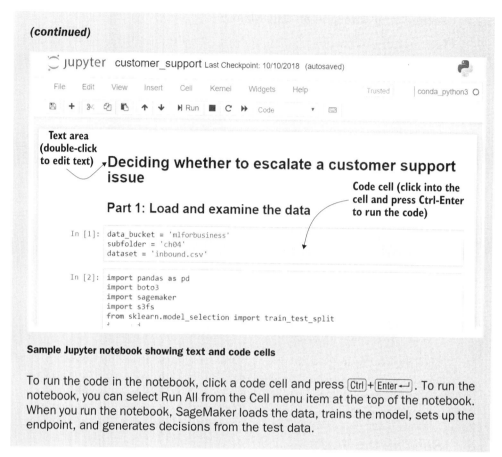

Sample Jupyter notebook showing text and code cells

To run the code in the notebook, click a code cell and press ⌈Ctrl⌉+⌈Enter ↵⌉. To run the notebook, you can select Run All from the Cell menu item at the top of the notebook. When you run the notebook, SageMaker loads the data, trains the model, sets up the endpoint, and generates decisions from the test data.

5.8.1   Part 1: Loading and examining the data

As in the previous three chapters, the first step is to say where you are storing the data. In listing 5.1, you need to change 'mlforbusiness' to the name of the bucket you created when you uploaded the data, then change the subfolder to the name of the subfolder on S3 where you want to store the data. If you named the S3 folder ch05, then you don't need to change the name of the folder. If you kept the name of the CSV file you uploaded earlier in the chapter, then you don't need to change the activities.csv line of code either. If you renamed the CSV file, then you need to update the filename with the name you changed it to. To run the code in the notebook cell, click the cell and press ⌈Ctrl⌉+⌈Enter ↵⌉.

Listing 5.1   Say where you are storing the data

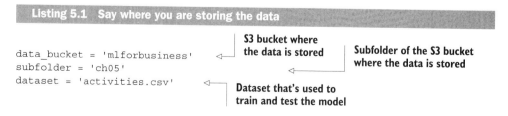

Next you'll import all of the Python libraries and modules that SageMaker uses to prepare the data, train the machine learning model, and set up the endpoint. The Python modules and libraries imported in listing 5.2 are the same as the imports you used in previous chapters.

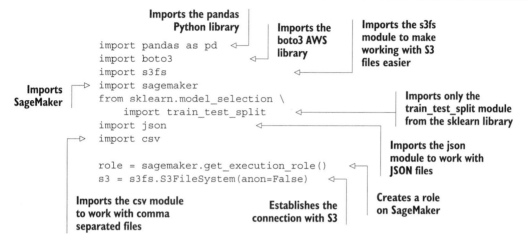

Listing 5.2 Importing the modules

The dataset contains invoice lines from all matters handled by your panel of lawyers over the past 3 months. The dataset has about 100,000 lines covering 2,000 invoices (50 lines per invoice). It contains the following columns:

- *Matter Number*—An identifier for each invoice. If two lines have the same number, it means that these are on the same invoice.
- *Firm Name*—The name of the law firm.
- *Matter Type*—The type of activity the invoice relates to.
- *Resource*—The resource that performs the activity.
- *Activity*—The activity performed by the resource.
- *Minutes*—How many minutes it took to perform the activity.
- *Fee*—The hourly rate for the resource.
- *Total*—The total fee.
- *Error*—Indicates whether the invoice line contains an error.

NOTE The Error column is not used during training because, in our scenario, this information is not known until you contact the law firm and determine whether the line was in error. This field is included here to allow you to determine how well your model is working.

Next, you'll load and view the data. In listing 5.3, you read the top 20 rows of the CSV data in activities.csv to display those in a pandas DataFrame. In this listing, you use a different way of displaying rows in the pandas DataFrame. Previously, you used the head() function to display the top 5 rows. In this listing, you use explicit numbers to display specific rows.

Listing 5.3   Loading and viewing the data

```
df = pd.read_csv(
    f's3://{data_bucket}/{subfolder}/{dataset}')
display(df[5:8])
```

Reads the S3 dataset
set in listing 5.1

Displays 3 rows of the
DataFrame (rows 5, 6, and 7)

In this example, the top 5 rows all show no errors. You can tell if a row shows an error by looking at the rightmost column, Error. Rows 5, 6, and 7 are displayed because they show two rows with Error = False and one row with Error = True. Table 5.2 shows the output of running display(df[5:8]).

Table 5.2   Dataset invoice lines display the three rows returned from running display(df[5:8]).

Row number	Matter Number	Firm Name	Matter Type	Resource	Activity	Minutes	Fee	Total	Error
5	0	Cox Group	Antitrust	Paralegal	Attend Court	110	50	91.67	False
6	0	Cox Group	Antitrust	Junior	Attend Court	505	150	1262.50	True
7	0	Cox Group	Antitrust	Paralegal	Attend Meeting	60	50	50.00	False

In listing 5.4, you use the pandas value_counts function to determine the error rate. You can see that out of 100,000 rows, about 2,000 have errors, which gives a 2% error rate. Note that in a real-life scenario, you won't know the error rate, so you would have to run a small project to determine your error rate by sampling lines from invoices.

Listing 5.4   Displaying the error rate

```
[id="esc
----
df['Error'].value_counts()
----
```

Displays the error rate:
False is no error; True
is an error.

The following listing shows the output from the code in listing 5.4.

Listing 5.5   Total number of tweets and the number of escalated tweets

```
False    103935
True      2030
Name: escalate, dtype: int64
```

The next listing shows the types of matters, resources, and activities.

Listing 5.6 Describing the data

```
print(f'Number of rows in dataset: {df.shape[0]}')
print()
print('Matter types:')
print(df['Matter Type'].value_counts())
print()
print('Resources:')
print(df['Resource'].value_counts())
print()
print('Activities:')
print(df['Activity'].value_counts())
```

The results of the code in listing 5.6 are shown in listing 5.7. You can see that there are 10 different matter types, ranging from Antitrust to Securities litigation; four different types of resources, ranging from Paralegal to Partner; and four different activity types, such as Phone Call, Attend Meeting, and Attend Court.

Listing 5.7 Viewing the data description

```
Number of rows in dataset: 105965

Matter types:
Antitrust              23922
Insolvency             16499
IPO                    14236
Commercial arbitration 12927
Project finance        11776
M&A                     6460
Structured finance      5498
Asset recovery          4913
Tax planning            4871
Securities litigation   4863
Name: Matter Type, dtype: int64

Resources:
Partner      26587
Junior       26543
Paralegal    26519
Senior       26316
Name: Resource, dtype: int64
*
Activities:
Prepare Opinion    26605
Phone Call         26586
Attend Court       26405
Attend Meeting     26369
Name: Activity, dtype: int64
```

The machine learning model uses these features to determine which invoice lines are potentially erroneous. In the next section, you'll work with these features to get them into the right shape for use in the machine learning model.

5.8.2   *Part 2: Getting the data into the right shape*

Now that you've loaded the data, you need to get the data into the right shape. This involves several steps:

- Changing the categorical data to numerical data
- Splitting the dataset into training data and validation data
- Removing unnecessary columns

The machine learning algorithm you'll use in this notebook is the Random Cut Forest algorithm. Just like the XGBoost algorithm you used in chapters 2 and 3, Random Cut Forest can't handle text values—everything needs to be a number. And, as you did in chapters 2 and 3, you'll use the pandas `get_dummies` function to convert each of the different text values in the Matter Type, Resource, and Activity columns and place a 0 or a 1 as the value in the column. For example, the rows shown in the three-column table 5.3 would be converted to a four column table.

Table 5.3   Data before applying the `get_dummies` function

Matter Number	Matter Type	Resource
0	Antitrust	Paralegal
0	Antitrust	Partner

The converted table (table 5.4) has four columns because an additional column gets created for each unique value in any of the columns. Given that there are two different values in the Resource column in table 5.3, that column is split into two columns: one for each type of resource.

Table 5.4   Data after applying the `get_dummies` function

Matter Number	Matter_Type_Antitrust	Resource_Paralegal	Resource_Partner
0	1	1	0
0	1	0	1

In listing 5.8, you create a pandas DataFrame called encoded_df by calling the `get_dummies()` function on the original pandas df DataFrame. Calling the `head()` function here returns the first three rows of the DataFrame.

Note that this can create very wide datasets, as every unique value becomes a column. The DataFrame you work with in this chapter increases from a 9-column table to a 24-column table. To determine how wide your table will be, you need to subtract the number of columns you are applying the `get_dummies` function to and add the number of unique elements in each column. So, your original 9-column table becomes a 6-column table once you subtract the 3 columns you apply the `get_dummies` function to. Then it expands to a 24-column table once you add 10 columns for each unique element in the Matter Type column and four columns each for the unique elements in the Resource and Activity columns.

Listing 5.8 Creating the train and validate data

```
encoded_df = pd.get_dummies(
    df,
    columns=['Matter Type','Resource','Activity'])
encoded_df.head(3)
```

Converts three columns into a column for each unique value

Displays the top three rows of the DataFrame

5.8.3 *Part 3: Creating training and validation datasets*

You now split the dataset into train and validation data. Note that with this notebook, you don't have any test data. In a real-world situation, the best way to test the data is often to compare your success at identifying errors *before* using the machine learning model with your success *after* you use the machine learning algorithm.

A test size of 0.2 instructs the function to place 80% of the data into a train Data-Frame and 20% into a validation DataFrame. If you are splitting a dataset into training and validation data, you typically will place 70% of your data into a training dataset, 20% into test, and 10% into validation. For the dataset in this chapter, you are just splitting the data into training and test datasets as, in Brett's data, there will be no validation data.

Listing 5.9 Creating training and validation datasets

```
train_df, val_df, _, _ = train_test_split(
    encoded_df,
    encoded_df['Error'],
    test_size=0.2,
    random_state=0)
print(
    f'{train_df.shape[0]} rows in training data')
```

Creates the training and validation datasets

Displays the number of rows in the training data

With that, the data is in a SageMaker session, and you are ready to start training the model.

5.8.4 *Part 4: Training the model*

In listing 5.10, you import the `RandomCutForest` function, set up the training parameters, and store the result in a variable called `rcf`. This all looks very similar to how you set up the training jobs in previous chapters, with the exception of the final two parameters in the `RandomCutForest` function.

The parameter `num_samples_per_tree` sets how many samples you include in each tree. Graphically, you can think of it as the number of dark dots per tree. If you have lots of samples per tree, your trees will get very large before the function creates a slice that contains only the target point. Large trees take longer to calculate than small trees. AWS recommends you start with 100 samples per tree, as that provides a good middle ground between speed and size.

The parameter `num_trees` is the number of trees (groups of dark dots). This parameter should be set to approximate the fraction of errors expected. In your dataset, about 2% (or 1/50) are errors, so you'll set the number of trees to 50. The final line of code in the following listing runs the training job and creates the model.

Listing 5.10 Training the model

```
from sagemaker import RandomCutForest

session = sagemaker.Session()

rcf = RandomCutForest(role=role,
                      train_instance_count=1,
                      train_instance_type='ml.m4.xlarge',
                      data_location=f's3://{data_bucket}/{subfolder}/',
                      output_path=f's3://{data_bucket}/{subfolder}/output',
                      num_samples_per_tree=100,          ◁──── Number of samples
                      num_trees=50)              ◁────────────── per tree

rcf.fit(rcf.record_set(train_df_no_result.values))    Number of trees
```

5.8.5 *Part 5: Hosting the model*

Now that you have a trained model, you can host it on SageMaker so it is ready to make decisions. If you have run this notebook already, you might already have an endpoint. To handle this, in the next listing, you delete any existing endpoints you have so you don't end up paying for a bunch of endpoints you aren't using.

Listing 5.11 Hosting the model: deleting existing endpoints

```
endpoint_name = 'suspicious-lines'      ◁──── So you don't create duplicate
try:                                           endpoints, name your endpoint.
    sess.delete_endpoint(
        sagemaker.predictor.RealTimePredictor(
            endpoint=endpoint_name).endpoint)   ◁──── Deletes existing endpoint
    print(                                             with that name
        'Warning: Existing endpoint deleted to make way for new endpoint.')
except:
    pass
```

Next, in listing 5.12, you create and deploy the endpoint. SageMaker is highly scalable and can handle very large datasets. For the datasets we use in this book, you only need a t2.medium machine to host your endpoint.

Listing 5.12 Hosting the model: setting machine size

```
rcf_endpoint = rcf.deploy(
    initial_instance_count=1,
    instance_type='ml.t2.medium'
)
```

Number of machines
to host your endpoint

Size of the machine

You now need to set up the code that takes the results from the endpoint and puts them in a format you can easily work with.

Listing 5.13 Hosting the model: converting to a workable format

```
from sagemaker.predictor import csv_serializer, json_deserializer

rcf_endpoint.content_type = 'text/csv'
rcf_endpoint.serializer = csv_serializer
rcf_endpoint.accept = 'application/json'
rcf_endpoint.deserializer = json_deserializer
```

5.8.6 *Part 6: Testing the model*

You can now compute anomalies on the validation data as shown in listing 5.14. Here you use the val_df_no_result dataset because it does not contain the Error column (just as the training data did not contain the Error column). You then create a Data-Frame called scores_df to hold the results from the numerical values returned from the rcf_endpoint.predict function. Then you'll combine the scores_df DataFrame with the val_df DataFrame so you can see the score from the Random Cut Forest algo-rithm associated with each row in the training data.

Listing 5.14 Adding scores to validation data

```
results = rcf_endpoint.predict(
    val_df_no_result.values)
scores_df = pd.DataFrame(results['scores'])
val_df = val_df.reset_index(drop=True)
results_df = pd.concat(
    [val_df, scores_df], axis=1)
results_df['Error'].value_counts()
```

Gets the results from the
val_df_no_result DataFrame

Creates a new
DataFrame with
the results

Resets the index of the val_df
DataFrame so it starts at zero

Concatenates the columns
in the val_df and the
scores_df DataFrames

Shows how many errors there
are in the val_df DataFrame

To combine the data, we used the pandas concat function in listing 5.14. This func-tion combines two DataFrames, using the index of the DataFrames. If the axis param-eter is 0, you will concatenate rows. If it is 1, you will concatenate columns.

Because we have just created the scores_df DataFrame, the index for the rows starts at 0 and goes up to 21,192 (as there are 21,193 rows in the val_df and scores_df Data-Frames). We then reset the index of the val_df DataFrame so that it also starts at 0. That way when we concatenate the DataFrames, the scores line up with the correct rows in the val_df DataFrame.

You can see from the following listing that there are 20,791 correct lines in the validation dataset (val_df) and 402 errors (based on the Errors column in the val_df DataFrame).

Listing 5.15   Reviewing erroneous lines

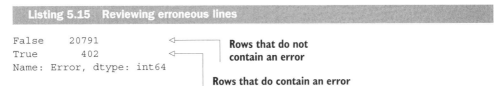

```
False    20791
True       402
Name: Error, dtype: int64
```

Rows that do not contain an error

Rows that do contain an error

Brett believes that he and his team catch about half the errors made by law firms and that this is sufficient to generate the behavior the bank wants from their lawyers: to bill accurately because they know that if they don't, they will be asked to provide additional supporting information for their invoices.

To identify the errors with scores in the top half of the results, you use the pandas median function to identify the median score of the errors and then create a DataFrame called results_above_cutoff to hold the results (listing 5.16). To confirm that you have the median, you can look at the value counts of the Errors column in the DataFrame to determine that there are 201 rows in the DataFrame (half the total number of errors in the val_df DataFrame).

The next listing calculates the number of rows where the score is greater than the median score.

Listing 5.16   Calculating errors greater than 1.5 (the median score)

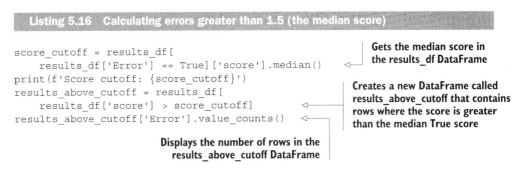

```
score_cutoff = results_df[
    results_df['Error'] == True]['score'].median()
print(f'Score cutoff: {score_cutoff}')
results_above_cutoff = results_df[
    results_df['score'] > score_cutoff]
results_above_cutoff['Error'].value_counts()
```

Gets the median score in the results_df DataFrame

Creates a new DataFrame called results_above_cutoff that contains rows where the score is greater than the median True score

Displays the number of rows in the results_above_cutoff DataFrame

And the next listing shows the number of true errors above the median score and the number of false positives.

Listing 5.17   Viewing false positives

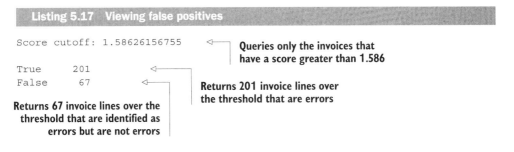

```
Score cutoff: 1.58626156755

True     201
False     67
```

Queries only the invoices that have a score greater than 1.586

Returns 201 invoice lines over the threshold that are errors

Returns 67 invoice lines over the threshold that are identified as errors but are not errors

Because you are looking at the value_counts of the Errors column, you can also see that for the 67 rows that did not contain errors, you will query the law firm. Brett tells you that this is a better hit rate than his team typically gets. With this information, you are able to prepare the two key ratios that allow you to describe how your model is performing. These two key ratios are *recall* and *precision*:

- Recall is the proportion of correctly identified errors over the total number of invoice lines with errors.
- Precision is the proportion of correctly identified errors over the total number of invoice lines predicted to be errors.

These concepts are easier to understand with examples. The key numbers in this analysis that allow you to calculate recall and precision are the following:

- There are 402 errors in the validation dataset.
- You set a cutoff to identify half the erroneous lines submitted by the law firms (201 lines).
- When you set the cutoff at this point, you misidentify 67 correct invoice lines as being erroneous.

Recall is the number of identified errors divided by the total number of errors. Because we decided to use the median score to determine the cutoff, the recall will always be 50%.

Precision is the number of correctly identified errors divided by the total number of errors predicted. The total number of errors predicted is 268 (201 + 67). The precision is 201 / 268, or 75%.

Now that you have defined the cutoff, you can set a column in the results_df Data-Frame that sets a value of True for rows with scores that exceed the cutoff and False for rows with scores that are less than the cutoff, as shown in the following listing.

Listing 5.18 Displaying the results in a pandas DataFrame

```
results_df['Prediction'] = \
    results_df['score'] > score_cutoff
results_df.head()
```

◁─── Sets the values in the Prediction column to True where the score is greater than the cutoff

◁─── Displays the results

The dataset now shows the results for each invoice line in the validation dataset.

Exercise:

1 What is the score for row 356 of the val_df dataset?
2 How would you submit this single row to the prediction function to return the score for only that row?

5.9   Deleting the endpoint and shutting down your notebook instance

It is important that you shut down your notebook instance and delete your endpoint. We don't want you to get charged for SageMaker services that you're not using.

5.9.1   Deleting the endpoint

Appendix D describes how to shut down your notebook instance and delete your endpoint using the SageMaker console, or you can do that with the code in this listing.

> **Listing 5.19   Deleting the notebook**

```
# Remove the endpoint (optional)
# Comment out this cell if you want the endpoint to persist after Run All
sagemaker.Session().delete_endpoint(rcf_endpoint.endpoint)
```

To delete the endpoint, uncomment the code in the listing, then click Ctrl + Enter ↵ to run the code in the cell.

5.9.2   Shutting down the notebook instance

To shut down the notebook, go back to your browser tab where you have SageMaker open. Click the Notebook Instances menu item to view all of your notebook instances. Select the radio button next to the notebook instance name as shown in figure 5.16, then click Stop on the Actions menu. It takes a couple of minutes to shut down.

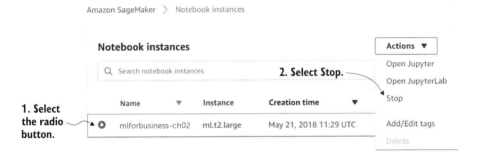

Figure 5.16   Shutting down the notebook

5.10   Checking to make sure the endpoint is deleted

If you didn't delete the endpoint using the notebook (or if you just want to make sure it is deleted), you can do this from the SageMaker console. To delete the endpoint, click the radio button to the left of the endpoint name, then click the Actions menu item and click Delete in the menu that appears.

When you have successfully deleted the endpoint, you will no longer incur AWS charges for it. You can confirm that all of your endpoints have been deleted when you see the text "There are currently no resources" displayed at the bottom of the Endpoints page (figure 5.17).

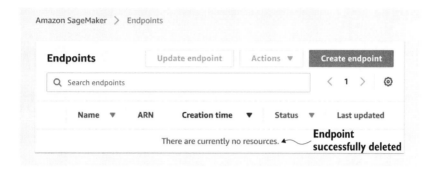

Figure 5.17   Verifying that you have successfully deleted the endpoint

Brett's team can now run each of the invoices they receive from their lawyers and determine within seconds whether they should query the invoice or not. Now Brett's team can focus on assessing the adequacy of the law firm's responses to their query rather than on whether an invoice should be queried. This will allow Brett's team to handle significantly more invoices with the same amount of effort.

Summary

- Identify what your algorithm is trying to achieve. In Brett's case in this chapter, the algorithm does not need to identify every erroneous line, it only needs to identify enough lines to drive the right behavior from the law firms.
- Synthetic data is data created by you, the analyst, as opposed to real data found in the real world. A good set of real data is more interesting to work with than synthetic data because it is typically more nuanced.
- Unsupervised machine learning can be used to solve problems where you don't have any trained data.
- The difference between a supervised algorithm and an unsupervised algorithm is that with an unsupervised algorithm, you don't provide any labeled data. You just provide the data, and the algorithm decides how to interpret it.
- Anomalies are data points that have something unusual about them.
- Random Cut Forest can be used to address the challenges inherent in identifying anomalies.
- Recall and precision are two of the key ratios you use to describe how your model is performing.

Forecasting your company's monthly power usage

This chapter covers

- Preparing your data for time-series analysis
- Visualizing data in your Jupyter notebook
- Using a neural network to generate forecasts
- Using DeepAR to forecast power consumption

Kiara works for a retail chain that has 48 locations around the country. She is an engineer, and every month her boss asks her how much energy they will consume in the next month. Kiara follows the procedure taught to her by the previous engineer in her role: she looks at how much energy they consumed in the same month last year, weights it by the number of locations they have gained or lost, and provides that number to her boss. Her boss sends this estimate to the facilities management teams to help plan their activities and then to Finance to forecast expenditure. The problem is that Kiara's estimates are always wrong—sometimes by a lot.

As an engineer, she reckons there must be a better way to approach this problem. In this chapter, you'll use SageMaker to help Kiara produce better estimates of her company's upcoming power consumption.

6.1   *What are you making decisions about?*

This chapter covers different material than you've seen in earlier chapters. In previous chapters, you used supervised and unsupervised machine learning algorithms to make decisions. You learned how each algorithm works and then you applied the algorithm to the data. In this chapter, you'll use a *neural network* to predict how much power Kiara's company will use next month.

Neural networks are much more difficult to intuitively understand than the machine learning algorithms we've covered so far. Rather than attempt to give you a deep understanding of neural networks in this chapter, we'll focus on how to explain the output from a neural network. Instead of a theoretical discussion of neural networks, you'll come out of this chapter knowing how to use a neural network to forecast time-series events and how to explain the results of the forecast. Rather than learning in detail the *why* of neural networks, you'll learn the *how*.

Figure 6.1 shows the predicted versus actual power consumption for one of Kiara's sites for a six-week period from mid-October 2018 to the end of November 2018. The site follows a weekly pattern with a higher usage on the weekdays and dropping very low on Sundays.

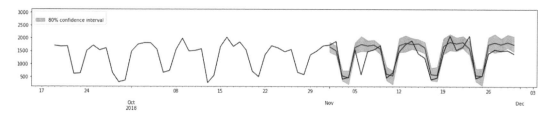

Figure 6.1   Predicted versus actual power consumption for November 2018 for one of Kiara's sites

The shaded area shows the range Kiara predicted with 80% accuracy. When Kiara calculates the average error for her prediction, she discovers it is 5.7%, which means that for any predicted amount, it is more likely to be within 5.7% of the predicted figure than not. Using SageMaker, you can do all of this without an in-depth understanding of how neural networks actually function. And, in our view, that's OK.

To understand how neural networks can be used for time-series forecasting, you first need to understand why time-series forecasting is a thorny issue. Once you understand this, you'll see what a neural network is and how a neural network can be applied to time-series forecasting. Then you'll roll up your sleeves, fire up SageMaker, and see it in action on real data.

> **NOTE** The power consumption data you'll use in this chapter is provided by BidEnergy (http://www.bidenergy.com), a company that specializes in power-usage forecasting and in minimizing power expenditure. The algorithms used

by BidEnergy are more sophisticated than you'll see in this chapter, but you'll get a feel for how machine learning in general, and neural networks in particular, can be applied to forecasting problems.

6.1.1   Introduction to time-series data

Time-series data consists of a number of observations at particular intervals. For example, if you created a time series of your weight, you could record your weight on the first of every month for a year. Your time series would have 12 observations with a numerical value for each observation. Table 6.1 shows what this might look like.

Table 6.1   Time-series data showing my (Doug's) weight in kilograms over the past year

Date	Weight (kg)
2018-01-01	75
2018-02-01	73
2018-03-01	72
2018-04-01	71
2018-05-01	72
2018-06-01	71
2018-07-01	70
2018-08-01	73
2018-09-01	70
2018-10-01	69
2018-11-01	72
2018-12-01	74

It's pretty boring to look at a table of data. It's hard to get a real understanding of the data when it is presented in a table format. Line charts are the best way to view data. Figure 6.2 shows the same data presented as a chart.

You can see from this time series that the date is on the left and my weight is on the right. If you wanted to record the time series of body weight for your entire family, for example, you would add a column for each of your family members. In table 6.2, you can see my weight and the weight of each of my family members over the course of a year.

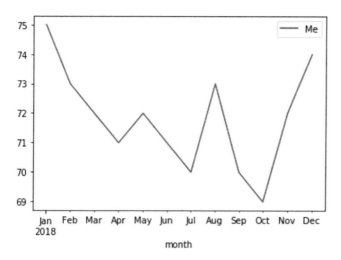

Figure 6.2　A line chart displays the same time-series data showing my weight in kilograms over the past year.

Table 6.2　Time-series data showing the weight in kilograms of family members over a year

Date	Me	Spouse	Child 1	Child 2
2018-01-01	75	52	38	67
2018-02-01	73	52	39	68
2018-03-01	72	53	40	65
2018-04-01	71	53	41	63
2018-05-01	72	54	42	64
2018-06-01	71	54	42	65
2018-07-01	70	55	42	65
2018-08-01	73	55	43	66
2018-09-01	70	56	44	65
2018-10-01	69	57	45	66
2018-11-01	72	57	46	66
2018-12-01	74	57	46	66

And, once you have that, you can visualize the data as four separate charts, as shown in figure 6.3.

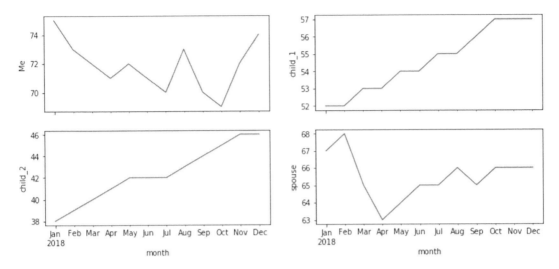

Figure 6.3   **Line charts display the same time-series data showing the weight in kilograms of members of a family over the past year.**

You'll see the chart formatted in this way throughout this chapter and the next. It is a common format used to concisely display time-series data.

6.1.2   *Kiara's time-series data: Daily power consumption*

Power consumption data is displayed in a manner similar to our weight data. Kiara's company has 48 different business sites (retail outlets and warehouses), so each site gets its own column when you compile the data. Each observation is a cell in that column. Table 6.3 shows a sample of the electricity data used in this chapter.

Table 6.3   Power usage data sample for Kiara's company in 30-minute intervals

Time	Site_1	Site_2	Site_3	Site_4	Site_5	Site_6
2017-11-01 00:00:00	13.30	13.3	11.68	13.02	0.0	102.9
2017-11-01 00:30:00	11.75	11.9	12.63	13.36	0.0	122.1
2017-11-01 01:00:00	12.58	11.4	11.86	13.04	0.0	110.3

This data looks similar to the data in table 6.2, which shows the weight of each family member each month. The difference is that instead of each column representing a family member, in Kiara's data, each column represents a site (office or warehouse location) for her company. And instead of each row representing a person's weight on the first day of the month, each row of Kiara's data shows how much power each site used on that day.

Now that you see how time-series data can be represented and visualized, you are ready to see how to use a Jupyter notebook to visualize this data.

6.2   Loading the Jupyter notebook for working with time-series data

To help you understand how to display time-series data in SageMaker, for the first time in this book, you'll work with a Jupyter notebook that does not contain a Sage-Maker machine learning model. Fortunately, because the SageMaker environment is simply a standard Jupyter Notebook server with access to SageMaker models, you can use SageMaker to run ordinary Jupyter notebooks as well. You'll start by downloading and saving the Jupyter notebook at

https://s3.amazonaws.com/mlforbusiness/ch06/time_series_practice.ipynb

You'll upload it to the same SageMaker environment you have used for previous chapters. Like you did for previous chapters, you'll set up a notebook on SageMaker. If you skipped the earlier chapters, follow the instructions in appendix C on how to set up SageMaker.

When you go to SageMaker, you'll see your notebook instances. The notebook instances you created for the previous chapters (or the one that you've just created by following the instructions in appendix C) will either say Open or Start. If it says Start, click the Start link and wait a couple of minutes for SageMaker to start. Once it displays Open Jupyter, select that link to open your notebook list (figure 6.4).

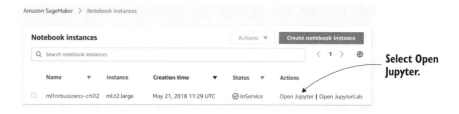

Figure 6.4   Viewing the Notebook instances list

Create a new folder for chapter 6 by clicking New and selecting Folder at the bottom of the dropdown list (figure 6.5). This creates a new folder called Untitled Folder.

To rename the folder, when you tick the checkbox next to Untitled Folder, you will see the Rename button appear. Click it and change the name to ch06. Click the ch06 folder and you will see an empty notebook list. Click Upload to upload the time_series _practice.ipynb notebook to the folder.

After uploading the file, you'll see the notebook in your list. Click it to open it. You are now ready to work with the time_series_practice notebook. But before we set up the time-series data for this notebook, let's look at some of the theory and practices surrounding time-series analysis.

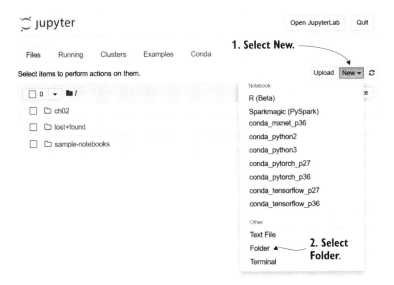

Figure 6.5   **Creating a new folder in SageMaker**

6.3   *Preparing the dataset: Charting time-series data*

Jupyter notebooks and pandas are excellent tools for working with time-series data. In the SageMaker neural network notebook you'll create later in this chapter, you'll use pandas and a data visualization library called *Matplotlib* to prepare the data for the neural network and to analyze the results. To help you understand how it works, you'll get your hands dirty with a time-series notebook that visualizes the weight of four different people over the course of a year.

To use a Jupyter notebook to visualize data, you'll need to set up the notebook to do so. As shown in listing 6.1, you first need to tell Jupyter that you intend to display some charts in this notebook. You do this with the line `%matplotlib inline`, as shown in line 1.

Listing 6.1   **Displaying charts**

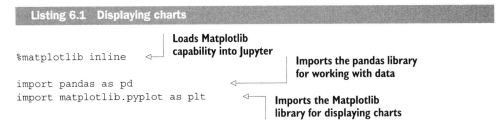

Matplotlib is a Python charting library, but there are lots of Python charting libraries that you could use. We have selected Matplotlib because it is available in the Python standard library and, for simple things, is easy to use.

The reason line 1 starts with a % symbol is that the line is an *instruction* to Jupyter, rather than a line in your code. It tells the Jupyter notebook that you'll be displaying charts, so it should load the software to do this into the notebook. This is called a *magic command.*

> ### The magic command: Is it really magic?
> Actually, it is. When you see a command in a Jupyter notebook that starts with % or with %%, the command is known as a magic command. Magic commands provide additional features to the Jupyter notebook, such as the ability to display charts or run external scripts. You can read more about magic commands at https://ipython .readthedocs.io/en/stable/interactive/magics.html.

As you can see in listing 6.1, after loading the Matplotlib functionality into your Jupyter notebook, you then imported the libraries: pandas and Matplotlib. (Remember that in line 1 of the listing, where you referenced %matplotlib inline, you did not import the Matplotlib library; line 3 is where you imported that library.)

After importing the relevant libraries, you then need to get some data. When working with SageMaker in the previous chapters, you loaded that data from S3. For this notebook, because you are just learning about visualization with pandas and Jupyter Notebook, you'll just create some data and send it to a pandas DataFrame, as shown in the next listing.

Listing 6.2 Inputting the time-series data

```
my_weight = [                                          Creates the dataset
    {'month': '2018-01-01', 'Me': 75},                 for data in figure 6.1
    {'month': '2018-02-01', 'Me': 73},
    {'month': '2018-03-01', 'Me': 72},
    {'month': '2018-04-01', 'Me': 71},
    {'month': '2018-05-01', 'Me': 72},
    {'month': '2018-06-01', 'Me': 71},
    {'month': '2018-07-01', 'Me': 70},
    {'month': '2018-08-01', 'Me': 73},
    {'month': '2018-09-01', 'Me': 70},
    {'month': '2018-10-01', 'Me': 69},                 Converts the dataset to
    {'month': '2018-11-01', 'Me': 72},                 a pandas DataFrame
    {'month': '2018-12-01', 'Me': 74}
]                                                      Sets the index of
df = pd.DataFrame(my_weight).set_index('month')        the DataFrame to a
df.index = pd.to_datetime(df.index)                    time series
df.head()                                              Displays the first five rows
```

Now, here's where the real magic lies. To display a chart, all you need to do is type the following line into the Jupyter notebook cell:

```
df.plot()
```

The Matplotlib library recognizes that the data is time-series data from the index type you set in line 3 of listing 6.2, so it just works. Magic! The output of the df.plot() command is shown in figure 6.6.

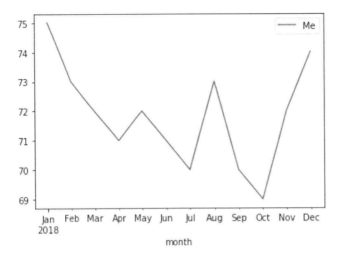

Figure 6.6 Time-series data returned by `df.plot` showing my weight in kilograms over the past year

To expand the data to include the weight of the entire family, you first need to set up the data. The following listing shows the dataset expanded to include data from every family member.

Listing 6.3 Inputting time-series data for the whole family

```
family_weight = [                                              ⊲──────┐  Creates the dataset
    {'month': '2018-01-01', 'Me': 75, 'spouse': 67,                      for the month and
        'ch_1': 52, 'ch_2': 38},                                         each person's weight
    {'month': '2018-02-01', 'Me': 73, 'spouse': 68,
        'ch_1': 52, 'ch_2': 39},
    {'month': '2018-03-01', 'Me': 72, 'spouse': 65,
        'ch_1': 53, 'ch_2': 40},
    {'month': '2018-04-01', 'Me': 71, 'spouse': 63,
        'ch_1': 53, 'ch_2': 41},
    {'month': '2018-05-01', 'Me': 72, 'spouse': 64,
        'ch_1': 54, 'ch_2': 42},
    {'month': '2018-06-01', 'Me': 71, 'spouse': 65,
        'ch_1': 54, 'ch_2': 42},
    {'month': '2018-07-01', 'Me': 70, 'spouse': 65,
        'ch_1': 55, 'ch_2': 42},
    {'month': '2018-08-01', 'Me': 73, 'spouse': 66,
        'ch_1': 55, 'ch_2': 43},
    {'month': '2018-09-01', 'Me': 70, 'spouse': 65,
        'ch_1': 56, 'ch_2': 44},
    {'month': '2018-10-01', 'Me': 69, 'spouse': 66,
        'ch_1': 57, 'ch_2': 45},
    {'month': '2018-11-01', 'Me': 72, 'spouse': 66,
        'ch_1': 57, 'ch_2': 46},
    {'month': '2018-12-01', 'Me': 74, 'spouse': 66,
        'ch_1': 57, 'ch_2': 46}
```

```
]
df2 = pd.DataFrame(
        family_weight).set_index('month')
df2.index = pd.to_datetime(df2.index)
df2.head()
```

**Converts the dataset to
a pandas DataFrame**

**Sets the index of the
DataFrame to a time series**

**Displays the first
five rows**

Displaying four charts in Matplotlib is a little more complex than displaying one chart. You need to first create an area to display the charts, and then you need to loop across the columns of data to display the data in each column. Because this is the first loop you've used in this book, we'll go into some detail about it.

6.3.1　Displaying columns of data with a loop

The loop is called a *for loop*, which means you give it a list (usually) and step through each item in the list. This is the most common type of loop you'll use in data analysis and machine learning because most of the things you'll loop through are lists of items or rows of data.

The standard way to loop is shown in the next listing. Line 1 of this listing defines a list of three items: A, B, and C. Line 2 sets up the loop, and line 3 prints each item.

Listing 6.4　Standard way to loop through a list

```
my_list = ['A', 'B', 'C']
for item in my_list:
    print(item)
```

**Creates a list
called my_list**

**Loops through
my_list**

**Prints each
item in the list**

Running this code prints A, B, and C, as shown next.

Listing 6.5　Standard output when you run the command to loop through a list

```
A
B
C
```

When creating charts with Matplotlib, in addition to looping, you need to keep track of how many times you have looped. Python has a nice way of doing this: it's called *enumerate*.

To enumerate through a list, you provide two variables to store the information from the loop and to wrap the list you are looping through. The enumerate function returns two such variables. The first variable is the count of how many times you've looped (starting with zero), and the second variable is the item retrieved from the list. Listing 6.6 shows listing 6.4 converted to an enumerated for loop.

Listing 6.6   Standard way to enumerate through a loop

```
my_list = ['A', 'B', 'C']
for i, item in enumerate(my_list):
    print(f'{i}. {item}')
```

Creates a list called my_list

Loops through my_list and stores the count in the i variable and the list item in the item variable

Prints the loop count (starting with zero) and each item in the list

Running this code creates the same output as that shown in listing 6.5 but also allows you to display how many items you have looped through in the list. To run the code, click the cell and press Ctrl+Enter↵. The next listing shows the output from using the enumerate function in your loop.

Listing 6.7   Output when enumerating through the loop

```
0. A
1. B
2. C
```

With that as background, you are ready to create multiple charts in Matplotlib.

6.3.2   Creating multiple charts

In Matplotlib, you use the subplots functionality to create multiple charts. To fill the subplots with data, you loop through each of the columns in the table showing the weight of each family member (listing 6.3) and display the data from each column.

Listing 6.8   Charting time-series data for the whole family

```
start_date = "2018-01-01"
end_date = "2018-12-31"
fig, axs = plt.subplots(
    2,
    2,
    figsize=(12, 5),
    sharex=True)
axx = axs.ravel()
for i, column in enumerate(df2.columns):
    df2[df2.columns[i]].loc[start_date:end_date].plot(
        ax=axx[i])
    axx[i].set_xlabel("month")
    axx[i].set_ylabel(column)
```

Sets the start date

Sets the end date

Creates the matplotlib to hold the four charts

Ensures the plots are stored as a series so you can loop through them

Loops through each of the columns of data

Sets the chart to display a particular column of data

Sets the y-axis label

Sets the x-axis label

In line 3 of listing 6.8, you state that you want to display a grid of 2 charts by 2 charts with a width of 12 inches and height of 5 inches. This creates four Matplotlib objects in a 2-by-2 grid that you can fill with data. You use the code in line 4 to turn the 2-by-2 grid into a list that you can loop through. The variable axx stores the list of Matplotlib subplots that you will fill with data.

When you run the code in the cell by clicking into the cell and pressing Ctrl + Enter ←,
you can see the chart, as shown in figure 6.7.

```
start_date = "2018-01-01"
end_date = "2018-12-31"
fig, axs = plt.subplots(2, 2, figsize=(12, 5), sharex=True)
axx = axs.ravel()
for i, column in enumerate(df2.columns):
    df2[df2.columns[i]].loc[start_date:end_date].plot(ax=axx[i])
    axx[i].set_xlabel("month")
    axx[i].set_ylabel(column)
```

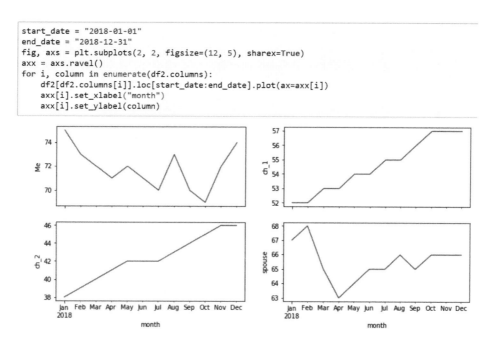

**Figure 6.7   Time-series data generated with code, showing the weight of family members over the
past year.**

So far in this chapter, you've looked at time-series data, learned how to loop through
it, and how to visualize it. Now you'll learn why neural networks are a good way to forecast time-series events.

6.4   *What is a neural network?*

Neural networks (sometimes referred to as *deep learning*) approach machine learning in a different way than traditional machine learning models such as XGBoost.
Although both XGBoost and neural networks are examples of supervised machine
learning, each uses different tools to tackle the problem. XGBoost uses an ensemble
of approaches to attempt to predict the target result, whereas a neural network uses
just one approach.

A neural network attempts to solve the problem by using layers of interconnected
neurons. The neurons take inputs in one end and push outputs to the other side. The
connections between the neurons have weights assigned to them. If a neuron receives
enough weighted input, then it *fires* and pushes the signal to the next layer of neurons
it's connected to.

DEFINITION   A neuron is simply a mathematical function that receives two or more inputs, applies a weighting to the inputs, and passes the result to multiple outputs if the weighting is above a certain threshold.

Imagine you're a neuron in a neural network designed to filter gossip based on how salacious it is or how true it is. You have ten people (the interconnected neurons) who tell you gossip, and if it is salacious enough, true enough, or a combination of the two, you'll pass it on to the ten people who you send gossip to. Otherwise, you'll keep it to yourself.

Also imagine that some of the people who send you gossip are not very trustworthy, whereas others are completely honest. (The trustworthiness of your sources changes when you get feedback on whether the gossip was true or not and how salacious it was perceived to be.) You might not pass on a piece of gossip from several of your least trustworthy sources, but you might pass on gossip that the most trusted people tell you, even if only one person tells you this gossip.

Now, let's look at a specific time-series neural network algorithm that you'll use to forecast power consumption.

What is DeepAR?

DeepAR is Amazon's time-series neural network algorithm that takes as its input related types of time-series data and automatically combines the data into a global model of all time series in a dataset. It then uses this global model to predict future events. In this way, DeepAR is able to incorporate different types of time-series data (such as power consumption, temperature, wind speed, and so on) into a single model that is used in our example to predict power consumption.

In this chapter, you are introduced to DeepAR, and you'll build a model for Kiara that uses historical data from her 48 sites. In chapter 7, you will incorporate other features of the DeepAR algorithm (such as weather patterns) to enhance your prediction.[a]

a   You can read more about DeepAR on this AWS site: https://docs.aws.amazon.com/sagemaker/latest/dg/deepar.html.

6.5   *Getting ready to build the model*

Now that you have a deeper understanding of neural networks and of how DeepAR works, you can set up another notebook in SageMaker and make some decisions. As you did in the previous chapters, you are going to do the following:

1   Upload a dataset to S3
2   Set up a notebook on SageMaker
3   Upload the starting notebook
4   Run it against the data

TIP If you're jumping into the book at this chapter, you might want to visit the appendixes, which show you how to do the following:

- Appendix A: sign up to AWS, Amazon's web service
- Appendix B: set up S3, AWS's file storage service
- Appendix C: set up SageMaker

6.5.1 Uploading a dataset to S3

To set up the dataset for this chapter, you'll follow the same steps as you did in appendix B. You don't need to set up another bucket though. You can just go to the same bucket you created earlier. In our example, we called the bucket mlforbusiness, but your bucket will be called something different.

When you go to your S3 account, you will see a list of your buckets. Clicking the bucket you created for this book, you might see the ch02, ch03, ch04, and ch05 folders if you created these in the previous chapters. For this chapter, you'll create a new folder called *ch06*. You do this by clicking Create Folder and following the prompts to create a new folder.

Once you've created the folder, you are returned to the folder list inside your bucket. There you will see you now have a folder called ch06.

Now that you have the ch06 folder set up in your bucket, you can upload your data file and start setting up the decision-making model in SageMaker. To do so, click the folder and download the data file at this link:

https://s3.amazonaws.com/mlforbusiness/ch06/meter_data.csv

Then upload the CSV file into the ch06 folder by clicking Upload. Now you're ready to set up the notebook instance.

6.5.2 Setting up a notebook on SageMaker

Just as we prepared the CSV data you uploaded to S3 for this scenario, we've already prepared the Jupyter notebook you'll use now. You can download it to your computer by navigating to this URL:

https://s3.amazonaws.com/mlforbusiness/ch06/energy_usage.ipynb

Once you have downloaded the notebook to your computer, you can upload it to the same SageMaker folder you used to work with the time_series_practice.ipynb notebook. (Click Upload to upload the notebook to the folder.)

6.6 Building the model

As in the previous chapters, you will go through the code in six parts:

1. Load and examine the data.
2. Get the data into the right shape.
3. Create training and validation datasets.

4 Train the machine learning model.

5 Host the machine learning model.

6 Test the model and use it to make decisions.

6.6.1   *Part 1: Loading and examining the data*

As in the previous chapters, the first step is to say where you are storing the data. To do that, you need to change 'mlforbusiness' to the name of the bucket you created when you uploaded the data, and rename its subfolder to the name of the subfolder on S3 where you want to store the data (listing 6.9).

If you named the S3 folder ch06, then you don't need to change the name of the folder. If you kept the name of the CSV file that you uploaded earlier in the chapter, then you don't need to change the meter_data.csv line of code. If you changed the name of the CSV file, then update meter_data.csv to the name you changed it to. To run the code in the notebook cell, click the cell and press $\boxed{Ctrl}$+$\boxed{Enter \leftarrow}$.

Listing 6.9   Say where you are storing the data

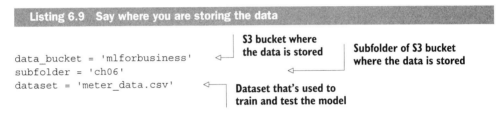

```
data_bucket = 'mlforbusiness'
subfolder = 'ch06'
dataset = 'meter_data.csv'
```

S3 bucket where the data is stored

Subfolder of S3 bucket where the data is stored

Dataset that's used to train and test the model

Many of the Python modules and libraries imported in listing 6.10 are the same as the imports you used in previous chapters, but you'll also use Matplotlib in this chapter.

Listing 6.10   Importing the modules

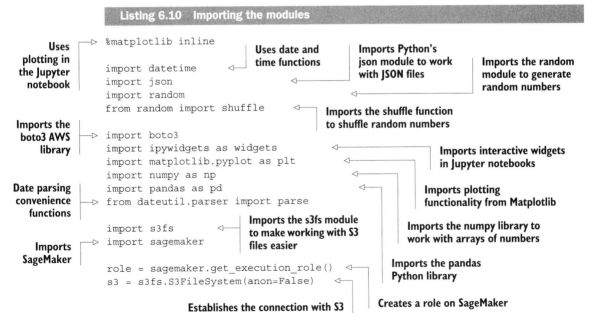

Uses plotting in the Jupyter notebook

```
%matplotlib inline

import datetime
import json
import random
from random import shuffle

import boto3
import ipywidgets as widgets
import matplotlib.pyplot as plt
import numpy as np
import pandas as pd
from dateutil.parser import parse

import s3fs
import sagemaker

role = sagemaker.get_execution_role()
s3 = s3fs.S3FileSystem(anon=False)
```

Uses date and time functions

Imports Python's json module to work with JSON files

Imports the random module to generate random numbers

Imports the shuffle function to shuffle random numbers

Imports the boto3 AWS library

Imports interactive widgets in Jupyter notebooks

Imports plotting functionality from Matplotlib

Date parsing convenience functions

Imports the s3fs module to make working with S3 files easier

Imports the numpy library to work with arrays of numbers

Imports SageMaker

Imports the pandas Python library

Establishes the connection with S3

Creates a role on SageMaker

Next, you'll load and view the data. In listing 6.11, you read in the CSV data and display the top 5 rows in a pandas DataFrame. Each row of the dataset shows 30-minute energy usage data for a 13-month period from November 1, 2017, to mid-December 2018. Each column represents one of the 48 retail sites owned by Kiara's company.

Listing 6.11 Loading and viewing the data

```
s3_data_path = \                                              Reads the S3 dataset
    f"s3://{data_bucket}/{subfolder}/data"
s3_output_path = \                                            Displays 3 rows of the
    f"s3://{data_bucket}/{subfolder}/output"                  DataFrame (rows 5, 6, and 7)
df = pd.read_csv(
    f's3://{data_bucket}/{subfolder}/meter_data.csv',
    index_col=0)
df.head()                       Reads in the meter data

                     Displays the top 5 rows
```

Table 6.4 shows the output of running `display(df[5:8])`. The table only shows the first 6 sites, but the dataset in the Jupyter notebook has all 48 sites.

Table 6.4 Power usage data in half-hour intervals

Index	Site_1	Site_2	Site_3	Site_4	Site_5	Site_6
2017-11-01 00:00:00	13.30	13.3	11.68	13.02	0.0	102.9
2017-11-01 00:30:00	11.75	11.9	12.63	13.36	0.0	122.1
2017-11-01 01:00:00	12.58	11.4	11.86	13.04	0.0	110.3

You can see that column 5 in table 6.4 shows zero consumption for the first hour and a half in November. We don't know if this is an error in the data or if the stores didn't consume any power during that period. We'll discuss the implications of this as you work through the analysis.

Let's take a look at the size of your dataset. When you run the code in listing 6.12, you can see that the dataset has 48 columns (one column per site) and 19,632 rows of 30-minute data usage.

Listing 6.12 Viewing the number of rows and columns

```
print(f'Number of rows in dataset: {df.shape[0]}')
print(f'Number of columns in dataset: {df.shape[1]}')
```

Now that you've loaded the data, you need to get the data into the right shape so you can start working with it.

6.6.2   *Part 2: Getting the data into the right shape*

Getting the data into the right shape involves several steps:

- Converting the data to the right interval
- Determining if missing values are going to create any issues
- Fixing any missing values if you need to
- Saving the data to S3

First, you will convert the data to the right interval. Time-series data from the power meters at each site is recorded in 30-minute intervals. The fine-grained nature of this data is useful for certain work, such as quickly identifying power spikes or drops, but it is not the right interval for our analysis.

For this chapter, because you are not combining this dataset with any other datasets, you could use the data with the 30-minute interval to run your model. However, in the next chapter, you will combine the historical consumption data with daily weather forecast predictions to better predict the consumption over the coming month. The weather data that you'll use in chapter 7 reflects weather conditions set at daily intervals. Because you'll be combining the power consumption data with daily weather data, it is best to work with the power consumption data using the same interval.

CONVERTING THE DATASET FROM 30-MINUTE INTERVALS TO DAILY INTERVALS

Listing 6.13 shows how to convert 30-minute data to daily data. The pandas library contains many helpful features for working with time-series data. Among the most helpful is the `resample` function, which easily converts time-series data in a particular interval (such as 30 minutes) into another interval (such as daily).

In order to use the `resample` function, you need to ensure that your dataset uses the date column as the index and that the index is in date-time format. As you might expect from its name, the index is used to reference a row in the dataset. So, for example, a dataset with the index of `1:30 AM 1 November 2017` can be referenced by `1:30 AM 1 November 2017`. The pandas library can take rows referenced by such indexes and convert them into other periods such as days, months, quarters, or years.

Listing 6.13   Converting data to daily figures

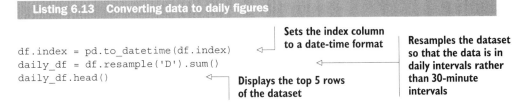

```
df.index = pd.to_datetime(df.index)      ◁── Sets the index column
daily_df = df.resample('D').sum()              to a date-time format
daily_df.head()      ◁──
```

Resamples the dataset so that the data is in daily intervals rather than 30-minute intervals

Displays the top 5 rows of the dataset

Table 6.5 shows the converted data in daily figures.

Table 6.5 Power usage data in daily intervals

Index	Site_1	Site_2	Site_3	Site_4	Site_5	Site_6
2017-11-01	1184.23	1039.1	985.95	1205.07	None	6684.4
2017-11-02	1210.9	1084.7	1013.91	1252.44	None	6894.3
2017-11-03	1247.6	1004.2	963.95	1222.4	None	6841

The following listing shows the number of rows and columns in the dataset as well as the earliest and latest dates.

Listing 6.14 Viewing the data in daily intervals

```
print(daily_df.shape)                                    ◁─── Prints the number of rows
print(f'Time series starts at {daily_df.index[0]} \          and columns in the dataset
and ends at {daily_df.index[-1]}')    ◁─┐
                                        └─ Displays the earliest date and
                                           latest date in the dataset
```

In the output, you can now see that your dataset has changed from 19,000 rows of 30-minute data to 409 rows of daily data, and the number of columns remains the same:

```
(409, 48)
Time series starts at 2017-11-01 00:00:00 and ends at 2018-12-14 00:00:00
```

HANDLING ANY MISSING VALUES IF REQUIRED

As you work with the pandas library, you'll come across certain gems that allow you to handle a thorny problem in an elegant manner. The line of code shown in listing 6.15 is one such instance.

Basically, the data you are using in this chapter, with the exception of the first 30 days, is in good shape. It is missing a few observations, however, representing a handful of missing data points. This doesn't impact the training of the data (DeepAR handles missing values well) but you can?t make predictions using data with missing values. To use this dataset to make predictions, you need to ensure there are no missing values. This section shows you how to do that.

> **NOTE** You need to make sure that the data you are using for your predictions is complete and has no missing values.

The pandas `fillna` function has the ability to forward fill missing data. This means that you can tell `fillna` to fill any missing value with the preceding value. But Kiara knows that most of their locations follow a weekly cycle. If one of the warehouse sites (that are closed on weekends) is missing data for one Saturday, and you forward fill the day from Friday, your data will not be very accurate. Instead, the one-liner in the next listing replaces a missing value with the value from 7 days prior.

Listing 6.15 Replacing missing values

```
daily_df = daily_df.fillna(daily_df.shift(7))
```

With that single line of code, you have replaced missing values with values from 7 days earlier.

VIEWING THE DATA

Time-series data is best understood visually. To help you understand the data better, you can create charts showing the power consumption at each of the sites. The code in listing 6.16 is similar to the code you worked with in the practice notebook earlier in the chapter. The primary difference is that, instead of looping through every site, you set up a list of sites in a variable called `indicies` and loop through that.

If you remember, in listing 6.16, you imported `matplotlib.pyplot as plt`. Now you can use all of the functions in `plt`. In line 2 of listing 6.16, you create a Matplotlib figure that contains a 2-by-5 grid. Line 3 of the listing tells Matplotlib that when you give it data to work with, it should turn the data into a single data series rather than an array.

In line 4, the indices are the column numbers of the sites in the dataset. Remember that Python is zero-based, so `0` would be site 1. These 10 sites display in the 2-by-5 grid you set up in line 2. To view other sites, just change the numbers and run the cell again.

Line 5 is a loop that goes through each of the indices you defined in line 4. For each item in an index, the loop adds data to the Matplotlib figure you created in line 2. Your figure contains a grid 2 charts wide by 5 charts long so it has room for 10 charts, which is the same as the number of indices.

Line 6 is where you put all the data into the chart. `daily_df` is the dataset that holds your daily power consumption data for each of the sites. The first part of the line selects the data that you'll display in the chart. Line 7 inserts the data into the plot. Lines 8 and 9 set the labels on the charts.

Listing 6.16   Creating charts to show each site over a period of months

Ensures that the data will be stored as a series

```
print('Number of time series:',daily_df.shape[1])
fig, axs = plt.subplots(
    5,
    2,
    figsize=(20, 20),
    sharex=True)
axx = axs.ravel()
indices = [0,1,2,3,4,5,40,41,42,43]
for i in indices:
    plot_num = indices.index(i)
    daily_df[daily_df.columns[i]].loc[
        "2017-11-01":"2018-01-31"].plot(
            ax=axx[plot_num])
    axx[plot_num].set_xlabel("date")
    axx[plot_num].set_ylabel("kW consumption")
```

Displays the number of columns in the daily_df dataset. This is 48, the total number of sites.

Creates the Matplotlib figure to hold the 10 charts (5 rows of 2 charts)

Identifies the 10 sites you want to chart

Loops through each of the sites

Gets each element, one by one, from the list indices

Sets the label for the x-axis

Sets the label for the y-axis

Sets the data in the plot to the site referenced by the variable indicies

Now that you can see what your data looks like, you can create your training and test datasets.

6.6.3 *Part 3: Creating training and testing datasets*

DeepAR requires the data to be in JSON format. JSON is a very common data format that can be read by people and by machines.

A hierarchical structure that you commonly use is the folder system on your computer. When you store documents relating to different projects you are working on, you might create a folder for each project and put the documents relating to each project in that folder. That is a hierarchical structure.

In this chapter, you will create a JSON file with a simple structure. Instead of project folders holding project documents (like the previous folder example), each element in your JSON file will hold daily power consumption data for one site. Also, each element will hold two additional elements, as shown in listing 6.17. The first element is start, which contains the date, and the second is target, which contains each day's power consumption data for the site. Because your dataset covers 409 days, there are 409 elements in the target element.

Listing 6.17 Sample JSON file

```json
{
    "start": "2017-11-01 00:00:00",
    "target": [
        1184.23,
        1210.9000000000003,
        1042.9000000000003,
        ...
        1144.2500000000002,
        1225.1299999999999
    ]
}
```

To create the JSON file, you need to take the data through a few transformations:

- Convert the data from a DataFrame to a list of series
- Withhold 30 days of data from the training dataset so you don't train the model on data you are testing against
- Create the JSON files

The first transformation is converting the data from a DataFrame to a list of data series, with each series containing the power consumption data for a single site. The following listing shows how to do this.

Listing 6.18 Converting a DataFrame to a list of series

Loops through the columns in the DataFrame

```python
daily_power_consumption_per_site = []
for column in daily_df.columns:
```

Creates an empty list to hold the columns in the DataFrame

```
    site_consumption = site_consumption.fillna(0)          ◁┐  Replaces any missing
    daily_power_consumption_per_site.append(                │  values with zeros
        site_consumption)                        ◁┐
                                                  │   Appends the
                                                  │   column to the list
print(f'Time series covers \
{len(daily_power_consumption_per_site[0])} days.')     ◁┐  Prints the number
print(f'Time series starts at \                         │  of days
{daily_power_consumption_per_site[0].index[0]}')    ◁┐
print(f'Time series ends at \                        │
{daily_power_consumption_per_site[0].index[-1]}')   ◁┐  Prints the start date
                                                     │   of the first site
                          Prints the end date of
                              the first site
```

In line 1 in the listing, you create a list to hold each of your sites. Each element of this list holds one column of the dataset. Line 2 creates a loop to iterate through the columns. Line 3 appends each column of data to the `daily_power_consumption_per _site` list you created in line 1. Lines 4 and 5 print the results so you can confirm that the conversion still has the same number of days and covers the same period as the data in the DataFrame.

Next, you set a couple of variables that will help you keep the time periods and intervals consistent throughout the notebook. The first variable is `freq`, which you set to D. *D* stands for day, and it means that you are working with daily data. If you were working with hourly data, you'd use H, and monthly data is M.

You also set your *prediction period*. This is the number of days out that you want to predict. For example, in this notebook, the training dataset goes from November 1, 2017, to October 31, 2018, and you are predicting power consumption for November 2018. November has 30 days, so you set the `prediction_length` to 30.

Once you have set the variables in lines 1 and 2 of listing 6.19, you then define the start and end dates in a timestamp format. *Timestamp* is a data format that stores dates, times, and frequencies as a single object. This allows for easy transformation from one frequency to another (such as daily to monthly) and easy addition and subtraction of dates and times.

In line 3, you set the `start_date` of the dataset to November 1, 2017, and the end date of the training dataset to the end of October 2018. The end date of the test dataset is 364 days later, and the end date of the training dataset is 30 days after that. Notice that you can simply add days to the original timestamp, and the dates are automatically calculated.

Listing 6.19   Setting the length of the prediction period

```
                            Sets frequency of the
                            time series to day
freq = 'D'          ◁┘                            Sets prediction
prediction_length = 30                 ◁┐         length to 30 days

start_date = pd.Timestamp(          Sets start_date as
    "2017-11-01 00:00:00",          November 1, 2017
    freq=freq)             ◁┘
```

```
end_training = start_date + 364
end_testing = end_training + prediction_length

print(f'End training: {end_training}, End testing: {end_testing}')
```

Sets the end of the training
dataset to October 31, 2018

Sets the end of the test
dataset to November 30, 2018

The DeepAR JSON input format represents each time series as a JSON object. In the simplest case (which you will use in this chapter), each time series consists of a start timestamp (start) and a list of values (target). The JSON input format is a JSON file that shows the daily power consumption for each of the 48 sites that Kiara is reporting on. The DeepAR model requires two JSON files: the first is the training data and the second is the test data.

Creating JSON files is a two-step process. First, you create a Python dictionary with a structure identical to the JSON file, and then you convert the Python dictionary to JSON and save the file.

To create the Python dictionary format, you loop through each of the daily_power _consumption_per_site lists you created in listing 6.18 and set the start variable and *target* list. Listing 6.20 uses a type of Python loop called a *list comprehension*. The code between the open and close curly brackets (line 2 and 5 of listing 6.20) marks the start and end of each element in the JSON file shown in listing 6.17. The code in lines 3 and 4 inserts the start date and a list of days from the training dataset.

Lines 1 and 7 mark the beginning and end of the list comprehension. The loop is described in line 6. The code states that the list ts will be used to hold each site as it loops through the daily_power_consumption_per_site list. That is why, in line 4, you see the variable ts[start_date:end_training]. The code ts[start_date:end _training] is a list that contains one site and all of the days in the range start_date to end_training that you set in listing 6.19.

Listing 6.20 Creating a Python dictionary in same structure as a JSON file

```
training_data = [
    {
        "start": str(start_date),
        "target": ts[
            start_date:end_training].tolist()
    }
    for ts in timeseries
]
test_data = [
    {
        "start": str(start_date),
        "target": ts[
            start_date:end_testing].tolist()
    }
    for ts in timeseries
]
```

Sets the start date

Sets the start of each dictionary object

Creates a list of dictionary objects to hold the training data

Creates a list of power consumption training data for one site

Sets the end of each dictionary object

Sets the end of the training data

List comprehension loop

Creates a list of power consumption test data for one site

Now that you have created two Python dictionaries called test_data and training_data, you need to save these as JSON files on S3 for DeepAR to work with. To do this, create a helper function that converts a Python dictionary to JSON and then apply that function to the test_data and training_data dictionaries, as shown in the following listing.

Listing 6.21 Saving the JSON files to S3

Creates a function that writes
the dictionary data to S3

Opens an S3
file object

Writes the
dictionary object
in JSON format

```
def write_dicts_to_s3(path, data):
    with s3.open(path, 'wb') as f:
        for d in data:
            f.write(json.dumps(d).encode("utf-8"))
            f.write("\n".encode('utf-8'))

write_dicts_to_s3(
    f'{s3_data_path}/train/train.json',
    training_data)
write_dicts_to_s3(
    f'{s3_data_path}/test/test.json',
    test_data)
```

Loops
through
the data

Writes a newline
character so that each
dictionary object starts
on a new line

Applies the function
to the training data

Applies the function
to the test data

Your training and test data are now stored on S3 in JSON format. With that, the data is in a SageMaker session and you are ready to start training the model.

6.6.4   *Part 4: Training the model*

Now that you have saved the data on S3 in JSON format, you can start training the model. As shown in the following listing, the first step is to set up some variables that you will hand to the estimator function that will build the model.

Listing 6.22 Setting up a server to train the model

Sets the path to save the
machine learning model

```
s3_output_path = \
    f's3://{data_bucket}/{subfolder}/output'
sess = sagemaker.Session()
image_name = sagemaker.amazon.amazon_estimator.get_image_uri(
    sess.boto_region_name,
    "forecasting-deepar",
    "latest")
```

Creates a variable
to hold the
SageMaker session

Tells AWS to use the
forecasting-deepar image
to create the model

Next, you hand the variables to the estimator (listing 6.23). This sets up the type of machine that SageMaker will fire up to create the model. You will use a single instance of a c5.2xlarge machine. SageMaker creates this machine, starts it, builds the model, and shuts it down automatically. The cost of this machine is about US$0.47 per hour. It will take about 3 minutes to create the model, which means it will cost only a few cents.

Listing 6.23 Setting up an estimator to hold training parameters

Creates the estimator
variable for the model

Applies the
SageMaker
session

Sets the
image

```
estimator = sagemaker.estimator.Estimator(
    sagemaker_session=sess,
    image_name=image_name,
    role=role,
    train_instance_count=1,
    train_instance_type='ml.c5.2xlarge',
    base_job_name='ch6-energy-usage',
    output_path=s3_output_path
)
```

Sets up a single instance
for the training machine

Sets the size of the machine
the model will be trained on

Nominates a name
for the job

Saves the model to the output
location you set up on S3

Gives the image a role
that allows it to run

Richie's note on SageMaker instance types

Throughout this book, you will notice that we have chosen to use the instance type ml.m4.xlarge for all training and inference instances. The reason behind this decision was simply that usage of these instance types was included in Amazon's free tier at the time of writing. (For details on Amazon's current inclusions in the free tier, see https://aws.amazon.com/free.)

For all the examples provided in this book, this instance is more than adequate. But what should you be using in your workplace if your problem is more complex and/or your dataset is much larger than the ones we have presented? There are no hard and fast rules, but here are a few guidelines:

- See the SageMaker examples on the Amazon website for the algorithm you are using. Start with the Amazon example as your default.
- Make sure you calculate how much your chosen instance type is actually costing you for training and inference (https://aws.amazon.com/sagemaker/pricing).
- If you have a problem with training or inference cost or time, don't be afraid to experiment with different instance sizes.
- Be aware that quite often a very large and expensive instance can actually cost less to train a model than a smaller one, as well as run in much less time.
- XGBoost runs in parallel when training on a compute instance but does not benefit at all from a GPU instance, so don't waste time on a GPU-based instance (p3 or accelerated computing) for training or inference. However, feel free to try an m5.24xlarge or m4.16xlarge in training. It might actually be cheaper!
- Neural-net-based models will benefit from GPU instances in training, but these usually should not be required for inference as these are exceedingly expensive.
- Your notebook instance is most likely to be memory constrained if you use it a lot, so consider an instance with more memory if this becomes a problem for you. Just be aware that you are paying for every hour the instance is running even if you are not using it!

Once you set up the estimator, you then need to set its parameters. SageMaker exposes several parameters for you. The only two that you need to change are the last two parameters shown in lines 7 and 8 of listing 6.24: `context_length` and `prediction_length`.

The *context length* is the minimum period of time that will be used to make a prediction. By setting this to 90, you are saying that you want DeepAR to use 90 days of data as a minimum to make its predictions. In business settings, this is typically a good value as it allows for the capture of quarterly trends. The *prediction length* is the period of time you are predicting. For this notebook, you are predicting November data, so you use the `prediction_length` of 30 days.

Listing 6.24 Inserting parameters for the estimator

Sets the batch size to 64 (leave this value as is)　　Sets the hyperparameters　　Sets the frequency to daily

```
estimator.set_hyperparameters(
    time_freq=freq,
    epochs="400",
    early_stopping_patience="40",
    mini_batch_size="64",
    learning_rate="5E-4",
    context_length="90",
    prediction_length=str(prediction_length)
)
```

Sets the epochs to 400 (leave this value as is)

Sets the early stopping to 40 (leave this value as is)

Sets the context length to 90 days

Sets the prediction length to 30 days

Sets the learning rate to 0.0005 (the decimal conversion of the exponential value 5E-4)

Now you train the model. This can take 5 to 10 minutes.

Listing 6.25 Training the model

Pulls in the training and test data to create the model　　Training data

Test data

```
%%time
data_channels = {
    "train": "{}/train/".format(s3_data_path),
    "test": "{}/test/".format(s3_data_path)
}
estimator.fit(inputs=data_channels, wait=True)
```

Runs the estimator function that creates the model

After this code runs, the model is trained, so now you can host it on SageMaker so it is ready to make decisions.

6.6.5 *Part 5: Hosting the model*

Hosting the model involves several steps. First, in listing 6.26, you delete any existing endpoints you have so you don't end up paying for a bunch of endpoints you aren't using.

Listing 6.26 Deleting existing endpoints

```
endpoint_name = 'energy-usage'
try:
    sess.delete_endpoint(
            sagemaker.predictor.RealTimePredictor(
                endpoint=endpoint_name).endpoint,
                delete_endpoint_config=True)
    print(
        'Warning: Existing endpoint deleted to make way for new endpoint.')
    from time import sleep
    sleep(10)
except:
    pass
```

Next is a code cell that you don't really need to know anything about. This is a helper class prepared by Amazon to allow you to review the results of the DeepAR model as a pandas DataFrame rather than as JSON objects. It is a good bet that in the future they will make this code part of the M library. For now, just run it by clicking into the cell and pressing Ctrl + Enter ↵.

You are now at the stage where you set up your endpoint to make predictions (listing 6.27). You will use an m5.large machine as it represents a good balance of power and price. As of March 2019, AWS charges 13.4 US cents per hour for the machine. So if you keep the endpoint up for a day, the total cost will be US$3.22.

Listing 6.27 Setting up the `predictor` class

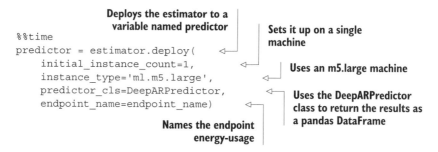

Deploys the estimator to a variable named predictor

Sets it up on a single machine

```
%%time
predictor = estimator.deploy(
    initial_instance_count=1,
    instance_type='ml.m5.large',
    predictor_cls=DeepARPredictor,
    endpoint_name=endpoint_name)
```

Uses an m5.large machine

Uses the DeepARPredictor class to return the results as a pandas DataFrame

Names the endpoint energy-usage

You are ready to start making predictions.

6.6.6 *Part 6: Making predictions and plotting results*

In the remainder of the notebook, you will do three things:

- Run a prediction for a month that shows the 50th percentile (most likely) prediction and also displays the range of prediction between two other percentiles. For example, if you want to show an 80% confidence range, the prediction will also show you the lower and upper range that falls within an 80% confidence level.

- Graph the results so that you can easily describe the results.
- Run a prediction across all the results for the data in November 2018. This data was not used to train the DeepAR model, so it will demonstrate how accurate the model is.

PREDICTING POWER CONSUMPTION FOR A SINGLE SITE

To predict power consumption for a single site, you just pass the site details to the predictor function. In the following listing, you are running the predictor against data from site 1.

Listing 6.28 Setting up the `predictor` class

```
predictor.predict(ts=daily_power_consumption_per_site[0]
                 [start_date+30:end_training],
              quantiles=[0.1, 0.5, 0.9]).head()
```
→ **Runs the predictor function against the first site**

Table 6.6 shows the result of running the prediction against site 1. The first column shows the day, and the second column shows the prediction from the 10th percentile of results. The third column shows the 50th percentile prediction, and the last column shows the 90th percentile prediction.

Table 6.6   Predicting power usage data for site 1 of Kiara's companies

Day	0.1	0.5	0.9
2018-11-01	1158.509766	1226.118042	1292.315430
2018-11-02	1154.938232	1225.540405	1280.479126
2018-11-03	1119.561646	1186.360962	1278.330200

Now that you have a way to generate predictions, you can chart the predictions.

CHARTING THE PREDICTED POWER CONSUMPTION FOR A SINGLE SITE

The code in listing 6.29 shows a function that allows you to set up charting. It is similar to the code you worked with in the practice notebook but has some additional complexities that allow you to display graphically the range of results.

Listing 6.29 Setting up a function that allows charting

```
def plot(              ←┐  Sets the argument
    predictor,          |  for the plot function
    target_ts,
    end_training=end_training,
    plot_weeks=12,
    confidence=80
):
    print(f"Calling served model to generate predictions starting from \
{end_training} to {end_training+prediction_length}")
```

```
low_quantile = 0.5 - confidence * 0.005
up_quantile = confidence * 0.005 + 0.5

plot_history = plot_weeks * 7

fig = plt.figure(figsize=(20, 3))
ax = plt.subplot(1,1,1)

prediction = predictor.predict(
    ts=target_ts[:end_training],
    quantiles=[
        low_quantile, 0.5, up_quantile])

target_section = target_ts[
    end_training-plot_history:\
    end_training+prediction_length]

target_section.plot(
    color="black",
    label='target')

ax.fill_between(
    prediction[str(low_quantile)].index,
    prediction[str(low_quantile)].values,
    prediction[str(up_quantile)].values,
    color="b",
    alpha=0.3,
    label=f'{confidence}% confidence interval'
)
prediction["0.5"].plot(
    color="b",
    label='P50')

ax.legend(loc=2)
ax.set_ylim(
    target_section.min() * 0.5,
    target_section.max() * 1.5)
```

Calculates the lower range

Calculates the upper range

Calculates the number of days based on the plot_weeks argument

Sets the size of the chart

Sets a single chart to display

The prediction function

Sets the actual values

Sets the color of the line for the actual values

Sets the color of the range

Sets the color of the prediction

Creates the legend

Sets the scale

Line 1 of the code creates a function called `plot` that lets you create a chart of the data for each site. The `plot` function takes three arguments:

- `predictor`—The predictor that you ran in listing 6.28, which generates predictions for the site
- `plot_weeks`—The number of weeks you want to display in your chart
- `confidence`—The confidence level for the range that is displayed in the chart

In lines 2 and 3 in listing 6.29, you calculate the confidence range you want to display from the confidence value you entered as an argument in line 1. Line 4 calculates the number of days based on the `plot_weeks` argument. Lines 5 and 6 set the size of the plot and the subplot. (You are only displaying a single plot.) Line 7 runs the `prediction` function on the site. Lines 8 and 9 set the date range for the chart and the color of the actual line. In line 10, you set the prediction range that will display in the chart, and in line 11 you define the prediction line. Finally, lines 12 and 13 set the legend and the scale of the chart.

> **NOTE**   In this function to set up charting, we use global variables that were set earlier in the notebook. This is not ideal but keeps the function a little simpler for the purposes of this book.

Listing 6.30 runs the function. The chart shows the actual and prediction data for a single site. This listing uses site 34 as the charted site, shows a period of 8 weeks before the 30-day prediction period, and defines a confidence level of 80%.

Listing 6.30   Running the function that creates the chart

```
         Sets the site for                Sets the number of weeks
              charting                     to include in the chart
site_id = 34            ◁
plot_weeks = 8          ◁         Sets the confidence
confidence = 80         ◁         level at 80%
plot(                   ◁         Runs the plot function
        predictor,
        target_ts=daily_power_consumption_per_site[
            site_id][start_date+30:],
        plot_weeks=plot_weeks,
        confidence=confidence
    )
```

Figure 6.8 shows the chart you have produced. You can use this chart to show the predicted usage patterns for each of Kiara's sites.

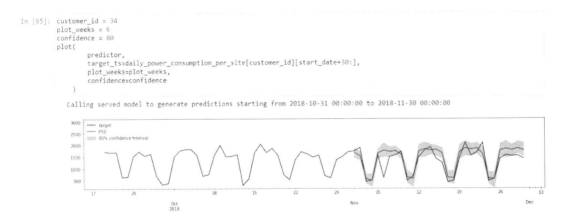

Figure 6.8   Chart showing predicted versus actual power consumption for November 2018, for one of Kiara's sites

CALCULATING THE ACCURACY OF THE PREDICTION ACROSS ALL SITES

Now that you can see one of the sites, it's time to calculate the error across all the sites. To express this, you use a Mean Absolute Percentage Error (MAPE). This function takes the difference between the actual value and the predicted value and divides it by the actual value. For example, if an actual value is 50 and the predicted value is 45, you'd subtract 45 from 50 to get 5, and then divide by 50 to get 0.1. Typically, this is expressed as a percentage, so you multiply that number by 100 to get 10%. So the MAPE of an actual value of 50 and a predicted value of 45 is 10%.

The first step in calculating the MAPE is to run the predictor across all the data for November 2018 and get the actual values (usages) for that month. Listing 6.31 shows how to do this.

In line 5, you see a function that we haven't used yet in the book: the `zip` function. This is a very useful piece of code that allows you to loop through two lists concurrently and do interesting things with the paired items from each list. In this listing, the interesting thing you'll do is to print the actual value compared to the prediction.

Listing 6.31 Running the predictor

```
predictions= []
for i, ts in enumerate(                        Loops through daily site
    daily_power_consumption_per_site):  ◁┘   power consumption

    print(i, ts[0])
    predictions.append(
        predictor.predict(
            ts=ts[start_date+30:end_training]   Runs predictions for the
            )['0.5'].sum())                 ◁   month of November

usages = [ts[end_training+1:end_training+30].sum() \
    for ts in daily_power_consumption_per_site]   ◁┘  Gets the usages

for p,u in zip(predictions,usages):             ◁
    print(f'Predicted {p} kwh but usage was {u} kwh,')   Prints usages
                                                         and predictions
```

The next listing shows the code that calculates the MAPE. Once the function is defined, you will use it to calculate the MAPE.

Listing 6.32 Calculating the Mean Absolute Percentage Error (MAPE)

```
def mape(y_true, y_pred):
    y_true, y_pred = np.array(y_true), np.array(y_pred)
    return np.mean(np.abs((y_true - y_pred) / y_true)) * 100
```

The following listing runs the MAPE function across all the usages and predictions for the 30 days in November 2018 and returns the mean MAPE across all the days.

Listing 6.33 Running the MAPE function

```
print(f'MAPE: {round(mape(usages, predictions),1)}%')
```

The MAPE across all the days is 5.7%, which is pretty good, given that you have not yet added weather data. You'll do that in chapter 7. Also in chapter 7, you'll get to work with a longer period of data so the DeepAR algorithm can begin to detect annual trends.

6.7   Deleting the endpoint and shutting down your notebook instance

It is important that you shut down your notebook instance and delete your endpoint. We don't want you to get charged for SageMaker services that you're not using.

6.7.1   Deleting the endpoint

Appendix D describes how to shut down your notebook instance and delete your endpoint using the SageMaker console, or you can do that with the following code.

Listing 6.34   Deleting the notebook

```
# Remove the endpoint (optional)
# Comment out this cell if you want the endpoint to persist after Run All
sagemaker.Session().delete_endpoint(rcf_endpoint.endpoint)
```

To delete the endpoint, uncomment the code in the listing, then click [Ctrl]+[Enter ←] to run the code in the cell.

6.7.2   Shutting down the notebook instance

To shut down the notebook, go back to your browser tab where you have SageMaker open. Click the Notebook Instances menu item to view all of your notebook instances. Select the radio button next to the notebook instance name as shown in figure 6.9, then select Stop from the Actions menu. It takes a couple of minutes to shut down.

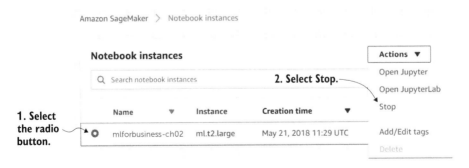

Figure 6.9   Shutting down the notebook

6.8 Checking to make sure the endpoint is deleted

If you didn't delete the endpoint using the notebook (or if you just want to make sure it is deleted), you can do this from the SageMaker console. To delete the endpoint, click the radio button to the left of the endpoint name, then click the Actions menu item and click Delete in the menu that appears.

When you have successfully deleted the endpoint, you will no longer incur AWS charges for it. You can confirm that all of your endpoints have been deleted when you see the text "There are currently no resources" displayed on the Endpoints page (figure 6.10).

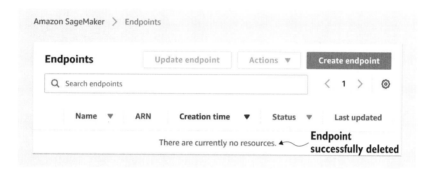

Figure 6.10   Endpoint deleted

Kiara can now predict power consumption for each site with a 5.7% MAPE and, as importantly, she can take her boss through the charts to show what she is predicting to occur in each site.

Summary

- Time-series data consists of a number of observations at particular intervals. You can visualize time-series data as line charts.
- Jupyter notebooks and the pandas library are excellent tools for transforming time-series data and for creating line charts of the data.
- Matplotlib is a Python charting library.
- Instructions to Jupyter begin with a % symbol. When you see a command in a Jupyter notebook that starts with % or with %%, it's known as a magic command.
- A `for` loop is the most common type of loop you'll use in data analysis and machine learning. The `enumerate` function lets you keep track of how many times you have looped through a list.
- A neural network (sometimes referred to as *deep learning*) is an example of supervised machine learning.
- You can build a neural network using SageMaker's DeepAR model.

- DeepAR is Amazon's time-series neural network algorithm that takes as its input related types of time-series data and automatically combines the data into a global model of all time series in a dataset to predict future events.
- You can use DeepAR to predict power consumption.

7

Improving your company's monthly power usage forecast

This chapter covers

- Adding additional data to your analysis
- Using pandas to fill in missing values
- Visualizing your time-series data
- Using a neural network to generate forecasts
- Using DeepAR to forecast power consumption

In chapter 6, you worked with Kiara to develop an AWS SageMaker DeepAR model to predict power consumption across her company's 48 sites. You had just a bit more than one year's data for each of the sites, and you predicted the temperature for November 2018 with an average percentage error of less that 6%. Amazing! Let's expand on this scenario by adding additional data for our analysis and filling in any missing values. First, let's take a deeper look at DeepAR.

7.1 DeepAR's ability to pick up periodic events

The DeepAR algorithm was able to identify patterns such as weekly trends in our data from chapter 6. Figure 7.1 shows the predicted and actual usage for site 33 in November. This site follows a consistent weekly pattern.

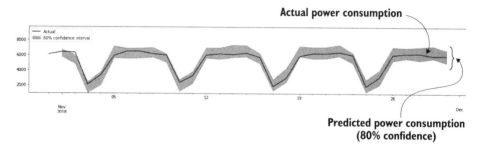

Figure 7.1   Predicted versus actual consumption from site 33 using the DeepAR model you built in chapter 6

You and Kiara are heroes. The company newsletter included a two-page spread showing you and Kiara with a large printout of your predictions for December. Unfortunately, when January came around, anyone looking at that photo would have noticed that your predictions weren't that accurate for December. Fortunately for you and Kiara, not many people noticed because most staff take some holiday time over Christmas, and some of the sites had a mandatory shutdown period.

"Wait a minute!" You and Kiara said at the same time as you were discussing why your December predictions were less accurate. "With staff taking time off and mandatory shut-downs, it's no wonder December was way off."

When you have rare but still regularly occurring events like a Christmas shutdown in your time-series data, your predictions will still be accurate, provided you have enough historical data for the machine learning model to pick up the trend. You and Kiara would need several years of power consumption data for your model to pick up a Christmas shutdown trend. But you don't have this option because the smart meters were only installed in November 2017. So what do you do?

Fortunately for you (and Kiara), SageMaker DeepAR is a neural network that is particularly good at incorporating several different time-series datasets into its forecasting. And these can be used to account for events in your time-series forecasting that your time-series data can't directly infer.

To demonstrate how this works, figure 7.2 shows time-series data covering a typical month. The x-axis shows days per month. The y-axis is the amount of power consumed on each day. The shaded area is the predicted power consumption with an 80%

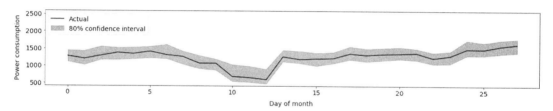

Figure 7.2   Actual versus predicted usage during a normal month

confidence interval. An 80% confidence interval means that 4 out of every 5 days will fall within this range. The black line shows the actual power consumption for that day. In figure 7.2, you can see that the actual power consumption was within the confidence interval for every day of the month.

Figure 7.3 shows a month with a shutdown from the 10th to the 12th day of the month. You can see that the actual power consumption dropped on these days, but the predicted power consumption did not anticipate this.

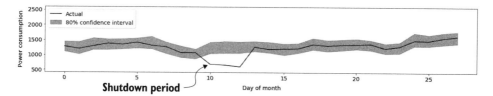

Figure 7.3   Actual versus predicted usage during a month with a shutdown

There are three possible reasons why the power consumption data during this shutdown was not correctly predicted. First, the shutdown *is* a regularly occurring event, but there is not enough historical data for the DeepAR algorithm to pick up the recurring event. Second, the shutdown *is not* a recurring event (and so can't be picked up in the historical data) but is an event that can be identified through other datasets. An example of this is a planned shutdown where Kiara's company is closing a site for a few days in December. Although the historical dataset won't show the event, the impact of the event on power consumption can be predicted if the model incorporated planned staff schedules as one of its time series. We'll discuss this more in the next section. Finally, the shutdown is not planned, and there is no dataset that could be incorporated to show the shutdown. An example of this is a work stoppage due to an employee strike. Unless your model can predict labor activism, there is not much your machine learning model can do to predict power consumption during these periods.

7.2   DeepAR's greatest strength: Incorporating related time series

To help the DeepAR model predict trends, you need to provide it with additional data that shows trends. As an example, you know that during the shutdown periods, only a handful of staff are rostered. If you could feed this data into the DeepAR algorithm, then it could use this information to predict power consumption during shutdown periods.[1]

---

[1] You can read more about DeepAR on the AWS site: https://docs.aws.amazon.com/sagemaker/latest/dg/deepar.html.

Figure 7.4 shows the number of staff rostered in a month during a shutdown. You can see that for most days, there are between 10 and 15 staff members at work, but on the 10th, 11th, and 12th, there are only 4 to 6 staff members.

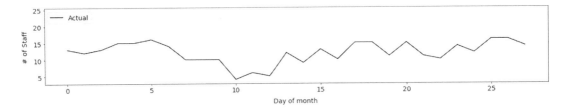

Figure 7.4   Number of staff rostered during a month with a shutdown

If you could incorporate this time series into the DeepAR model, you would better predict upcoming power consumption. Figure 7.5 shows the prediction when you use both historical consumption and rostering data in your DeepAR model.

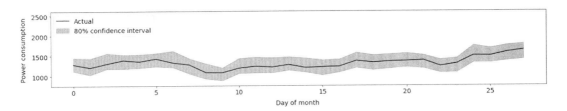

Figure 7.5   Power consumption predictions incorporating historical and staff roster data

In this chapter, you'll learn how to incorporate additional datasets into your DeepAR model to improve the accuracy of the model in the face of known upcoming events that are either not periodic or are periodic, but you don't have enough historical data for the model to incorporate into its predictions.

7.3   *Incorporating additional datasets into Kiara's power consumption model*

In chapter 6, you helped Kiara build a DeepAR model that predicted power consumption across each of the 41 sites owned by her company. The model worked well when predicting power consumption in November, but performed less well when predicting December's consumption because some of the sites were on reduced operating hours or shut down altogether.

Additionally, you noticed that there were seasonal fluctuations in power usage that you attributed to changes in temperature, and you noticed that different types of sites had different usage patterns. Some types of sites were closed every weekend, whereas others operated consistently regardless of the day of the week. After discussing this with Kiara, you realized that some of the sites were retail sites, whereas others were industrial or transport-related areas.

In this chapter, the notebook you'll build will incorporate this data. Specifically, you'll add the following datasets to the power consumption metering data you used in chapter 6:

- *Site categories*—Indicates retail, industrial, or transport site
- *Site holidays*—Indicates whether a site has a planned shutdown
- *Site maximum temperatures*—Lists the maximum temperature forecast for each site each day

Then you'll train the model using these three datasets.

Different types of datasets

The three datasets used in this chapter can be classified into two types of data:

- *Categorical*—Information about the site that doesn't change. The dataset site categories, for example, contains categorical data. (A site is a retail site and will likely always be a retail site.)
- *Dynamic*—Data that changes over time. Holidays and forecasted maximum temperatures are examples of dynamic data.

When predicting power consumption for the month of December, you'll use a schedule of planned holidays for December and the forecasted temperature for that month.

7.4 Getting ready to build the model

As in previous chapters, you need to do the following to set up another notebook in SageMaker and fine tune your predictions:

1. From S3, download the notebook we prepared for this chapter.
2. Set up the folder to run the notebook on AWS SageMaker.
3. Upload the notebook to AWS SageMaker.
4. Download the datasets from your S3 bucket.
5. Create a folder in your S3 bucket to store the datasets.
6. Upload the datasets to your AWS S3 bucket.

Given that you've followed these steps in each of the previous chapters, we'll move quickly through them in this chapter.

7.4.1 Downloading the notebook we prepared

We prepared the notebook you'll use in this chapter. You can download it from this location:

https://s3.amazonaws.com/mlforbusiness/ch07/energy_consumption_additional_datasets.ipynb

Save this file on your computer. In step 3, you'll upload it to SageMaker.

7.4.2   Setting up the folder on SageMaker

Go to AWS SageMaker at https://console.aws.amazon.com/sagemaker/home, and select Notebook Instances from the left-hand menu. If your instance is stopped, you'll need to start it. Once it is started, click Open Jupyter.

This opens a new tab and shows you a list of folders in SageMaker. If you have been following along in earlier chapters, you will have a folder for each of the earlier chapters. Create a new folder for this chapter. We've called our folder ch07.

7.4.3   Uploading the notebook to SageMaker

Click the folder you've just created, and click Upload to upload the notebook. Select the notebook you downloaded in step 1, and upload it to SageMaker. Figure 7.6 shows what your SageMaker folder might look like after uploading the notebook.

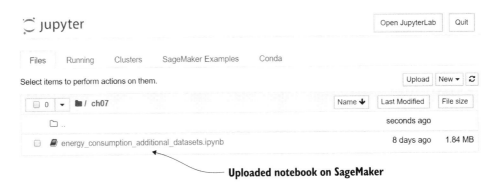

Figure 7.6   Viewing the uploaded energy_consumption_additional_datasets notebook on S3

7.4.4   Downloading the datasets from the S3 bucket

We stored the datasets for this chapter in one of our S3 buckets. You can download each of the datasets by clicking the following links:

- *Meter data*—https://s3.amazonaws.com/mlforbusiness/ch07/meter_data_daily.csv
- *Site categories*—https://s3.amazonaws.com/mlforbusiness/ch07/site_categories.csv
- *Site holidays*—https://s3.amazonaws.com/mlforbusiness/ch07/site_holidays.csv
- *Site maximums*—https://s3.amazonaws.com/mlforbusiness/ch07/site_maximums.csv

The power consumption data you'll use in this chapter is provided by BidEnergy (http://www.bidenergy.com), a company that specializes in power-usage forecasting and in minimizing power expenditure. The algorithms used by BidEnergy are more sophisticated than you'll see in this chapter, but you'll still get a feel for how machine learning in general, and neural networks in particular, can be applied to forecasting problems.

7.4.5 Setting up a folder on S3 to hold your data

In AWS S3, go to the bucket you created to hold your data in earlier chapters, and create another folder. You can see a list of your buckets at this link:

https://s3.console.aws.amazon.com/s3/buckets

The bucket we are using to hold our data is called mlforbusiness. Your bucket will be called something else (a name of your choosing). Once you click into your bucket, create a folder to store your data, naming it something like *ch07*.

7.4.6 Uploading the datasets to your AWS bucket

After creating the folder on S3, upload the datasets you downloaded in step 4. Figure 7.7 shows what your S3 folder might look like.

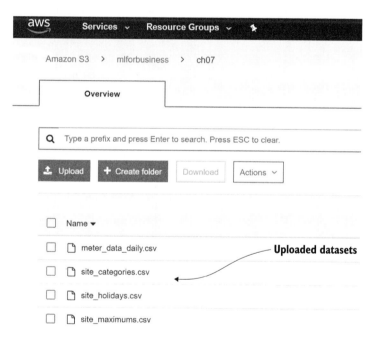

Figure 7.7   Viewing the uploaded CSV datasets on S3

7.5   Building the model

With the data uploaded to S3 and the notebook uploaded to SageMaker, you can now start to build the model. As in previous chapters, you'll go through the following steps:

1 Set up the notebook.
2 Import the datasets.
3 Get the data into the right shape.
4 Create training and test datasets.
5 Configure the model and build the server.
6 Make predictions and plot results.

7.5.1   Part 1: Setting up the notebook

Listing 7.1 shows your notebook setup. You will need to change the values in line 1 to the name of the S3 bucket you created on S3, then change line 2 to the subfolder of that bucket where you saved the data. Line 3 sets the location of the training and test data created in this notebook, and line 4 sets the location where the model is stored.

Listing 7.1   Setting up the notebook

```
data_bucket = 'mlforbusiness'          ◁─── S3 bucket where the data is stored
subfolder = 'ch07'                     ◁─── Subfolder of the bucket where the data is stored
s3_data_path = \
    f"s3://{data_bucket}/{subfolder}/data"     ◁─── Path where training and test data will be stored
s3_output_path = \
    f"s3://{data_bucket}/{subfolder}/output"   ◁─── Path where model will be stored
```

The next listing imports the modules required by the notebook. This is the same as the imports used in chapter 6, so we won't review these here.

Listing 7.2   Importing Python modules and libraries

```
%matplotlib inline

from dateutil.parser import parse
import json
import random
import datetime
import os

import pandas as pd
import boto3
import s3fs
import sagemaker
import numpy as np
import pandas as pd
import matplotlib.pyplot as plt
```

```
role = sagemaker.get_execution_role()
s3 = s3fs.S3FileSystem(anon=False)
s3_data_path = f"s3://{data_bucket}/{subfolder}/data"
s3_output_path = f"s3://{data_bucket}/{subfolder}/output"
```

With that done, you are now ready to import the datasets.

7.5.2 Part 2: Importing the datasets

Unlike other chapters, in this notebook, you'll upload four datasets for the meter, site categories, holidays, and maximum temperatures. The following listing shows how to import the meter data.

Listing 7.3 Importing the meter data

```
daily_df = pd.read_csv(
    f's3://{data_bucket}/{subfolder}/meter_data_daily.csv',
    index_col=0,
    parse_dates=[0])
daily_df.index.name = None
daily_df.head()
```

The meter data you use in this chapter has a few more months of observations. In chapter 6, the data ranged from October 2017 to October 2018. This dataset contains meter data from November 2017 to February 2019.

Listing 7.4 Displaying information about the meter data

```
print(daily_df.shape)
print(f'timeseries starts at {daily_df.index[0]} \
and ends at {daily_df.index[-1]}')
```

Listing 7.5 shows how to import the site categories data. There are three types of sites:

- Retail
- Industrial
- Transport

Listing 7.5 Displaying information about the site categories

```
category_df = pd.read_csv
    (f's3://{data_bucket}/{subfolder}/site_categories.csv',
    index_col=0
    ).reset_index(drop=True)
print(category_df.shape)
print(category_df.Category.unique())
category_df.head()
```

In listing 7.6, you import the holidays. Working days and weekends are marked with a 0; holidays are marked with a 1. There is no need to mark all the weekends as holidays because DeepAR can pick up that pattern from the site meter data. Although you don't have enough site data for DeepAR to identify annual patterns, DeepAR can work out the pattern if it has access to a dataset that shows holidays at each of the sites.

Listing 7.6 Displaying information about holidays for each site

```
holiday_df = pd.read_csv(
    f's3://{data_bucket}/{subfolder}/site_holidays.csv',
    index_col=0,
    parse_dates=[0])
print(holiday_df.shape)
print(f'timeseries starts at {holiday_df.index[0]} \
and ends at {holiday_df.index[-1]}')
holiday_df.loc['2018-12-22':'2018-12-27']
```

Listing 7.7 shows the maximum temperature reached each day for each of the sites. The sites are located in Australia, so energy usage increases as temperatures rise in the summer due to air conditioning; whereas, in more temperate climates, energy usage increases more as temperatures drop below zero degrees centigrade in the winter due to heating.

Listing 7.7 Displaying information about maximum temperatures for each site

```
max_df = pd.read_csv(
    f's3://{data_bucket}/{subfolder}/site_maximums.csv',
    index_col=0,
    parse_dates=[0])
print(max_df.shape)
print(f'timeseries starts at {max_df.index[0]} \
and ends at {max_df.index[-1]}')
```

With that, you are finished loading data into your notebook. To recap, for each site for each day from November 1, 2018, to February 28, 2019, you loaded data from CSV files for

- Energy consumption
- Site category (Retail, Industrial, or Transport)
- Holiday information (1 represents a holiday and 0 represents a working day or normal weekend)
- Maximum temperatures reached on the site

You will now get the data into the right shape to train the DeepAR model.

7.5.3 *Part 3: Getting the data into the right shape*

With your data loaded into DataFrames, you can now get each of the datasets ready for training the DeepAR model. The shape of each of the datasets is the same: each site is represented by a column, and each day is represented by a row.

In this section, you'll ensure that there are no problematic missing values in each of the columns and each of the rows. DeepAR is very good at handling missing values in training data but cannot handle missing values in data it uses for predictions. To ensure that you don't have annoying errors when running predictions, you fill in missing values in your prediction range. You'll use November 1, 2018, to January 31, 2019, to train the data, and you'll use December 1, 2018, to February 28, 2019, to test the model. This means that for your prediction range, there cannot be any missing data from December 1, 2018, to February 28, 2019. The following listing replaces any zero values with `None` and then checks for missing energy consumption data.

Listing 7.8 Checking for missing energy consumption data

```
daily_df = daily_df.replace([0],[None])
daily_df[daily_df.isnull().any(axis=1)].index
```

You can see from the output that there are several days in November 2018 with missing data because that was the month the smart meters were installed, but there are no days with missing data after November 2018. This means you don't need to do anything further with this dataset because there's no missing prediction data.

The next listing checks for missing category data. Again, there is no missing category data, so you can move on to holidays and missing maximum temperatures.

Listing 7.9 Checking for missing category data and holiday data

```
print(f'{len(category_df[category_df.isnull().any(axis=1)])} \
sites with missing categories.')
print(f'{len(holiday_df[holiday_df.isnull().any(axis=1)])} \
days with missing holidays.')
```

The following listing checks for missing maximum temperature data. There are several days without maximum temperature values. This is a problem, but one that can be easily solved.

Listing 7.10 Checking for missing maximum temperature data

```
print(f'{len(max_df[max_df.isnull().any(axis=1)])} \
days with missing maximum temperatures.')
```

The next listing uses the `interpolate` function to fill in missing data for a time series. In the absence of other information, the best way to infer missing values for a temperature time series like this is straight line interpolation based on time.

Listing 7.11 Fixing missing maximum temperature data

```
max_df = max_df.interpolate(method='time')        ⟵  Interpolates
print(f'{len(max_df[max_df.isnull().any(axis=1)])} \      missing values
days with missing maximum temperatures. Problem solved!')
```

To ensure you are looking at data similar to the data we used in chapter 6, take a look at the data visually. In chapter 6, you learned about using Matplotlib to display multiple plots. As a refresher, listing 7.12 shows the code for displaying multiple plots. Line 1 sets the shape of the plots as 6 rows by 2 columns. Line 2 creates a series that can be looped over. Line 3 sets which 12 sites will be displayed. And lines 4 through 7 set the content of each plot.

Listing 7.12 Fixing missing maximum temperature data

```
print('Number of timeseries:',daily_df.shape[1])
fig, axs = plt.subplots(
    6,                          Sets the shape as 6
    2,                          rows by 2 columns
    figsize=(20, 20),                               Sets which sites will
    sharex=True)            Creates a series from    display in the plots
axx = axs.ravel()           the 6 x 2 plot table
indices = [0,1,2,3,26,27,33,39,42,43,46,47]                  Loops through the list
for i in indices:                                            of sites and gets each
    plot_num = indices.index(i)                              site number
    daily_df[daily_df.columns[i]].loc[
        "2017-11-01":"2019-02-28"       Gets the data
        ].plot(ax=axx[plot_num])        for the plot      Sets the x-axis
    axx[plot_num].set_xlabel("date")                        label for the plot
    axx[plot_num].set_ylabel("kW consumption")
                                                          Sets the y-axis
                                                          label for the plot
```

Figure 7.8 shows the output of listing 7.12. In the notebook, you'll see an additional eight charts because the shape of the plot is 6 rows and 2 columns of plots.

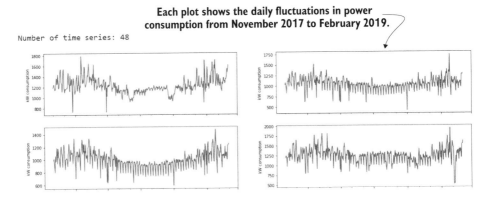

Figure 7.8 Site plots showing temperature fluctuations from November 2017 to February 2019

With that complete, you can start preparing the training and test datasets.

7.5.4 *Part 4: Creating training and test datasets*

In the previous section, you loaded each of the datasets into pandas DataFrames and fixed any missing values. In this section, you'll turn the DataFrames into lists to create the training and test data.

Listing 7.13 converts the category data into a list of numbers. Each of the numbers 0 to 2 represents one of these categories: Retail, Industrial, or Transport.

```
cats = list(category_df.Category.astype('category').cat.codes)
print(cats)
```

The next listing turns the power consumption data into a list of lists. Each site is a list, and there are 48 of these lists.

```
usage_per_site = [daily_df[col] for col in daily_df.columns]
print(f'timeseries covers {len(usage_per_site[0])} days.')
print(f'timeseries starts at {usage_per_site[0].index[0]}')
print(f'timeseries ends at {usage_per_site[0].index[-1]}')
usage_per_site[0][:10]
```

Displays the first 10 days of power consumption from site 0

The next listing repeats this for holidays.

```
hols_per_site = [holiday_df[col] for col in holiday_df.columns]
print(f'timeseries covers {len(hols_per_site[0])} days.')
print(f'timeseries starts at {hols_per_site[0].index[0]}')
print(f'timeseries ends at {hols_per_site[0].index[-1]}')
hols_per_site[0][:10]
```

And the next listing repeats this for maximum temperatures.

```
max_per_site = [max_df[col] for col in max_df.columns]
print(f'timeseries covers {len(max_per_site[0])} days.')
print(f'timeseries starts at {max_per_site[0].index[0]}')
print(f'timeseries ends at {max_per_site[0].index[-1]}')
max_per_site[0][:10]
```

With the data formatted as lists, you can split it into training and test data and then write the files to S3. Listing 7.17 sets the start date for both testing and training as November 1, 2017. It then sets the end date for training as the end of January 2019, and the end date for testing as 28 days later (the end of February 2019).

```
freq = 'D'
prediction_length = 28

start_date = pd.Timestamp("2017-11-01", freq=freq)
end_training = pd.Timestamp("2019-01-31", freq=freq)
end_testing = end_training + prediction_length

print(f'End training: {end_training}, End testing: {end_testing}')
```

Just as you did in chapter 6, you now create a simple function, shown in the next listing, that writes each of the datasets to S3. In listing 7.19, you'll apply the function to the test data and training data.

Listing 7.18   Creating a function that writes data to S3

```
def write_dicts_to_s3(path, data):
    with s3.open(path, 'wb') as f:
        for d in data:
            f.write(json.dumps(d).encode("utf-8"))
            f.write("\n".encode('utf-8'))
```

The next listing creates the training and test datasets. DeepAR requires categorical data to be separated from dynamic features. Notice how this is done in the next listing.

Listing 7.19   Creating training and test datasets

```
training_data = [
    {
        "cat": [cat],                                   Categorical data for
                                                        site categories
        "start": str(start_date),
        "target": ts[start_date:end_training].tolist(),
        "dynamic_feat": [
            hols[
                start_date:end_training
                ].tolist(),                             Dynamic data
            maxes[                                      for holidays
                start_date:end_training
                ].tolist(),                             Dynamic data
        ] # Note: List of lists                         for maximum
    }                                                   temperatures
    for cat, ts, hols, maxes in zip(
        cats,
        usage_per_site,
        hols_per_site,
        max_per_site)
]

test_data = [
    {
        "cat": [cat],
        "start": str(start_date),
        "target": ts[start_date:end_testing].tolist(),
        "dynamic_feat": [
            hols[start_date:end_testing].tolist(),
            maxes[start_date:end_testing].tolist(),
        ] # Note: List of lists
    }
    for cat, ts, hols, maxes in zip(
        cats,
        usage_per_site,
        hols_per_site,
        max_per_site)
]
```

```
write_dicts_to_s3(f'{s3_data_path}/train/train.json', training_data)
write_dicts_to_s3(f'{s3_data_path}/test/test.json', test_data)
```

In this chapter, you set up the notebook in a slightly different way than you have in previous chapters. This chapter is all about how to use additional datasets such as site category, holidays, and max temperatures to enhance the accuracy of time series predictions.

To allow you to see the impact of these additional datasets on the prediction, we have prepared a commented-out notebook cell that creates and tests the model without using the additional datasets. If you are interested in seeing this result, you can uncomment that part of the notebook and run the entire notebook again. If you do so, you will see that, without using the additional datasets, the MAPE (Mean Average Percentage Error) for February is 20%! Keep following along in this chapter to see what it drops to when the additional datasets are incorporated into the model.

7.5.5 Part 5: Configuring the model and setting up the server to build the model

Listing 7.20 sets the location on S3 where you will store the model and determines how SageMaker will configure the server that will build the model. At this point in the process, you would normally set a random seed to ensure that each run through the DeepAR algorithm generates a consistent result. At the time of this writing, there is an inconsistency in SageMaker's DeepAR model—the functionality is not available. It doesn't impact the accuracy of the results, only the consistency of the results.

> #### Listing 7.20 Setting up the SageMaker session and server to create the model

```
s3_output_path = f's3://{data_bucket}/{subfolder}/output'
sess = sagemaker.Session()
image_name = sagemaker.amazon.amazon_estimator.get_image_uri(
    sess.boto_region_name,
    "forecasting-deepar",
    "latest")

data_channels = {
    "train": f"{s3_data_path}/train/",
    "test": f"{s3_data_path}/test/"
}
```

Listing 7.21 is used to calculate the MAPE of the prediction. It is calculated for each day you are predicting by subtracting the predicted consumption each day from the actual consumption and dividing it by the predicted amount (and, if the number is negative, making it positive). You then take the average of all of these amounts.

For example, if on three consecutive days, you predicted consumption of 1,000 kilowatts of power, and the actual consumption was 800, 900, and 1,150 kilowatts, the MAPE would be the average of (200 / 800) + (100 / 900) + (150 / 1150) divided by three. This equals 0.16, or 16%.

Listing 7.21 Calculating MAPE

```
def mape(y_true, y_pred):
    y_true, y_pred = np.array(y_true), np.array(y_pred)
    return np.mean(np.abs((y_true - y_pred) / y_true)) * 100
```

Listing 7.22 is the standard SageMaker function for creating a DeepAR model. You do not need to modify this function. You just need to run it as is by clicking `Ctrl`+`Enter ←` while in the notebook cell.

Listing 7.22 The DeepAR `predictor` function used in chapter 6

```
class DeepARPredictor(sagemaker.predictor.RealTimePredictor):

    def __init__(self, *args, **kwargs):
        super().__init__(
            *args,
            content_type=sagemaker.content_types.CONTENT_TYPE_JSON,
            **kwargs)

    def predict(
            self,
            ts,
            cat=None,
            dynamic_feat=None,
            num_samples=100,
            return_samples=False,
            quantiles=["0.1", "0.5", "0.9"]):x
        prediction_time = ts.index[-1] + 1
        quantiles = [str(q) for q in quantiles]
        req = self.__encode_request(
            ts,
            cat,
            dynamic_feat,
            num_samples,
            return_samples,
            quantiles)
        res = super(DeepARPredictor, self).predict(req)
        return self.__decode_response(
            res,
            ts.index.freq,
            prediction_time,
            return_samples)

    def __encode_request(
            self,
            ts,
            cat,
            dynamic_feat,
            num_samples,
            return_samples,
            quantiles):
        instance = series_to_dict(
            ts,
```

```
                cat if cat is not None else None,
                dynamic_feat if dynamic_feat else None)
            configuration = {
                "num_samples": num_samples,
                "output_types": [
                    "quantiles",
                    "samples"] if return_samples else ["quantiles"],
                "quantiles": quantiles
            }
            http_request_data = {
                "instances": [instance],
                "configuration": configuration
            }
            return json.dumps(http_request_data).encode('utf-8')

    def __decode_response(
            self,
            response,
            freq,
            prediction_time,
            return_samples):
        predictions = json.loads(
            response.decode('utf-8'))['predictions'][0]
        prediction_length = len(next(iter(
                predictions['quantiles'].values()
            )))
        prediction_index = pd.DatetimeIndex(
            start=prediction_time,
            freq=freq,
            periods=prediction_length)
        if return_samples:
            dict_of_samples = {
                    'sample_' + str(i): s for i, s in enumerate(
                        predictions['samples'])
                }
        else:
            dict_of_samples = {}
        return pd.DataFrame(
            data={**predictions['quantiles'],
            **dict_of_samples},
            index=prediction_index)

    def set_frequency(self, freq):
        self.freq = freq

def encode_target(ts):
    return [x if np.isfinite(x) else "NaN" for x in ts]

def series_to_dict(ts, cat=None, dynamic_feat=None):
    # Given a pandas.Series, returns a dict encoding the timeseries.
    obj = {"start": str(ts.index[0]), "target": encode_target(ts)}
    if cat is not None:
        obj["cat"] = cat
    if dynamic_feat is not None:
        obj["dynamic_feat"] = dynamic_feat
    return obj
```

Just as in chapter 6, you now need to set up the estimator and then set the parameters for the estimator. SageMaker exposes several parameters for you. The only two that you need to change are the first two parameters shown in lines 1 and 2 of listing 7.23: `context_length` and `prediction_length`.

The *context length* is the minimum period of time that will be used to make a prediction. By setting this value to 90, you are saying that you want DeepAR to use 90 days of data as a minimum to make its predictions. In business settings, this is typically a good value because it allows for the capture of quarterly trends. The *prediction length* is the period of time you are predicting. In this notebook, you are predicting February data, so you use the `prediction_length` of 28 days.

Listing 7.23 Setting up the estimator

```
%%time
estimator = sagemaker.estimator.Estimator(
    sagemaker_session=sess,
    image_name=image_name,
    role=role,
    train_instance_count=1,
    train_instance_type='ml.c5.2xlarge', # $0.476 per hour as of Jan 2019.
    base_job_name='ch7-energy-usage-dynamic',
    output_path=s3_output_path
)

estimator.set_hyperparameters(
    context_length="90",
    prediction_length=str(prediction_length),
    time_freq=freq,
    epochs="400",
    early_stopping_patience="40",
    mini_batch_size="64",
    learning_rate="5E-4",
    num_dynamic_feat=2,
)

estimator.fit(inputs=data_channels, wait=True)
```

Sets the context length to 90 days

Sets the prediction length to 28 days

Sets the frequency to daily

Sets the epochs to 400 (leave this value as is)

Sets the early stopping to 40 (leave this value as is)

Sets the batch size to 64 (leave this value as is)

Sets the number of dynamic features to 2 for holidays and temperature (leave this as is)

Sets the learning rate to 0.0005 (the decimal conversion of the exponential value 5E-4)

Listing 7.24 creates the endpoint you'll use to test the predictions. In the next chapter, you'll learn how to expose that endpoint to the internet, but for this chapter, just like the preceding chapters, you'll hit the endpoint using code in the notebook.

Listing 7.24 Setting up the endpoint

```
endpoint_name = 'energy-usage-dynamic'

try:
    sess.delete_endpoint(
        sagemaker.predictor.RealTimePredictor(
```

```
                    endpoint=endpoint_name).endpoint)
        print(
            'Warning: Existing endpoint deleted to make way for new endpoint.')
        from time import sleep
        sleep(30)
except:
    pass
```

Now it's time to build the model. The following listing creates the model and assigns it to the variable `predictor`.

Listing 7.25 Building and deploying the model

```
%%time
predictor = estimator.deploy(
    initial_instance_count=1,
    instance_type='ml.m5.large',
    predictor_cls=DeepARPredictor,
    endpoint_name=endpoint_name)
```

7.5.6 *Part 6: Making predictions and plotting results*

Once the model is built, you can run the predictions against each of the days in February. First, however, you'll test the predictor as shown in the next listing.

Listing 7.26 Checking the predictions from the model

```
predictor.predict(
    cat=[cats[0]],
    ts=usage_per_site[0][start_date+30:end_training],
    dynamic_feat=[
            hols_per_site[0][start_date+30:end_training+28].tolist(),
            max_per_site[0][start_date+30:end_training+28].tolist(),
        ],
    quantiles=[0.1, 0.5, 0.9]
).head()
```

Now that you know the predictor is working as expected, you're ready run it across each of the days in February 2019. But before you do that, to allow you to calculate the MAPE, you'll create a list called *usages* to store the actual power consumption for each site for each day in February 2019. When you run the predictions across each day in February, you store the result in a list called *predictions*.

Listing 7.27 Getting predictions for all sites during February 2019

```
usages = [
    ts[end_training+1:end_training+28].sum() for ts in usage_per_site]

predictions= []
for s in range(len(usage_per_site)):
    # call the end point to get the 28 day prediction
    predictions.append(
```

```
        predictor.predict(
            cat=[cats[s]],
            ts=usage_per_site[s][start_date+30:end_training],
            dynamic_feat=[
                hols_per_site[s][start_date+30:end_training+28].tolist(),
                max_per_site[s][start_date+30:end_training+28].tolist(),
            ]
        )['0.5'].sum()
    )

for p,u in zip(predictions,usages):
    print(f'Predicted {p} kwh but usage was {u} kwh.')
```

Once you have the usage list and the predictions list, you can calculate the MAPE by running the mape function you created in listing 7.21.

Listing 7.28   Calculating MAPE

```
print(f'MAPE: {round(mape(usages, predictions),1)}%')
```

Listing 7.29 is the same plot function you saw in chapter 6. The function takes the usage list and creates predictions in the same way you did in listing 7.27. The difference in the plot function here is that it also calculates the lower and upper predictions at an 80% confidence level. It then plots the actual usage as a line and shades the area within the 80% confidence threshold.

Listing 7.29   Displaying plots of sites

```
def plot(
    predictor,
    site_id,
    end_training=end_training,
    plot_weeks=12,
    confidence=80
):
    low_quantile = 0.5 - confidence * 0.005
    up_quantile = confidence * 0.005 + 0.5
    target_ts = usage_per_site[site_id][start_date+30:]
    dynamic_feats = [
            hols_per_site[site_id][start_date+30:].tolist(),
            max_per_site[site_id][start_date+30:].tolist(),
        ]

    plot_history = plot_weeks * 7

    fig = plt.figure(figsize=(20, 3))
    ax = plt.subplot(1,1,1)

    prediction = predictor.predict(
        cat = [cats[site_id]],
        ts=target_ts[:end_training],
```

```
        dynamic_feat=dynamic_feats,
        quantiles=[low_quantile, 0.5, up_quantile])

    target_section = target_ts[
        end_training-plot_history:end_training+prediction_length]
    target_section.plot(color="black", label='target')

    ax.fill_between(
        prediction[str(low_quantile)].index,
        prediction[str(low_quantile)].values,
        prediction[str(up_quantile)].values,
        color="b",
        alpha=0.3,
        label=f'{confidence}% confidence interval'
    )

    ax.set_ylim(target_section.min() * 0.5, target_section.max() * 1.5)
```

The following listing runs the `plot` function you created in listing 7.29.

Listing 7.30 Plotting several sites and the February predictions

```
indices = [2,26,33,39,42,47,3]
for i in indices:
    plot_num = indices.index(i)
    plot(
        predictor,
        site_id=i,
        plot_weeks=6,
        confidence=80
```

Figure 7.9 shows the predicted results for several sites. As you can see, the daily prediction for each time series falls within the shaded area.

One of the advantages of displaying the data in this manner is that it is easy to pick out sites where you haven't predicted accurately. For example, if you look at site 3, the last site in the plot list in figure 7.10, you can see that there was a period in February with almost no power usage, when you predicted it would have a fairly high usage. This provides you with an opportunity to improve your model by including additional datasets.

When you see a prediction that is clearly inaccurate, you can investigate what happened during that time and determine if there is some data source that you could incorporate into your predictions. If, for example, this site had a planned maintenance shutdown in early February and this shutdown was not already included in your holiday data, if you can get your hands on a schedule of planned maintenance shutdowns, then you can easily incorporate that data in your model in the same way that you incorporated the holiday data.

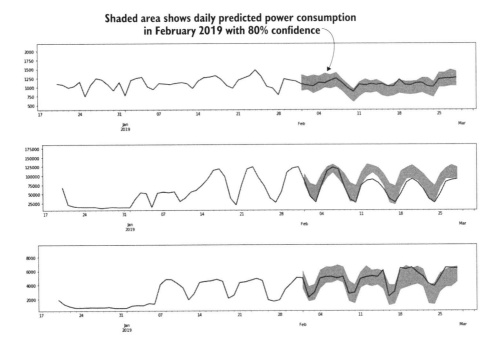

Figure 7.9   Site plots showing predicted usage for February 2019

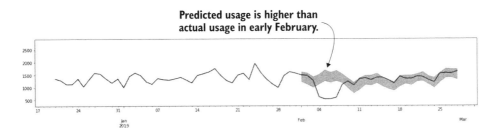

Figure 7.10   Predicted usage for site 3 is incorrect in early February.

7.6   *Deleting the endpoint and shutting down your notebook instance*

As always, when you are no longer using the notebook, remember to shut down the notebook and delete the endpoint. We don't want you to get charged for SageMaker services that you're not using.

7.6.1   *Deleting the endpoint*

To delete the endpoint, uncomment the code in listing 7.31, then click Ctrl+Enter↵ to run the code in the cell.

Listing 7.31 Deleting the endpoint

```
# Remove the endpoints
# Comment out these cells if you want the endpoint to persist after Run All
# sess.delete_endpoint('energy-usage-baseline')
# sess.delete_endpoint('energy-usage-dynamic')
```

7.6.2 Shutting down the notebook instance

To shut down the notebook, go back to your browser tab where you have SageMaker open. Click the Notebook Instances menu item to view all of your notebook instances. Select the radio button next to the notebook instance name, as shown in figure 7.11, then select Stop from the Actions menu. It takes a couple of minutes to shut down.

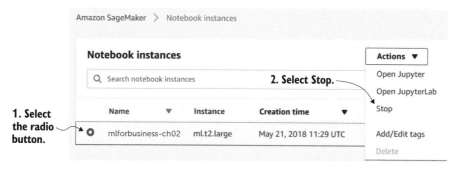

Figure 7.11 Shutting down the notebook

7.7 Checking to make sure the endpoint is deleted

If you didn't delete the endpoint using the notebook (or if you just want to make sure it is deleted), you can do this from the SageMaker console. To delete the endpoint, click the radio button to the left of the endpoint name, then click the Actions menu item and click Delete in the menu that appears.

When you have successfully deleted the endpoint, you will no longer incur AWS charges for it. You can confirm that all of your endpoints have been deleted when you see the text "There are currently no resources" displayed on the Endpoints page (figure 7.12).

Kiara can now predict power consumption for each site with a 6.9% MAPE, even for months with a number of holidays or predicted weather fluctuations.

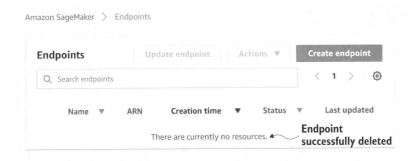

Figure 7.12   Confirm that all endpoints were deleted.

Summary

- Past usage is not always a good predictor of future usage.
- DeepAR is a neural network algorithm that is particularly good at incorporating several different time-series datasets into its forecasting, thereby accounting for events in your time-series forecasting that your time-series data can't directly infer.
- The datasets used in this chapter can be classified into two types of data: categorical and dynamic. Categorical data is information about the site that doesn't change, and dynamic data is data that changes over time.
- For each day in your prediction range, you calculate the Mean Average Prediction Error (MAPE) for the time-series data by defining the function mape.
- Once the model is built, you can run the predictions and display the results in multiple time-series charts to easily visualize the predictions.

Part 3

Moving machine learning into production

The final part of this book shows you how to serve your machine learning models over the web without setting up any servers or other infrastructure.

The book concludes with two case studies showing how companies are running machine learning projects in their own operations and how they are changing their workforce to take advantage of the opportunities created by machine learning and automation.

Serving predictions over the web

This chapter covers

- Setting up SageMaker to serve predictions over the web
- Building and deploying a serverless API to deliver SageMaker predictions
- Sending data to the API and receiving predictions via a web browser

Until now, the machine learning models you built can be used only in SageMaker. If you wanted to provide a prediction or a decision for someone else, you would have to submit the query from a Jupyter notebook running in SageMaker and send them the results. This, of course, is not what AWS intended for SageMaker. They intended that your users would be able to access predictions and decisions over the web. In this chapter, you'll enable your users to do just that.

> **Serving tweets**
>
> In chapter 4, you helped Naomi identify which tweets should be escalated to her support team and which tweets could be handled by an automated bot. One of the things you didn't do for Naomi was provide a way for her to send tweets to the machine learning model and receive a decision as to whether a tweet should be escalated. In this chapter, you will rectify that.

8.1   Why is serving decisions and predictions over the web so difficult?

In each of the previous chapters, you created a SageMaker model and set up an endpoint for that model. In the final few cells of your Jupyter Notebook, you sent test data to the endpoint and received the results. You have only interacted with the SageMaker endpoint from within the SageMaker environment. In order to deploy the machine learning model on the internet, you need to expose that endpoint to the internet.

Until recently, this was not an easy thing to do. You first needed to set up a web server. Next, you coded the API that the web server would use, and finally, you hosted the web server and exposed the API as a web address (URL). This involved lots of moving parts and was not easy to do. Nowadays, all this is much easier.

In this chapter, you'll tackle the problem of creating a web server and hosting the API in a way that builds on many of the skills relating to Python and AWS that you've learned in previous chapters. At present, you can serve web applications without worrying about the complexities of setting up a web server. In this chapter, you'll use AWS Lambda as your web server (figure 8.1).

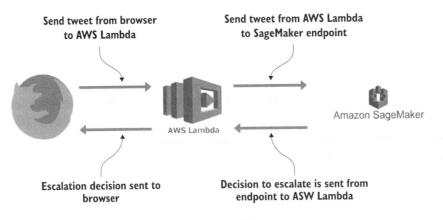

Send tweet from browser to AWS Lambda

Send tweet from AWS Lambda to SageMaker endpoint

AWS Lambda

Amazon SageMaker

Escalation decision sent to browser

Decision to escalate is sent from endpoint to ASW Lambda

Figure 8.1   Sending a tweet from a browser to SageMaker

AWS Lambda is a server that boots on demand. Every tweet you send to the SageMaker endpoint creates a server that sends the tweet and receives the response, and then shuts down once it's finished. This sounds like it might be slow from reading that description, but it's not. AWS Lambda can start and shut down in a few milliseconds. The advantage when serving your API is that you're paying for the Lambda server only when it is serving decisions from your API. For many APIs, this is a much more cost-effective model than having a permanent, dedicated web server waiting to serve predictions from your API.

> **Serverless computing**
>
> Services like AWS Lambda are often called *serverless*. The term serverless is a misnomer. When you are serving an API on the internet, by definition it cannot be serverless. What serverless refers to is the fact that somebody else has the headache of running your server.

8.2 Overview of steps for this chapter

This chapter contains very little new code. It's mostly configurations. To help follow along throughout the chapter, you'll see a list of steps and where you are in the steps. The steps are divided into several sections:

1 Set up the SageMaker endpoint.
2 Configure AWS on your local computer.
3 Create a web endpoint.
4 Serve decisions.

With that as an introduction, let's get started.

8.3 The SageMaker endpoint

Up to this point, you have interacted with your machine learning models using a Jupyter notebook and the SageMaker endpoint. When you interact with your models in this manner, it hides some of the distinctions between the parts of the system.

The SageMaker endpoint can also serve predictions to an API, which can then be used to serve predictions and decisions to users over the web. This configuration works because it is a safe environment. You can't access the SageMaker endpoint unless you're logged into Jupyter Notebook, and anyone who is logged into the Notebook server has permission to access the endpoint.

When you move to the web, however, things are a little more wild. You don't want just anyone hitting on your SageMaker endpoint, so you need to be able to secure the endpoint and make it available only to those who have permission to access it.

Why do you need an API endpoint in addition to the SageMaker endpoint? SageMaker endpoints don't have any of the required components to allow them to be safely exposed to the wilds of the internet. Fortunately, there are lots of systems that can handle this for you. In this chapter, you'll use AWS's infrastructure to create a serverless web application configured to serve predictions and decisions from the SageMaker endpoint you set up in chapter 4. To do so, you'll follow these steps:

1 Set up the SageMaker endpoint by
  a Starting SageMaker
  b Uploading a notebook
  c Running a notebook
2 Configure AWS on your local computer.
3 Create a web endpoint.
4 Serve decisions.

To begin, you need to start SageMaker and create an endpoint for the notebook. The notebook you'll use is the same as the notebook you used for chapter 4 (customer _support.ipynb), except it uses a different method for normalizing the tweet text. Don't worry if you didn't work through that chapter or don't have the notebook on SageMaker anymore, we'll walk you through how to set it up.

8.4 Setting up the SageMaker endpoint

Like each of the other chapters, you'll need to start SageMaker (detailed in appendix C). For your convenience, that's summarized here. First, go to the SageMaker service on AWS by clicking this link:

https://console.aws.amazon.com/sagemaker/home

Then, start your notebook instance. Figure 8.2 shows the AWS Notebook instances page. Click the Start action.

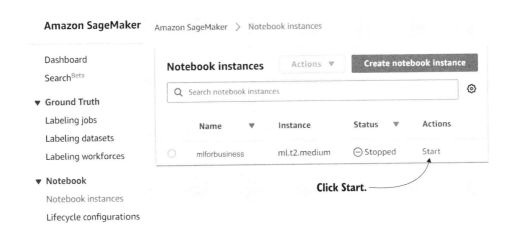

Figure 8.2   Starting a SageMaker instance

In a few minutes, the page refreshes and a link to Open Jupyter appears, along with an InService status message. Figure 8.3 shows the AWS Notebook Instances page after the notebook instance is started.

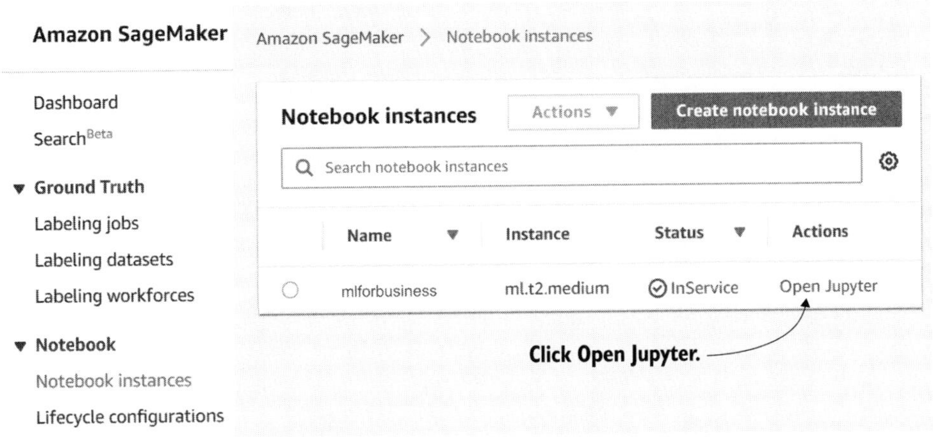

Figure 8.3 Opening Jupyter

The next section shows you how to upload the notebook and data for this chapter. But what are the differences between the notebook used in chapter 4 and the notebook used in chapter 8?

In this chapter, even though you are deciding which tweets to escalate as you did in chapter 4, you will create a new notebook rather than reuse the notebook for chapter 4. The reason for this is that we want to be able to pass the text of the tweet as a URL in the address bar of the browser (so we don't have to build a web form to enter the text of the tweet). This means that the text of the tweet can't contain any characters that are not permitted to be typed in the address bar of the browser. As this is not how we built the model in chapter 4, we need to train a new model in this chapter.

The notebook we create in this chapter is exactly the same as the notebook in chapter 4, except that it uses a library called *slugify* to preprocess the tweet rather than NLTK. Slugify is commonly used to turn text into website URLs. In addition to providing a lightweight mechanism to normalize text, it also allows the tweets to be accessed as URLs.

8.4.1 Uploading the notebook

Start by downloading the Jupyter notebook to your computer from this link:

https://s3.amazonaws.com/mlforbusiness/ch08/customer_support_slugify.ipynb

Now, in the notebook instance shown in figure 8.4, create a folder to store the notebook by clicking New on the Files page and selecting the Folder menu item as shown in figure 8.5. The new folder will hold all of your code for this chapter.

Figure 8.6 shows the new folder after you click it. Once in the folder, you see an Upload button on the top right of the page. Clicking this button opens a file selection

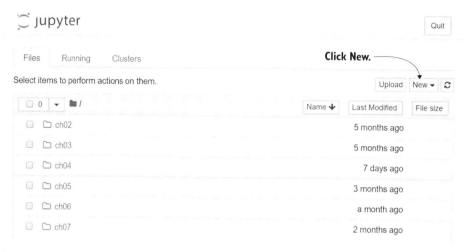

Figure 8.4   Creating a new notebook folder: Step 1

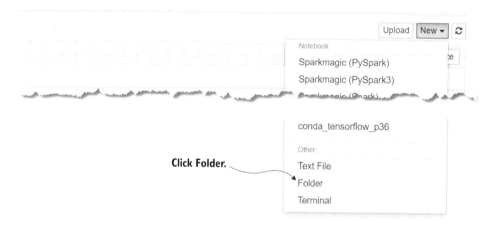

Figure 8.5   Creating a new notebook folder: Step 2

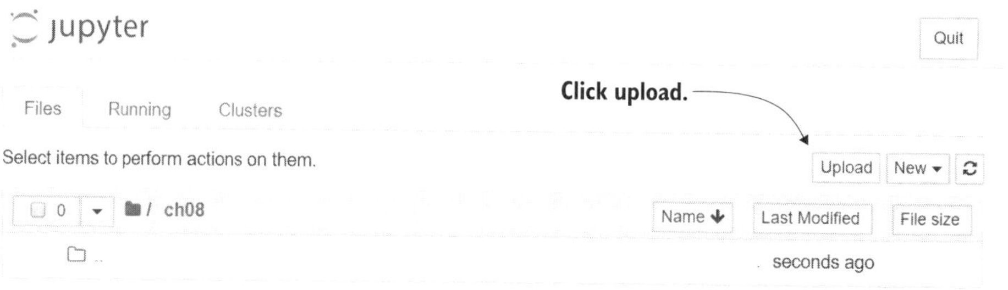

Figure 8.6   Uploading the notebook to a new notebook folder

window. Navigate to the location where you downloaded the Jupyter notebook, and upload it to the notebook instance.

Figure 8.7 shows the notebook you have uploaded to SageMaker.

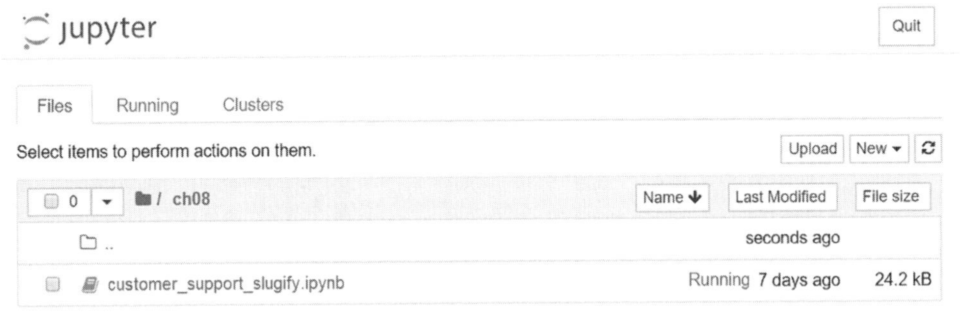

Figure 8.7   Verifying that the notebook customer_support_slugify.ipynb was uploaded to your SageMaker folder

8.4.2   Uploading the data

Even though you can't reuse the notebook from chapter 4, you can reuse the data. If you set up the notebook and the data for chapter 4, you can use that dataset; skip ahead to section 8.4.3, "Running the notebook and creating the endpoint." If you didn't do that, follow the steps in this section.

If you didn't set up the notebook and the data for chapter 4, download the dataset from this location:

https://s3.amazonaws.com/mlforbusiness/ch04/inbound.csv

Save this file to a location on your computer. You won't do anything with this file other than upload it to S3, so you can use your downloads directory or some other temporary folder.

Now, head to AWS S3, the AWS file storage service, by clicking this link:

https://s3.console.aws.amazon.com/s3/home

Once there, create or navigate to the S3 bucket where you are keeping the data for this book (see appendix B if you haven't created an S3 bucket yet).

In your bucket, you can see any folders you have created. If you haven't done so already, create a folder to hold the data for chapter 4 by clicking Create Folder. (We are setting up the data for chapter 4 because this chapter uses the same data as that chapter. You may as well store the data as in chapter 4, even if you haven't worked through the content of that chapter.) Figure 8.8 shows the folder structure you might have if you have followed all the chapters in this book.

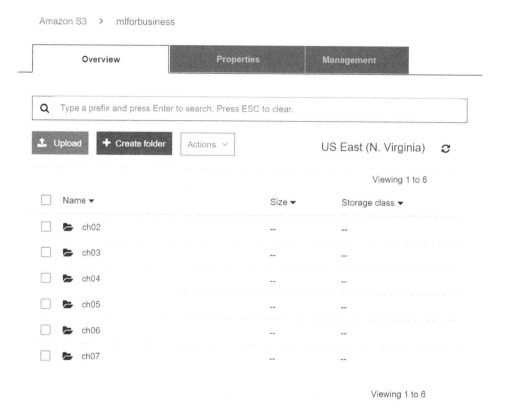

Figure 8.8   Example of what your S3 folder structure might look like

Inside the folder, click Upload on the top left of the page, find the CSV data file you just saved, and upload it. After you have done so, you'll see the inbound.csv file listed in the folder (figure 8.9). Keep this page open because you'll need to get the location of the file when you run the notebook.

You now have a Jupyter notebook set up on SageMaker and data loaded onto S3. You are ready to begin to build and deploy your model in preparation for serving predictions over the web.

8.4.3   *Running the notebook and creating the endpoint*

Now that you have a Jupyter notebook instance running and uploaded your data to S3, run the notebook and create the endpoint. You do this by selecting Cell from the menu and then clicking Run All (figure 8.10).

Figure 8.9 Example of what your S3 bucket might look like once you have uploaded the CSV data

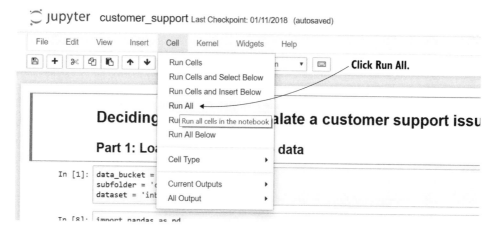

Figure 8.10 Running all cells in the notebook

After 5 minutes or so, all the cells in the notebook will have run, and you will have created an endpoint. You can see that all the cells have run by scrolling to the bottom of the notebook and checking for a value in the second-to-last cell (below the Test the Model heading) as shown in figure 8.11.

Test the Model

```
In [19]:  tweet = "Help me I'm very disappointed!"

          tokenized_tweet = [' '.join(nltk.word_tokenize(tweet))]
          payload = {"instances" : tokenized_tweet}
          response = text_classifier.predict(json.dumps(payload))
          escalate = pd.read_json(response)
          escalate
```

```
Out[19]:
              label           prob
          0  [__label__1]  [0.9999783039093011]
```

Notebook has completed if the output of this cell has a value.

Figure 8.11   Confirming that all cells in the notebook have run

Once you have run the notebook, you can view the endpoint by clicking the Endpoints link as shown in figure 8.12.

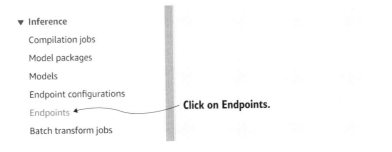

Click on Endpoints.

Figure 8.12   Navigating to Endpoints to view your current endpoints

Here you will see the ARN (Amazon Resource Name) of the endpoint you have created. You will need this when you set up the API endpoint. Figure 8.13 shows an example of what your endpoint might look like.

Now, you can set up the serverless API endpoint. The API endpoint is the URL or web address that you will send the tweets to. You will set up the endpoint on AWS serverless technology, which is called AWS Lambda. In order for AWS Lambda to know what to do, you will install the Chalice Python library.

Chalice is a library built by AWS to make it easy to use Python to serve an API endpoint. You can read more about Chalice here: https://chalice.readthedocs.io/en/latest/.

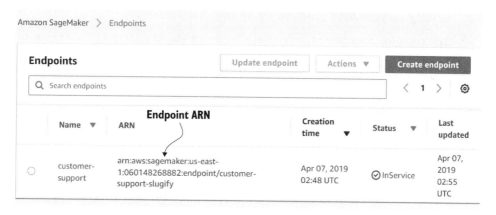

Figure 8.13 Example of what your endpoint ARN might look like

8.5   *Setting up the serverless API endpoint*

To review where you are at in the process, you have just set up a SageMaker endpoint that is ready to serve decisions about whether to escalate a tweet to your support team. Next, you'll set Chalice, the serverless API endpoint as follows:

1. Set up the SageMaker endpoint.
2. Configure AWS on your local computer by
   a. Creating credentials
   b. Installing the credentials on your local computer
   c. Configuring the credentials
3. Create a web endpoint.
4. Serve decisions.

It's somewhat ironic that the first thing you need to do to set up a serverless API endpoint is set up software on your computer. The two applications you need are Python (version 3.6 or higher) and a text editor.

Instructions for installing Python are in appendix E. Although installing Python used to be tricky, it's become much easier for Windows operating systems with the inclusion of Python in the Microsoft Windows Store. And installing Python on Apple computers has been made easier for some time now by the Homebrew package manager.

As we mentioned, you'll also need a text editor. One of the easiest editors to set up is Microsoft's Visual Studio Code (VS Code). It runs on Windows, macOS, and Linux. You can download VS Code here: https://code.visualstudio.com/.

Now that you are set up to run Python on your computer, and you have a text editor, you can start setting up the serverless endpoint.

8.5.1   *Setting up your AWS credentials on your AWS account*

To access the SageMaker endpoint, your serverless API needs to have permission to do so. And because you are writing code on your local computer rather than in a Sage-Maker notebook (as you have done for each of the previous chapters in the book), your local computer also needs permission to access the SageMaker endpoint and your AWS account. Fortunately, AWS provides a simple way to do both.

First, you need to create credentials in your AWS account. To set up credentials, click the AWS username in the top right of the browser from any AWS page (figure 8.14).

Figure 8.14   Creating AWS credentials

In the page that opens, there's a Create access key button that allows you to create an *access key*, which is one of the types of credentials you can use to access your AWS account. Click this button.

Figure 8.15 shows the AWS user interface for creating an access key. After clicking this button, you will be able to download your security credentials as a CSV file.

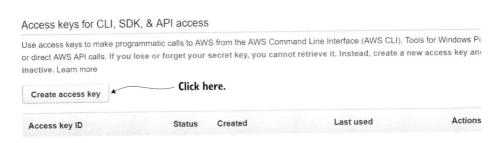

Figure 8.15   Creating an AWS access key

NOTE You are presented with your one and only opportunity to download your keys as a CSV file.

Download the CSV file and save it somewhere on your computer where only you have access (figure 8.16). Anyone who gets this key can use your AWS account.

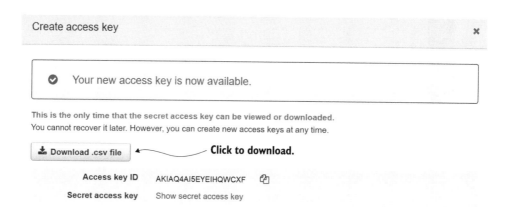

Figure 8.16 Downloading the AWS access key

With the access key downloaded to your computer, you can set up your local computer to access AWS. We'll cover that next.

8.5.2 Setting up your AWS credentials on your local computer

To set up your local computer to access AWS, you need to install two AWS Python libraries on your local computer. This section will walk you through how to install these libraries from VS Code, but you can use any terminal application such as Bash on Unix or macOS, or PowerShell on Windows.

First, create a folder on your computer that you will use for saving your code. Then open VS Code and click the Open Folder button as shown in figure 8.17.

Create a new folder on your computer to hold the files for this chapter. Once you have done so, you can start installing the Python libraries you'll need.

The code you'll write on your local computer needs Python libraries in the same way SageMaker needs Python libraries to run. The difference between your local computer and SageMaker is that SageMaker has the libraries you need already installed, whereas on your computer, you may need to install the libraries yourself.

In order to install the Python libraries on your computer, you need to open a terminal shell. This is a way to enter commands into your computer using only the keyboard. Opening a terminal window in VS Code is done by pressing Ctrl + ⇧ Shift. Alternatively, you can open a terminal window from VS Code by selecting Terminal from the menu bar and then selecting New Terminal.

Figure 8.17   Opening a folder in VS Code

A terminal window appears at the bottom of VS Code, ready for you to type into. You can now install the Python libraries you need to access SageMaker.

The first library you will install is called boto3. This library helps you interact with AWS services. SageMaker itself uses boto3 to interact with services such as S3. To install boto3, in the terminal window, type

```
pip install boto3
```

Next, you'll need to install the command-line interface (CLI) library that lets you stop and start an AWS service from your computer. It also allows you to set up credentials that you have created in AWS. To install the AWS CLI library, type

```
pip install awscli
```

With both boto3 and the CLI library installed, you can now configure your credentials.

8.5.3   *Configuring your credentials*

To configure your AWS credentials, run the following command at the prompt in the terminal window:

```
aws configure
```

You are asked for your AWS Access Key ID and the AWS Secret Access Key you downloaded earlier. You are also asked for your AWS region. Figure 8.18 shows how to locate your SageMaker region.

Figure 8.18 shows the address bar of a web browser when you are logged into Sage-Maker. The address shows which region your SageMaker service is located in. Use this

Figure 8.18 Locating your SageMaker region

region when you configure the AWS credentials. Note that you can leave the Default output format blank.

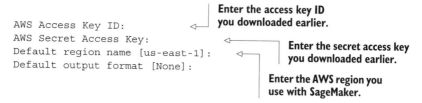

You've completed the configuration of AWS on your local computer. To recap, you set up the SageMaker endpoint, then you configured AWS on your local computer. Now you will create the web endpoint that allows you to serve decisions regarding which tweets to escalate to Naomi's support team. Let's update where we are in the process:

1 Set up the SageMaker endpoint.
2 Configure AWS on your local computer.
3 Create a web endpoint by
   a Installing Chalice
   b Writing endpoint code
   c Configuring permissions
   d Updating requirements.txt
   e Deploying Chalice
4 Serve decisions

8.6 Creating the web endpoint

You are at the point in the chapter that amazed us when we first used AWS to serve an API endpoint. You are going to create a serverless function using an AWS technology called a Lambda function (https://aws.amazon.com/lambda/), and configure the API using an AWS technology called the Amazon API Gateway (https://aws.amazon .com/api-gateway/). Then you'll deploy the SageMaker endpoint so it can used by anyone, anywhere. And you will do it in only a few lines of code. Amazing!

8.6.1   *Installing Chalice*

Chalice (https://github.com/aws/chalice) is open source software from Amazon that automatically creates and deploys a Lambda function and configures an API gateway endpoint for you. During configuration, you will create a folder on your computer to store the Chalice code. Chalice will take care of packaging the code and installing it in your AWS account. It can do this because, in the previous section, you configured your AWS credentials using the AWS CLI.

The easiest way to get started is to navigate to an empty folder on your computer. Right-click the folder to open a menu, and then click Open with Code as shown in figure 8.19. Alternatively, you can open this folder from VS Code in the same way you did in figure 8.17. Neither way is better than the other—use whichever approach you prefer.

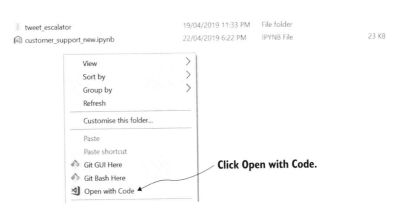

Figure 8.19   Opening the VS Code editor in a folder

To install Chalice, once you have opened VS Code, go to the terminal window like you did when you configured the AWS CLI, and type this command:

```
pip install chalice
```

Depending on the permissions you have on your computer, if this produces an error, you might need to type this command:

```
pip install --user chalice
```

Just like the AWS CLI you used earlier, this command creates a CLI application on your system. Now you're all set to use Chalice.

Using Chalice is straightforward. There are two main commands:

- `new-project`
- `deploy`

To create a new project named tweet_escalator, run the following command at the prompt:

```
chalice new-project tweet_escalator
```

If you look in the folder you opened VS Code from, you will see a folder called tweet_escalator that contains some files that Chalice automatically created. We'll discuss these files shortly, but first, let's deploy a Hello World application.

In the terminal window, you'll see that after running `chalice new-project tweet_escalator`, you're still in the folder you opened VS Code from. To navigate to the tweet_escalator folder, type

```
cd tweet_escalator
```

You'll see that you are now in the folder tweet_escalator:

```
c:\\mlforbusiness\ch08\tweet_escalator
```

Now that you are in the tweet_escalator folder, you can type `chalice deploy` to create a Hello World application:

```
c:\\mlforbusiness\ch08\tweet_escalator chalice deploy
```

Chalice will then automatically create a Lambda function on AWS, set up the permissions to run the application (known as an *IAM role*), and configure a Rest endpoint using AWS Gateway. Here's Chalice's process:

- Create a deployment package
- Create an IAM role (`tweet_escalator-dev`)
- Create a Lambda function (`tweet_escalator-dev`)
- Create a Rest API

The resources deployed by Chalice are

- Lambda ARN (arn:aws:lambda_us-east-1:3839393993:function:tweet_escalator-dv)
- Rest API URL (https://eyeueiwwo.execute-api.us-east-1.amazonaws.com/api/)

You can run the Hello World application by clicking the Rest API URL shown in the terminal. Doing so opens a web browser and displays `{"hello":"world"}` in JSON, as shown in figure 8.20.

← → C 🔒 https://g8lqvzw5mj.execute-api.us-east-1.amazonaws.com/api/

`{"hello":"world"}`

Figure 8.20 Hello World

Congratulations! Your API is now up and running and you can see the output in your web browser.

8.6.2   *Creating a Hello World API*

Now that you have the Hello World application working, it's time to configure Chalice to return decisions from your endpoint. Figure 8.21 shows the files that Chalice automatically created when you typed `chalice new-project tweet_escalator`. Three important components are created:

- A .chalice folder that contains the configuration files. The only file in this folder that you will need to modify is the policy-dev.json file, which sets the permissions that allow the Lambda function to call the SageMaker endpoint.
- An app.py file that contains the code that runs when the endpoint is accessed (such as when you view it in your web browser).
- A requirements.txt file that lists any Python libraries that your application needs to run.

← → ∨ ↑ ▯ > This PC > Desktop > 2019_projects > hudgeon > code_ch08 > tweet_escalator

Name

▯ .chalice ◄――――― **1. Set permissions.**
▯ __pycache__
▯ chalicelib ――――― **2. Configure application.**
▯ app.py ◄
▯ requirements.txt ◄――― **3. List software to install.**

Figure 8.21   Screenshot of the Chalice folder on your computer

Listing 8.1 shows the code in the app.py file that Chalice creates automatically. The app only needs a name, a route, and a function to work.

Listing 8.1   Chalice's default app.py code

```python
from chalice import Chalice

app = Chalice(app_name='tweet_escalator')

@app.route('/')
def index():
    return {'hello': 'world'}
```

Imports Chalice, the library that creates the Lambda function and API gateway

Sets the name of the app

Sets the default route

Defines the function that runs when the default route is hit

Sets the value that gets returned by the function and displayed in the web browser

In listing 8.1, the name of the app (line 2) is the name that is used to identify the Lambda function and API gateway on AWS. The route (line 3) identifies the URL location that runs the function. And the function (line 4) is the code that is run when the URL location is accessed.

Accessing URLs

There are many ways to access a URL. In this chapter, we'll access the URL simply by typing the URL in the address bar of a browser. More commonly, when you are invoking a SageMaker endpoint, you will access the URL location from another application. For example, you would implement an app in the ticketing system that Naomi's support team uses when responding to tweets. Then the app would send the tweet to the URL location and read the response returned. And finally, if the response returned recommends that the tweet be escalated, then it would be routed to a particular support channel in your ticketing system.

Building this application is beyond the scope of this book. In this chapter, you will just set up the URL location that invokes the SageMaker endpoint and displays an escalation recommendation in a web browser.

8.6.3 Adding the code that serves the SageMaker endpoint

You can keep the Hello World code you just created and use it as the basis for your code that will serve the SageMaker endpoint. For now, at the bottom of the Hello World code, add two blank lines and enter the code shown in listing 8.2. The full code listing can be downloaded from this link: https://s3.amazonaws.com/mlforbusiness/ch08/app.py.

Listing 8.2 The default app.py code

```
@app.route('/tweet/{tweet}')              ◁———— Defines the route
def return_tweet(tweet):          ◁—┐ Sets up the function
    tokenized_tweet = [
        slugify(tweet, separator=' ')]     ◁———— Tokenizes the tweet
    payload = json.dumps(
        {"instances" : tokenized_tweet})    ◁———— Sets up the payload

    endpoint_name = 'customer-support-slugify'   ◁—┐ Identifies the
                                                    │ SageMaker endpoint

    runtime = boto3.Session().client(
        service_name='sagemaker-runtime',
        region_name='us-east-1')            ◁—┐ Prepares the
                                               │ endpoint
    response = runtime.invoke_endpoint(
        EndpointName=endpoint_name,
        ContentType='application/json',      ┌ Invokes the endpoint
        Body=payload)             ◁—┘ and gets the response
```

```
response_list = json.loads(
    response['Body'].read().decode())          ◁──────┤  Converts the
response = response_list[0]              ◁──┐              response to a list
                                            │  Gets the first
                                               item in the list
if '1' in response['label'][0]:    ◁──┐
    escalate = 'Yes'                    │
else:                                   │  Sets escalate decision
    escalate = 'No'                        to Yes or No

full_response = {                ◁──┤  Sets the full
    'Tweet': tweet,                     response format
    'Tokenised tweet': tokenized_tweet,
    'Escalate': escalate,
    'Confidence': response['prob'][0]
}
return full_response        ◁────────  Returns the response
```

Just like the @app.route you set in line 3 of listing 8.1, you start your code by defining the route that will be used. Instead of defining the route as / as you did earlier, in line 1 of listing 8.2, you set the route as /tweet/{tweet}/. This tells the Lambda function to watch for anything that hits the URL path /tweet/ and submit anything it sees after that to the SageMaker endpoint, for example, if Chalice creates an endpoint for you at

```
https://ifs1qanztg.execute-api.us-east-1.amazonaws.com/api/
```

When you go to this endpoint, it returns {"hello": "world"}. Similarly, the code in line 1 of listing 8.2 would send I am angry to the SageMaker endpoint when you access this endpoint:

```
https://ifs1qanztg.execute-api.us-east-1.amazonaws.com/api/tweet/i-am-angry
```

The code {tweet} tells Chalice to put everything it sees at the end of the URL into a variable called tweet. In the function you see in line 2, you are using the variable tweet from line 1 as your input to the function.

Line 3 slugifies the tweet using the same function that the Jupyter notebook uses. This ensures that the tweets you send to the SageMaker endpoint are normalized using the same approach that was used to train the model. Line 4 reflects the code in the Jupyter notebook to create the payload that gets sent to the SageMaker endpoint. Line 5 is the name of the SageMaker endpoint you invoke. Line 6 ensures that the endpoint is ready to respond to a tweet sent to it, and line 7 sends the tweet to the SageMaker endpoint.

Line 8 receives the response. The SageMaker endpoint is designed to take in a list of tweets and return a list of responses. For our application in this chapter, you are only sending a single tweet, so line 9 returns just the first result. Line 10 converts the escalate decision from 0 or 1 to No or Yes, respectively. And finally, line 11 defines the response format, and line 12 returns the response to the web browser.

8.6.4 Configuring permissions

At this point, your Chalice API still cannot access your AWS Lambda function. You need to give the AWS Lambda function permission to access your endpoint. Your Hello World Lambda function worked without configuring permissions because it did not use any other AWS resources. The updated function needs access to AWS SageMaker, or it will give you an error.

Chalice provides a file called policy-dev.json, which sets permissions. You'll find it in the .chalice folder that's located in the same folder as the app.py file you've just worked on. Once you navigate into the .chalice folder, you'll see the policy-dev.json file. Open it in VS Code and replace the contents with the contents of listing 8.3.

> **NOTE** If you don't want to type or copy and paste, you can download the policy-dev.json file here: https://s3.amazonaws.com/mlforbusiness/ch08/policy-dev.json.

Listing 8.3   Contents of policy-dev.json

```
{
    "Version": "2012-10-17",
    "Statement": [
        {
            "Sid": "VisualEditor0",
            "Effect": "Allow",
            "Action": [
                "logs:CreateLogStream",
                "logs:PutLogEvents",
                "logs:CreateLogGroup"
            ],
            "Resource": "arn:aws:logs:*:*:*"
        },
        {
            "Sid": "VisualEditor1",
            "Effect": "Allow",
            "Action": "sagemaker:InvokeEndpoint",     ◁── Adds permission to
            "Resource": "*"                                invoke a SageMaker
        }                                                  endpoint
    ]
}
```

Your API now has permission to invoke the SageMaker endpoint. There is still one more step to do before you can deploy the code to AWS.

8.6.5 Updating requirements.txt

You need to instruct the Lambda function to install the slugify so it can be used by the application. To do this, you add the line in listing 8.4 to the requirements.txt file located in the same folder as the app.py file.

> **NOTE** You can download the file here: https://s3.amazonaws.com/mlforbusiness/ch08/requirements.txt.

Listing 8.4 Contents of requirements.txt

```
python-slugify
```

The requirements.txt update is the final step you need to do before you are ready to deploy Chalice.

8.6.6 Deploying Chalice

At last, it's time to deploy your code so that you can access your endpoint. In the terminal window in VS Code, from the tweet_escalator folder, type:

```
chalice deploy
```

This regenerates your Lambda function on AWS with a few additions:

- The Lambda function now has permission to invoke the SageMaker endpoint.
- The Lambda function has installed the slugify library so it can be used by the function.

8.7 Serving decisions

To recap, in this chapter, you have set up the SageMaker endpoint, configured AWS on your computer, and created and deployed the web endpoint. Now you can start using it. We're finally at the last step in the process:

1 Set up the SageMaker endpoint.
2 Configure AWS on your local computer.
3 Create a web endpoint.
4 Serve decisions.

To view your API, click the Rest API URL link that is shown in your terminal window after you run `chalice deploy` (figure 8.22). This still brings up the Hello World page because we didn't change the output (figure 8.23).

```
- Rest API URL: https://g8lqvzw5mj.execute-api.us-east-1.amazonaws.com/api/
```

Figure 8.22   The Rest API URL used to access the endpoint in a web browser.

```
←  →  C     🔒 https://g8lqvzw5mj.execute-api.us-east-1.amazonaws.com/api/
```

```
{"hello":"world"}
```

Figure 8.23   Hello World, again

To view the response to a tweet, you need to enter the route in the address bar of your browser. An example of the route you need to add is shown in figure 8.24. At the end of the URL in the address bar of your browser (after the final /), you type `tweet/the-text-of-the-tweet-with-dashes-instead-of-spaces` and press ‎Enter↵‎.

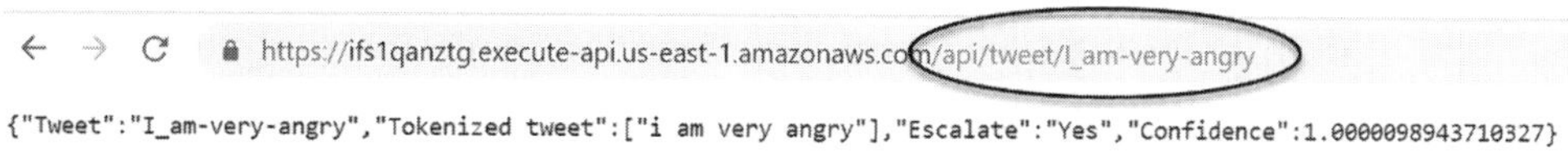

← → C   🔒 https://ifs1qanztg.execute-api.us-east-1.amazonaws.com/api/tweet/I_am-very-angry

```
{"Tweet":"I_am-very-angry","Tokenized tweet":["i am very angry"],"Escalate":"Yes","Confidence":1.0000098943710327}
```

Figure 8.24 Tweet response: I am very angry

The response displayed on the web page now changes from {`"hello"`: `"world"`} to

```
{"Tweet":"I-am-very-angry","Tokenized tweet":["i am very angry"],
    "Escalate":"Yes","Confidence":1.0000098943710327}
```

The response shows the tweet it pulled from the address bar, the tokenized tweet after running it through slugify, the recommendation on whether to escalate the tweet or not (in this case the answer is Yes), and the confidence of the recommendation.

To test additional phrases, simply type them into the address bar. For example, entering `thanks-i-am-happy-with-your-service` generates the response shown in figure 8.25. As expected, the recommendation is to not escalate this tweet.

← → C   🔒 ute-api.us-east-1.amazonaws.com/api/tweet/thanks-i-am-happy-with-your-service ☆

```
{"Tweet":"thanks-i-am-happy-with-your-service","Tokenized tweet":["thanks i am happy with your
service"],"Escalate":"No","Confidence":1.0000100135803223}
```

Figure 8.25 Tweet response: I am happy with your service

It is interesting to see the results for negating a tweet such as turning "I am very angry" to "I am not angry." You might expect that the API would recommend not escalating this, but that is often not the case. Figure 8.26 shows the response to this tweet. You can see it still recommends escalation, but its confidence is much lower— down to 52%.

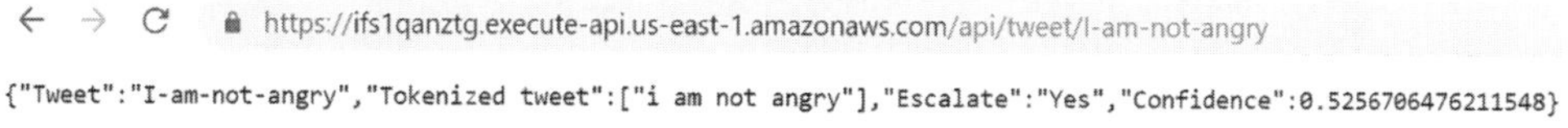

← → C   🔒 https://ifs1qanztg.execute-api.us-east-1.amazonaws.com/api/tweet/I-am-not-angry

```
{"Tweet":"I-am-not-angry","Tokenized tweet":["i am not angry"],"Escalate":"Yes","Confidence":0.5256706476211548}
```

Figure 8.26 Tweet response: I am not angry

To see why it was escalated, you need to look at the data source for the tweets. When you look at the negated tweets, you see that many of the tweets were labeled Escalate because the negated phrase was part of a longer tweet that expressed frustration. For example, a common tweet pattern was for a person to tweet "I'm not angry, I'm just disappointed."

Summary

- In order to deploy a machine learning model on the internet, you need to expose that endpoint to the internet. Nowadays, you can serve web applications containing your model without worrying about the complexities of setting up a web server.
- AWS Lambda is a web server that boots on demand and is a much more cost-effective way to serve predictions from your API.
- The SageMaker endpoint can also serve predictions to an API, which can then be used to serve predictions and decisions to users over the web, and you can secure the endpoint and make it available only to those who have permission to access it.
- To pass the text of the tweet as a URL, the text of the tweet can't contain any characters that are not permitted to be typed in the address bar of the browser.
- You set up a SageMaker endpoint with slugify (rather than NLTK) to normalize tweets. Slugify is commonly used to turn text into website URLs.
- You set up the serverless API SageMaker endpoint on AWS serverless technology, which is called AWS Lambda. In order for AWS Lambda to know what to do, you install the Chalice Python library.
- To access the SageMaker endpoint, your serverless API needs to have permission to do so. Using Microsoft's Visual Studio Code (VS Code), you set up credentials in your AWS account by creating an access key, then setting up your AWS credentials on your local computer.
- You set up the AWS command-line interface (CLI) and boto3 libraries on your local computer so you can work with AWS resources from your local machine.
- To create a serverless function, you learned about AWS Lambda functions and the AWS API Gateway services and how easy it is to use them with Chalice.
- You deployed an API that returns recommendations about whether to escalate a tweet to Naomi's support team.

Case studies

9

This chapter covers

- Review of the topics in this book
- How two companies using machine learning improved their business
  - Case study 1: Implementing a single machine learning project in your company
  - Case study 2: Implementing machine learning at the heart of everything your company does

Throughout the book, you have used AWS SageMaker to build solutions to common business problems. The solutions have covered a broad range of scenarios and approaches:

- Using XGBoost supervised learning to solve an approval routing challenge
- Reformatting data so that you could use XGBoost again, but this time to predict customer churn
- Using BlazingText and Natural Language Processing (NLP) to identify whether a tweet should be escalated to your support team
- Using unsupervised Random Cut Forest to decide whether to query a supplier's invoice

- Using DeepAR to predict power consumption based on historical trends
- Adding datasets such as weather forecasts and scheduled holidays to improve DeepAR's predictions

In the previous chapter, you learned how to serve your predictions and decisions over the web using AWS's serverless technology. Now, we'll wrap it all up with a look at how two different companies are implementing machine learning in their business.

In chapter 1, we put forward our view that we are on the cusp of a massive surge in business productivity and that this surge is going to be due in part to machine learning. Every company wants to be more productive, but they find it's difficult to achieve this goal. Until the advent of machine learning, if a company wanted to become more productive, they needed to implement and integrate a range of best-in-class software or change their business practices to conform exactly to how their ERP (Enterprise Resource Planning) system worked. This greatly slows the pace of change in your company because your business either comprises a number of disparate systems, or it's fitted with a straightjacket (also known as your ERP system). With machine learning, a company can keep many of their operations in their core systems and use machine learning to assist with automating decisions at key points in the process. Using this approach, a company can maintain a solid core of systems yet still take advantage of the best available technology.

In each of the chapters from 2 through 7, we looked at how machine learning could be used to make a decision at a particular point in a process (approving purchase orders, reconnecting with customers at risk of churning, escalating tweets, and reviewing invoices), and how machine learning can be used to generate predictions based on historical data combined with other relevant datasets (power consumption prediction based on past usage and other information such as forecasted weather and upcoming holidays).

The two case studies we look at in this chapter show several different perspectives when adopting machine learning in business. The first case study follows a labor-hire company as it uses machine learning to automate a time-consuming part of its candidate interview process. This company is experimenting with machine learning to see how it can solve various challenges in their business. The second case study follows a software company that already has machine learning at its core but wants to apply it to speed up more of its workflow. Let's jump in and look at how the companies in these case studies use machine learning to enhance their business practices.

9.1   *Case study 1: WorkPac*

WorkPac is Australia's largest privately held labor-hire company. Every day, tens of thousands of workers are contracted out across thousands of clients. And every day, to maintain a suitable pool of candidates, WorkPac has teams of people interviewing candidates.

The interview process can be thought of as a pipeline where candidates go into a funnel at the top and are categorized into broad categories as they progress down the funnel. Recruiters who are experts in a particular category apply metadata to the candidates so they can be filtered based on skills, experience, aptitude, and interest. Applying these filters allows the right pool of candidates to be identified for each open position.

Figure 9.1 shows a simplified view of the categorization process. Candidate resumes go into the top of the funnel and are classified into different job categories.

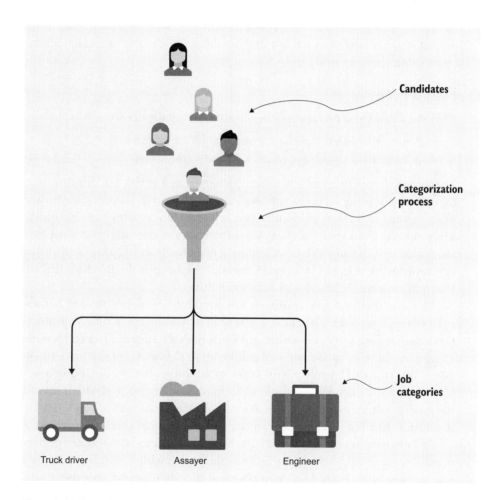

Figure 9.1   Funnel to categorize candidates into different types of jobs

The anticipated benefit of automating the categorization funnel is that it frees up time for recruiters to focus on gathering metadata about candidates rather than classifying candidates. An additional benefit of using a machine learning model to perform the classification is that, as a subsequent phase, some of the metadata gathering can also be automated.

Before implementing the machine learning application, when a candidate submits their resume through WorkPac's candidate portal, it's categorized by a generalist recruiter and potentially passed on to a specialist recruiter for additional metadata. After passing through this process, the candidate would then be available for other recruiters to find. For example, if the candidate was classified as a truck driver, then recruiters looking to fill a truck driver role would be able to find this candidate.

Now that WorkPac has implemented the machine learning application, the initial classification is performed by a machine learning algorithm. The next phase of this project is to implement a chat bot that can elicit some of the metadata, further freeing up valuable recruiter time.

9.1.1   *Designing the project*

WorkPac considered two approaches to automating the classification of candidates:

- A simple keyword classification system for candidates
- A machine learning approach to classify candidates

The keyword classification system was perceived as low risk but also low reward. Like the approval-routing scenario you looked at in chapter 2, *keyword classification* requires ongoing time and effort to identify new keywords. For example, if Caterpillar releases a new mining truck called a 797F, WorkPac has to update their keyword list to associate that term with truck driver. Adopting a machine learning approach ensures that as new vehicles are released by manufacturers, for example, the machine learning model learns to associate 797F vehicles with truck drivers.

The machine learning approach was perceived as higher reward but also higher risk because it would be WorkPac's first time delivering a machine learning project. A machine learning project is a different beast than a standard IT project. With a typical IT project, there are standard methodologies to define the project and the outcomes. When you run an IT project, you know in advance what the final outcome will look like. You have a map, and you follow the route to the end. But with a machine learning project, you're more like an explorer. Your route changes as you learn more about the terrain. Machine learning projects are more iterative and less predetermined.

To help overcome these challenges, WorkPac retained the services of Blackbook.ai to assist them. Blackbook.ai is an automation and machine learning software company that services other businesses. WorkPac and Blackbook.ai put together a project plan that allowed them to build trust in the machine learning approach by delivering the solution in stages. The stages this project progressed through are typical of machine learning automation projects in general:

- *Stage 1*—Prepare and test the model to validate that decisions can be made using machine learning.
- *Stage 2*—Implement proof of concept (POC) around the workflow.
- *Stage 3*—Embed the process into the company's operations.

9.1.2   Stage 1: Preparing and testing the model

Stage 1 involved building a machine learning model to classify existing resumes. WorkPac had more than 20 years of categorized resume data, so they had plenty of data to use for training. Blackbook.ai used OCR technology to extract text from the resumes and trained the model on this text. Blackbook.ai had enough data that they were able to balance out the classes by selecting equal numbers of resumes across each of the job categories. After training and tuning the model, the model was able to hit an F Score of 0.7, which was deemed to be suitable for this activity.

F scores

An *F score* (also known as an F1 score) is a measure of the performance of a machine learning model. In chapter 3, you learned how to create a confusion matrix showing the number of false positive and false negative predictions. An F score is another way of summarizing the results of a machine learning model. An example is the best way to see how an F score is calculated.

The following table summarizes the results of a machine learning algorithm that made 50 predictions. The algorithm was attempting to predict whether a particular candidate should be classified as a truck driver, assayer, or engineer.

Table 9.1   Data table showing candidate predictions

	Prediction (truck driver)	Prediction (assayer)	Prediction (engineer)	Total
Actual (truck driver)	**11**	4	0	15
Actual (assayer)	4	**9**	2	15
Actual (engineer)	3	3	**14**	20
Total	18	16	16	**50**

The top row of the table indicates that out of 15 candidates who were actually truck drivers, the algorithm correctly predicted that 11 were truck drivers and incorrectly predicted that 4 were assayers. The algorithm did not incorrectly predict that any truck drivers were engineers. Likewise for the second row (Assayer), the algorithm correctly predicted that nine assayer candidates were indeed assayers, but it incorrectly predicted that four truck drivers were assayers and two engineers were assayers. If you look at the top row (the actual truck driver), you would say that 11 out of 15 predictions were correct. This is known as the *precision* of the algorithm. A result of 11/15 means the algorithm has a precision of 73% for truck drivers.

You can also look at each column of data. If you look at the first column, Prediction (truck driver), you can see that the algorithm predicted 18 of the candidates were truck drivers. Out of 18 predictions, it got 11 right and 7 wrong. It predicted 4 assayers were truck drivers and 3 engineers were assayers. This is known as the *recall* of the algorithm. The algorithm correctly recalls 11 out of 18 predictions (61%).

(continued)

From this example, the importance of both precision and recall can be seen. The precision result of 73% looks pretty good, but the results look less favorable when you consider that only 61% of its truck driver predictions are correct. The F score reduces this number to a single value using the following formula:

((Precision * Recall) / (Precision + Recall)) * 2

Using the values from the table, the calculation is

((.73 * .61) / (.73 + .61)) * 2 = 0.66

so the F score of the first row is 0.66. Note that if you average the F scores across a table for a multiclass algorithm (as in this example), the result will typically be close to the precision. But it's useful to look at the F score for each class to see if any of these have wildly different recall results.

During this stage, Blackbook.ai developed and honed their approach for transforming resumes into data that could be fed into their machine learning model. In the model development phase, a number of the steps in this process were manual, but Blackbook.ai had a plan to automate each of these steps. After achieving an F score in excess of 0.7 and armed with a plan for automating the process, Blackbook.ai and WorkPac moved on to stage 2 of the project.

9.1.3   *Stage 2: Implementing proof of concept (POC)*

The second stage involves building a POC that incorporates the machine learning model into WorkPac's workflow. Like many business process-improvement projects involving machine learning, this part of the project took longer than the machine learning component. From a risk perspective, this part of the project was a standard IT project.

In this stage, Blackbook.ai built a workflow that took resumes uploaded from candidates, classified the resumes, and presented the resumes and the results of the classification to a small number of recruiters in the business. Blackbook.ai then took feedback from the recruiters and incorporated recommendations into the workflow. Once the workflow was approved, they moved on to the final stage of the project—implementation and rollout.

9.1.4   *Stage 3: Embedding the process into the company's operations*

The final stage of the project was to roll out the process across all of WorkPac. This is typically time consuming as it involves building error-catching routines that allow the process to function in production, and training staff in the new process. Although time consuming, this stage can be low risk, providing the feedback from the stage 2 users is positive.

9.1.5   Next steps

Now that resumes are being automatically classified, WorkPac can build and roll out chatbots that are trained on a particular job type to get metadata from candidates (such as work history and experience). This allows their recruiters to focus their efforts on the highest-value aspects of their jobs, rather than spending time gathering information about the candidates.

9.1.6   Lessons learned

One of the time-consuming aspects of a machine learning project is getting the data to feed the model. In this case, the data was locked away in resume documents in PDF format. Rather than spending time building their own OCR data-extraction service, Blackbook.ai solved this problem by using a commercial resume data-extraction service. This allowed them to get started right away at a low cost. If the cost of this service becomes too high down the track, a separate business case can be prepared to replace the OCR service with an in-house application.

To train the machine learning model, Blackbook.ai also required metadata about the existing documents. Getting this metadata required information to be extracted from WorkPac's systems using SQL queries, and it was time consuming to get this data from WorkPac's internal teams. Both WorkPac and Blackbook.ai agreed this should have been done in a single workshop rather than as a series of requests over time.

9.2   Case study 2: Faethm

Faethm is a software company with artificial intelligence (AI) at its core. At the heart of Faethm's software is a system that predicts what a company (or country) could look like several years from now, based on the current structure of its workforce and the advent of emerging technologies like machine learning, robotics, and automation. Faethm's data science team accounts for more than a quarter of their staff.

9.2.1   AI at the core

What does it mean to have AI at the core of the company? Figure 9.2 shows how Faethm's platform is constructed. Notice how every aspect of the platform is designed to drive data to Faethm's AI engine.

Faethm combines their two main data models—Technology Adoption Model and Workforce Attribution Model—with client data in their AI engine to predict how a company will change over the coming years.

9.2.2   Using machine learning to improve processes at Faethm

This case study doesn't focus on how Faethm's AI engine predicts how a company will change over the coming years. Instead, it focuses on a more operational aspect of their business: how can it onboard new customers faster and more accurately? Specifically, how can it more accurately match their customers' workforce to Faethm's job

Figure 9.2   Every aspect of Faethm's operating model drives data toward its AI engine.

categorization? This process fits section 4, Contextual Client Data, which is shown in Faethm's Platform Construct (figure 9.2).

Figure 9.3 shows a company's organizational structure being converted to Faethm's job classification. Correctly classifying jobs is important because the classified jobs serve as a starting point for Faethm's modeling application. If the jobs do not reflect their customer's current workforce, the end result will not be correct.

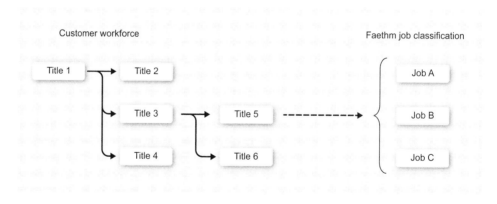

Figure 9.3   Job description categorization funnel

At first glance, this looks like a challenge similar to what WorkPac faced, in that both Faethm and WorkPac are classifying jobs. The key difference is the incoming data: WorkPac has 20 years of labeled resume data, whereas Faethm has only a few years of job title data. So Faethm broke the project down into four stages:

- *Stage 1*—Get the data
- *Stage 2*—Identify features
- *Stage 3*—Validate the results
- *Stage 4*—Implement in production

9.2.3   Stage 1: Getting the data

When Faethm started operations in 2017, the team manually categorized their customers' job title data. Over time, it developed several utility tools to speed up the process, but categorizing the job titles for incoming clients still required manual effort from expert staff. Faethm wanted to use its considerable machine learning expertise to automate this process.

Faethm decided to use SageMaker's BlazingText algorithm. This was due, in part, to the fact that BlazingText handles out-of-vocabulary words by creating vectors from sub-words.

> **What are out-of-vocabulary words?**
>
> As discussed in chapter 4, BlazingText turns words into a string of numbers called a *vector*. The vector represents not only a word, but also the different contexts it appears in. If the machine learning model only creates vectors from whole words, then it cannot do anything with a word that it hasn't been specifically trained on.
>
> With job titles, there are lots of words that might not appear in training data. For example, the model might be trained to recognize gastroenterologist and neuroradiologist, but it can stumble when it comes across a gastrointestinal radiologist. BlazingText's sub-word vectors allow the model to handle words like gastrointestinal radiologist, for example, because it creates vectors from *gas*, *tro*, *radio*, and *logist*, even though these terms are only sub-words of any of the words the model is trained on.

The first problem Faethm needed to surmount was getting sufficient training data. Instead of waiting until it had manually classified a sufficient number of clients, Faethm used its utility tools to create a large number of classified job titles similar to, but not exactly the same as, existing companies. This pool of companies formed the training dataset.

> **Training data**
>
> You might not have to worry about labeling your data. WorkPac was able to use undersampling and oversampling to balance their classes because they had 20 years of labeled data. When you are looking at machine learning opportunities in your business, you might find yourself in a similar position in that the processes most amenable to implementing machine learning are those that have been done by a person for a long time, and you have their historical decisions to use as training data.

An additional complication with Faethm's data was that their classes were imbalanced. Some of the jobs they classified into titles had hundreds of samples (Operations Manager, for example). Others had only one. To address this imbalance, Faethm adjusted the weighting of each category (like you did using XGBoost in chapter 3). Now armed with a large labeled dataset, Faethm could begin building the model.

9.2.4   *Stage 2: Identifying the features*

Once they had the data, Faethm looked at other features that might be relevant for classifying job titles into roles. Two features found to be important in the model were industry and salary. For example, an analyst in a consulting firm or bank is usually a different role than an analyst in a mining company, and an operations manager earning $50,000 per year is likewise a different role than an operations manager earning $250,000 per year.

By requesting the anonymised employee_id of each employee's manager, Faethm was able to construct two additional features: first, the ratio of employees with each title who have direct reports; and second, the ratio of employees with each title who have managers reporting to them. The addition of these two features resulted in a further significant improvement in accuracy.

9.2.5   *Stage 3: Validating the results*

After building the model in SageMaker, Faethm was able to automatically categorize a customer's workforce into jobs that serve as inputs into Faethm's predictive model. Faethm then classified the workforce using its human classifiers and identified the anomalies. After several rounds of tuning and validation, Faethm was able to move the process into production.

9.2.6   *Stage 4: Implementing in production*

Implementing the algorithm in production was simply a matter of replacing the human decision point with the machine learning algorithm. Instead of making the decision, Faethm's expert staff spend their time validating the results. As it takes less time to validate than it does to classify, their throughput is greatly improved.

9.3   *Conclusion*

In the case studies, you progressed from a company taking its first steps in machine learning to a company with machine learning incorporated into everything it does. The goal of this book has been to provide you with the context and skills to use machine learning in your business.

Throughout the book, we provided examples of how machine learning can be applied at decision points in your business activities so that a person doesn't have to be involved in those processes. By using a machine learning application, rather than a human, to make decisions, you get the dual benefits of a more consistent and a more robust result than when using rules-based programming.

In this chapter, we have shown different perspectives on machine learning from companies using machine learning today. In your company, each of the following perspectives is helpful in evaluating which problems you should tackle and why.

9.3.1 Perspective 1: Building trust

WorkPac and Blackbook.ai made sure that the projects had achievable and measurable outcomes, delivered in bite-sized chunks throughout the project. These companies also made sure they reported progress regularly, and they weren't overpromising during each phase. This approach allowed the project to get started without requiring a leap of faith from WorkPac's executive team.

9.3.2 Perspective 2: Getting the data right

There are two ways to read the phrase *Getting the data right*. Both are important. The first way to read the phrase is that the data needs to be as accurate and complete as possible. The second way to read the phrase is that you need to correctly build the process for extracting the data and feeding it into the machine learning process.

When you move into production, you need to be able to seamlessly feed data into your model. Think about how you are going to do this and, if possible, set this up in your training and testing processes. If you automatically pull your data from source systems during development, that process will be well tested and robust when you move to production.

9.3.3 Perspective 3: Designing your operating model to make the most of your machine learning capability

Once you have the ability to use machine learning in your company, you should think about how to you can use this functionality in as many places as possible and how you can get as many transactions as possible flowing through the models. Faethm's first question when considering a new initiative was probably, "How can this feed our AI engine?" In your company, when looking at a new business opportunity, you'll want to ask, "How can this new opportunity fit into our existing models or be used to bolster our current capability?"

9.3.4 Perspective 4: What does your company look like once you are using machine learning everywhere?

As you move from your first machine learning projects to using machine learning everywhere, your company will look very different. In particular, the shape of your workforce will change. Preparing your workforce for this change is key to your success.

Armed with these perspectives and the skills you picked up as you've worked your way through the chapters in this book, we hope you are ready to tackle processes within your own company. If you are, then we've achieved what we set out to do, and we wish you every success.

Summary

- You followed WorkPac as they embarked on their first machine learning project.
- You saw how Faethm, an experienced machine learning company, incorporated machine learning into yet another of its processes.

appendix A
Signing up for Amazon AWS

AWS is Amazon's cloud service. At the time of writing this book, it has a larger share of the cloud service market than either Microsoft or Google, its two biggest competitors.

AWS consists of a large number of services ranging from servers to storage to specialized machine learning applications for text and images. In fact, one of the most difficult aspects of using a cloud service is understanding what each of the components does. While you are encouraged to explore the breadth of AWS services, for this book, we are only going to use two of them: S3 (AWS's file storage service) and SageMaker (AWS's machine learning platform).

This appendix takes you through setting up an AWS account, appendix B takes you through setting up and using S3, and appendix C takes you through setting up and using SageMaker. If you have an AWS account already, skip this appendix and go to appendix B, which shows you how to configure S3.

You'll need to provide your credit card number to get an AWS account, but you won't be charged until you exceed your free tier limits.

NOTE You should be able to do all the exercises in this book without going over the free tier limits offered to new accounts.

A.1 Signing up for AWS

To sign up for AWS, go to the following link:

https://portal.aws.amazon.com/billing/signup

Once there, click Sign Up and walk through the prompts. The first form (figure A.1) asks you for an email address, a password, and a username.

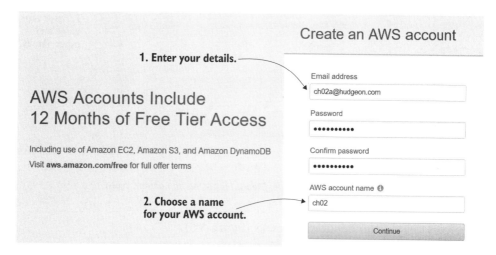

Figure A.1   Creating an AWS account: Step 1 (entering an email address, a password, and a username)

Next, choose an account type (we used Personal for this book) and information about your location (figure A.2).

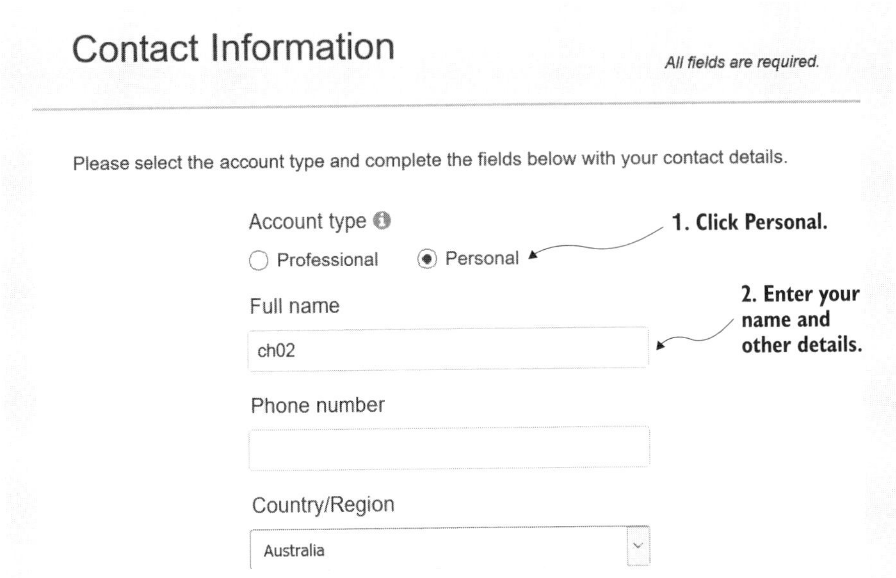

Contact Information

All fields are required.

Please select the account type and complete the fields below with your contact details.

Account type ⓘ

○ Professional   ⊙ Personal ◄   **1. Click Personal.**

Full name   **2. Enter your
                                               name and
ch02   other details.**

Phone number

Country/Region

Australia

Figure A.2   Creating an AWS account: Step 2 (choosing an account type)

Next, enter your credit card details (figure A.3).

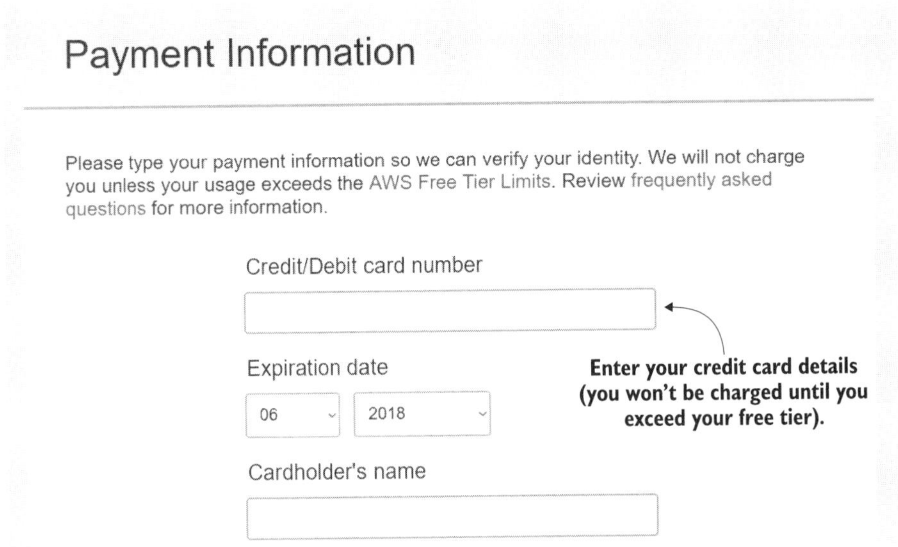

Payment Information

Please type your payment information so we can verify your identity. We will not charge you unless your usage exceeds the AWS Free Tier Limits. Review frequently asked questions for more information.

Credit/Debit card number

Expiration date   **Enter your credit card details
                                     (you won't be charged until you
06   2018   exceed your free tier).**

Cardholder's name

Figure A.3   Creating an AWS account: Step 3 (entering credit card details)

The next pages' forms relate to verifying your account. Likely, as a provider of compute services, AWS is subject to attempts by technically savvy users trying to get free services. Accordingly, there are a few steps to the verification process. The first verification step is a security check by typing annoyingly displayed characters (figure A.4).

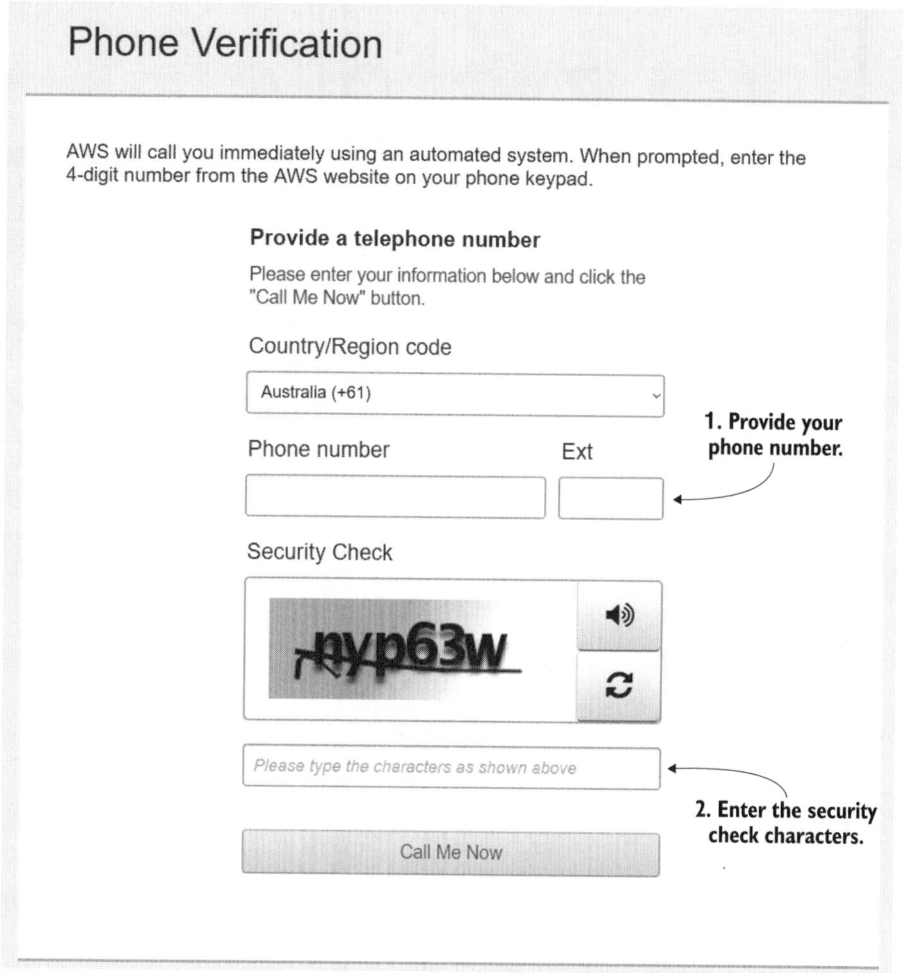

Figure A.4   Verifying your account information: matching captcha characters

Clicking Call Me Now kicks off the second verification step, where you'll receive an automated call from AWS. It will ask you to key in the four-digit code that is displayed on the page (figure A.5).

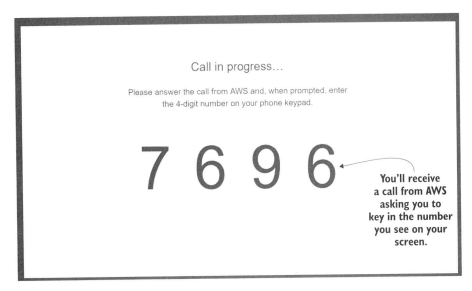

Figure A.5   Verifying your account information: entering the four-digit code

You're now verified. You can continue on to the next step (figure A.6).

Figure A.6   Creating an AWS account: Step 4 (identity verification confirmation)

Next, you select the plan you want (figure A.7). The Free plan will suffice for working through this book.

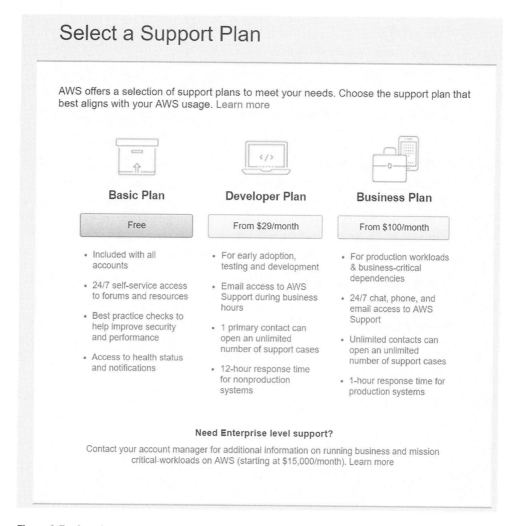

Figure A.7   Creating an AWS account: Step 5 (selecting a support plan)

Congratulations, you're now signed up (figure A.8). You can sign into the AWS console and move on to appendix B to learn how to set up S3 (AWS's file storage service) and SageMaker (AWS's machine learning service). But first a word on AWS charges.

Click to sign in.

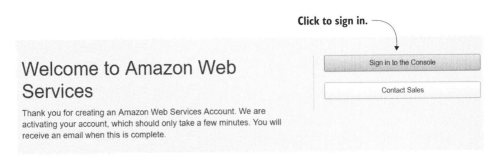

Figure A.8 Creating an AWS account: Success!

A.2   *AWS Billing overview*

AWS charges by the second for using resources such as SageMaker, the machine learning service we use in the book. When you open a new AWS account, for the first 12 months, you get free use of the resources you will need to work through the exercises in this book. There are limits on the amount of resources available to you; but the free tier will be sufficient to complete all the exercises in this book.

> **NOTE** You can get up-to-date pricing information for AWS services on this page: https://aws.amazon.com/sagemaker/pricing/.

If you have an existing AWS account, you will be charged for your use of AWS resources. However, if you are careful to ensure you shut down your resources when you are not using them, you can complete all the exercises in this book spending only US$10–$20 on AWS resources.

appendix B
Setting up and using S3 to store files

S3 is AWS's file storage system. Throughout this book, you'll use S3 to store your data files for machine learning and your machine learning models after you create them in SageMaker. This appendix walks you through how to set up a bucket to hold your code for the examples in this book.

> **NOTE** If you haven't already signed up for Amazon Web Services, go to appendix A, which provides detailed information on how to do this.

To log into the AWS console, go to http://console.aws.amazon.com, and enter your email address and password. Once you have logged in, you will see an AWS Services heading. In the text box under AWS Services, type S3 to find the S3 service, then press Enter↵ on your keyboard.

AWS uses the concept of *buckets* to identify where you store your files. The first thing you'll do when you go to S3 is to set up a bucket to store your files for this book. If you have already created your bucket, when you go to S3, you should see a bucket list that shows your bucket (figure B.1).

You'll create a folder in this bucket for each of the datasets you work with in this book. This is good practice for all of your work. Use buckets to separate your work by who should have access to it, and use folders to separate your datasets.

B.1 Creating and setting up a bucket in S3

You can think of a bucket as a top-level folder in a directory. AWS calls them buckets because they are globally unique. This means that you cannot have a bucket with the same name as a bucket someone else has created. The advantage of this is that each bucket can be assigned a unique address on the web and can be navigated

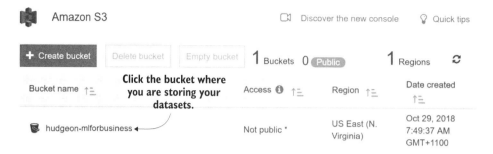

Figure B.1   List of buckets in S3 used to store the code and data used in this book

to by anyone who knows the name of the bucket (of course, you would need to give them access to the bucket before they could get to the bucket or see anything in it). When you first open the S3 service in a new account, you are notified that you don't have any buckets (figure B.2).

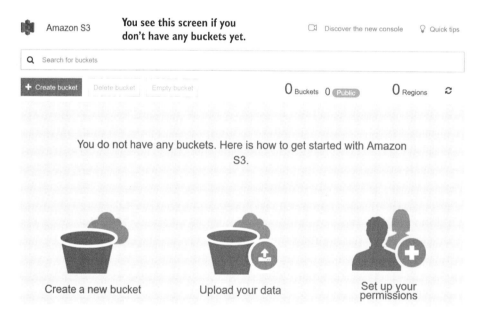

Figure B.2   S3 Dashboard before you have created any buckets

To create your first bucket, click Create Bucket. You are now asked to provide information about your bucket. A wizard walks you through four steps:

- Name your bucket.
- Set properties for your bucket.
- Set permissions.
- Review settings.

B.1.1 Step 1: Naming your bucket

Figure B.3 shows step 1 of the wizard that helps you create your bucket.

In this step, you name your bucket and say what region you want your bucket in. For the purposes of the exercises in this book, create a bucket name that is something unique (like your name) followed by *mlforbusiness*. If someone has already created a bucket with the same name, you might need to add some random numbers after your name.

> **NOTE** The name of your bucket can only contain characters that can appear in a valid web address. This means it can't contain spaces. It is also common practice to use a dash (-) to separate words.

Change the region to US East (N. Virginia). SageMaker is in the process of being rolled out across all regions, but it is not available in all regions yet. So, for the purposes of this book, use US East.

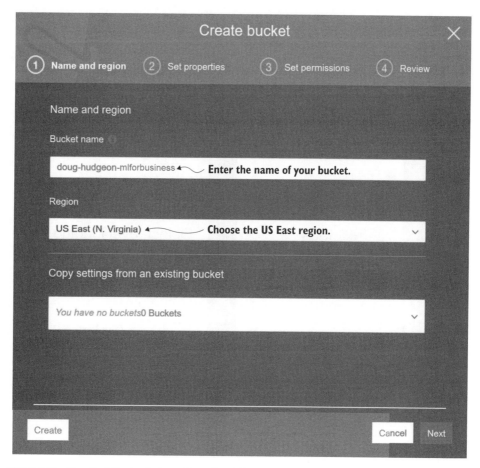

Figure B.3   Step 1 of the bucket creation wizard: Name your bucket

AWS regions such as US East do not refer to where you can access the services from. It refers to where the AWS servers physically reside. When you select US East as the region, it means that you can use the AWS S3 bucket from anywhere, but that the server sits somewhere on the east coast of the United States (North Virginia to be more precise).

B.1.2   Step 2: Setting properties for your bucket

Next, you need to set properties for your bucket. Figure B.4 shows step 2. This is where you say how you want files in the bucket to be versioned, logged, and tagged. No need to change anything here, so click Next.

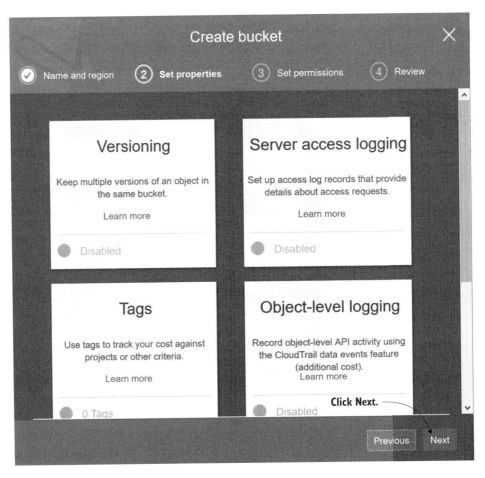

Figure B.4   Step 2 of the bucket creation wizard: Set properties

B.1.3 Step 3: Setting permissions

Permissions allow you to determine who can access your bucket. Figure B.5 shows step 3. For most purposes, you probably only want yourself to access your bucket, so you can leave the permissions as they are set by default. Click Next on this page too.

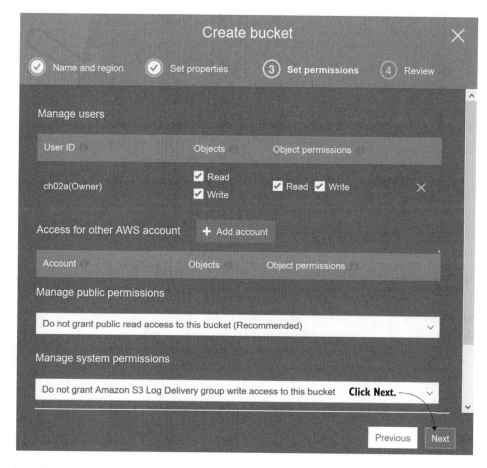

Figure B.5 Step 3 of the bucket creation wizard: Set permissions

B.1.4 Step 4: Reviewing settings

Here you can check your settings and make any required changes, as shown in figure B.6. If you followed the previous instructions, you don't need to make any changes, so click Create Bucket.

Once you click Submit, you are taken back to S3. Figure B.7 shows the bucket you have just created. Now that you have a bucket set up, you can set up folders in your bucket.

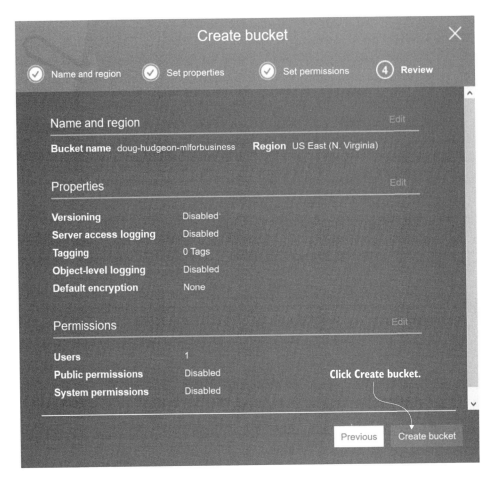

Figure B.6   Step 4 of the bucket creation wizard: Review settings

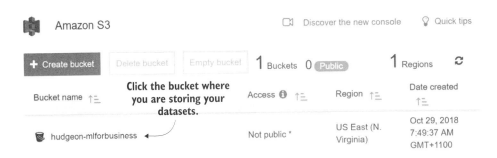

Figure B.7   List of buckets in S3 including the bucket you just created

B.2　Setting up folders in S3

In the previous section, you created a bucket to hold all of your files and code for this book. In this section, you set up a folder to hold your files and code for chapter 2. Once you get the hang of this, you can easily set up folders for the other chapters.

You can think of a bucket in S3 as a top-level folder. The folder that you'll create in this appendix is a subfolder of that top-level folder.

In this book, you'll see terminology such as "a folder" when describing the contents of a bucket, but this terminology is not entirely accurate. In reality, there is no such thing as a folder in an S3 bucket. It looks like there is in the user interface, but an S3 bucket doesn't actually store things hierarchically.

It is more accurate to say that a bucket in S3 is a web location that you can easily restrict access to. Every file that sits in that S3 bucket sits at the top level of the bucket. When you create a folder in S3, it looks like a folder, but it is simply a file stored at the top level of a bucket named in such a way that it looks like a folder.

For example, in the bucket you set up in this appendix, you will create a folder called ch02 and put in it a file called orders_with_predicted_value.csv. In reality, you are just creating a file of that name in your bucket. To use more accurate terminology, the file name is a *key*, and the file contents are a *value*. So a bucket is just a web location that stores key/value pairs.

You are going to create a separate folder within the bucket you just created for each of the machine learning datasets you work with. To begin with, click Create Bucket, and then click Create Folder and name it ch02, as shown in figure B.8.

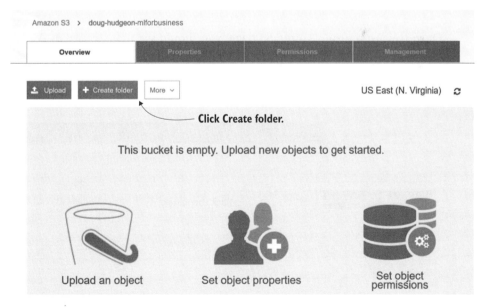

Figure B.8　Create a folder in S3.

After you've named your bucket (figure B.9), click Save.

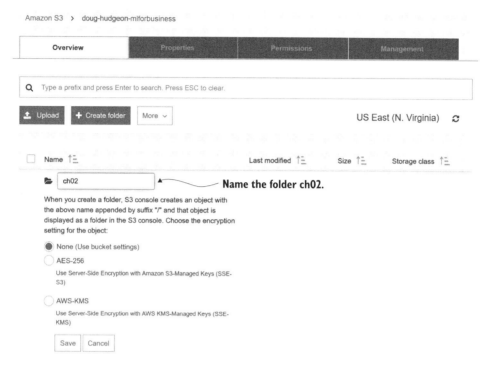

Figure B.9   Name the folder in S3.

Once you are returned to the S3 page, you should see that you are in the bucket you just created, and you have a folder called ch02, as shown in figure B.10.

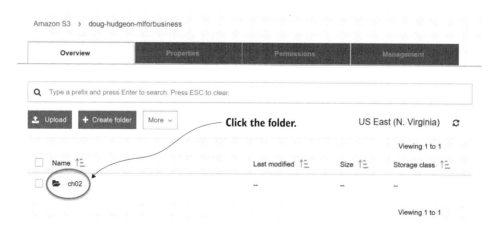

Figure B.10   Click into the folder in S3.

Now that you have a folder set up in S3, you can upload your data file and start setting up the prediction model in SageMaker.

B.3   *Uploading files to S3*

To upload your data file, after clicking the folder, download the data file at this link:

https://s3.amazonaws.com/mlforbusiness/ch02/orders_with_predicted_value.csv

Then upload it into the ch02 folder by clicking Upload, as shown in figure B.11.

Figure B.11   Upload the data into S3.

Once you have uploaded the file, it will appear in S3 (figure B.12).

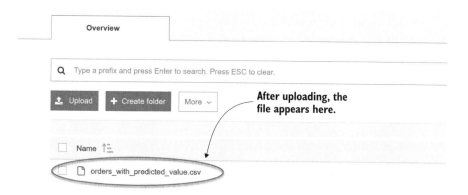

Figure B.12   Dataset listing on S3

In the next appendix, you will learn how to set up AWS SageMaker.

appendix C
Setting up and using AWS SageMaker to build a machine learning system

SageMaker is Amazon's environment for building and deploying machine learning models. Let's look at the functionality it provides. SageMaker is revolutionary because it

- Serves as your development environment in the cloud so you don't have to set up a development environment on your computer
- Uses a preconfigured machine learning model on your data
- Uses inbuilt tools to validate the results of the machine learning model
- Hosts your machine learning model
- Automatically sets up an endpoint that takes in new data and returns predictions

C.1 Setting up

To begin, you need to set your AWS region to a region provided by SageMaker. Figure C.1 shows the dropdown menu you use to select an AWS region to deploy SageMaker into. Set this region to US East (N. Virginia).

The SageMaker interface lets you work with four main components:

- *Dashboard*—Your SageMaker home
- *Notebook instances*—An EC2 server that hosts your notebook

- *Models*—The machine learning models that you create in the Jupyter notebook
- *Endpoints*—An EC2 server that hosts your model and allows you to make predictions

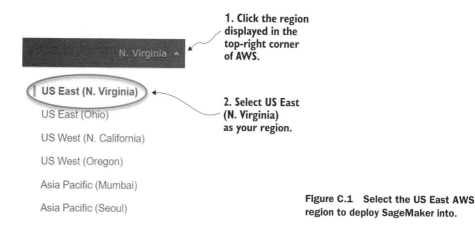

1. Click the region displayed in the top-right corner of AWS.

2. Select US East (N. Virginia) as your region.

Figure C.1   Select the US East AWS region to deploy SageMaker into.

First, you'll set up SageMaker to work with your data. The next section takes you through how to do this. Then, you'll see how to start using SageMaker and how to upload the file you'll work with in chapter 2. You'll also learn how to access the file.

C.2   Starting at the Dashboard

When you first navigate to the SageMaker service, you can see a workflow that contains an orange button that reads Create Notebook Instance. Click it to set up a server to run your Jupyter notebooks.

C.3   Creating a notebook instance

Figure C.2 shows the fields you need to complete to set up your notebook instance. The first field sets your notebook instance name. You'll use the same instance name as you work through all the chapters in the book. We've called ours *mlforbusiness*.

Next is the notebook instance type (the type of AWS server that will run your Jupyter notebook). This sets the size of the server that your notebook will use. For the datasets you'll use in this book, a medium-sized server is sufficient, so select ml.t2.medium.

The third setting is the IAM role. It's best to create a new role to run your notebook instance. Click Create New Role, give it permission to access any S3 Bucket by selecting the option with that label, and click Create Role. After this, you can accept all the rest of the defaults.

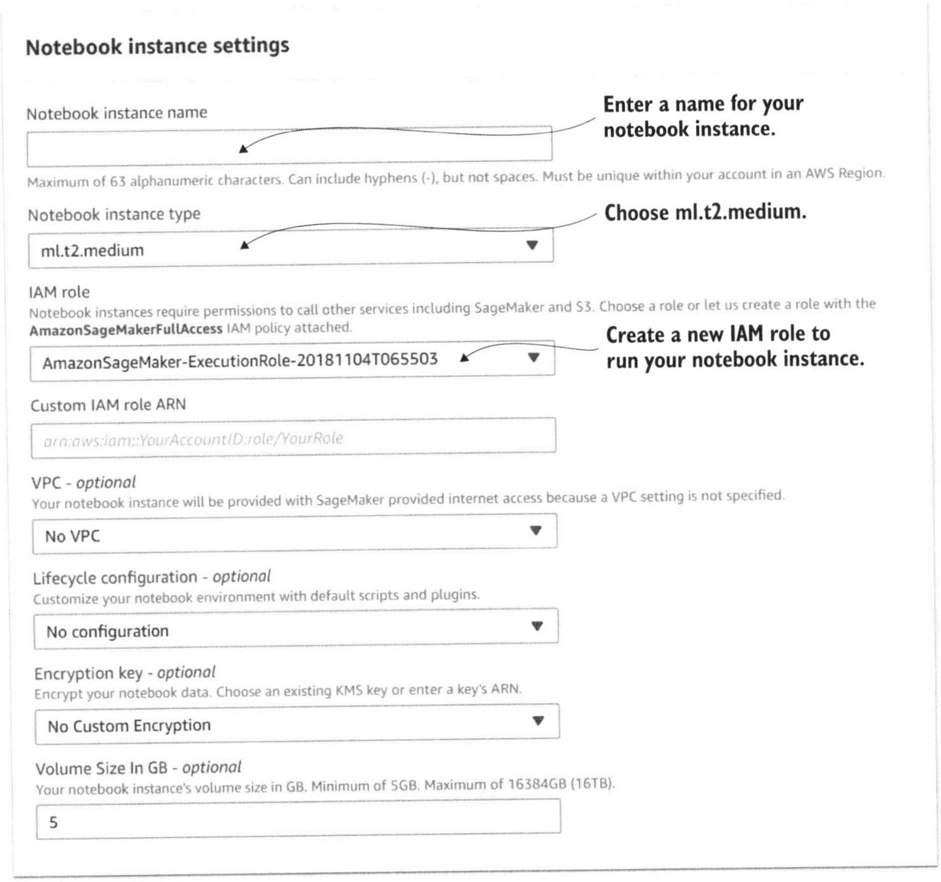

Notebook instance settings

Notebook instance name

> **Enter a name for your notebook instance.**

Maximum of 63 alphanumeric characters. Can include hyphens (-), but not spaces. Must be unique within your account in an AWS Region.

Notebook instance type

> **Choose ml.t2.medium.**

ml.t2.medium ▼

IAM role

Notebook instances require permissions to call other services including SageMaker and S3. Choose a role or let us create a role with the **AmazonSageMakerFullAccess** IAM policy attached.

AmazonSageMaker-ExecutionRole-20181104T065503 ▼

> **Create a new IAM role to run your notebook instance.**

Custom IAM role ARN

arn:aws:iam::YourAccountID:role/YourRole

VPC - *optional*

Your notebook instance will be provided with SageMaker provided internet access because a VPC setting is not specified.

No VPC ▼

Lifecycle configuration - *optional*

Customize your notebook environment with default scripts and plugins.

No configuration ▼

Encryption key - *optional*

Encrypt your notebook data. Choose an existing KMS key or enter a key's ARN.

No Custom Encryption ▼

Volume Size In GB - *optional*

Your notebook instance's volume size in GB. Minimum of 5GB. Maximum of 16384GB (16TB).

5

Figure C.2   To create a new instance, you need to complete three fields of information: the name of the instance, the instance type, and the IAM role.

AWS and resources

AWS servers come in a variety of sizes. Unless you are on the Free plan (which you can be on for 12 months after signing up), AWS charges you for the computer resources you use; this includes AWS servers. Fortunately, they charge you by the second. But you might want to make sure that you use the smallest servers you can get away with.

For the exercises in this book, the ml.t2.medium server is sufficient for working with our datasets. At the time of writing, the cost of this server is less than US$0.05 per hour. You can view current prices by clicking this link: https://aws.amazon.com/ec2/pricing/on-demand.

C.4   Starting the notebook instance

You will now see your notebook instance in a list. The status should say Pending for about 5 mins while SageMaker sets up the EC2 server for you. To avoid unexpected charges from AWS, remember to come back here and click the Stop link that appears under Actions once the EC2 server is ready to go.

When you see Open appear under Actions, click it. A Jupyter notebook launches in another tab. You are a few steps away from your completing your (first) machine learning model.

C.5   Uploading the notebook to the notebook instance

When the notebook instance starts, you'll see a table of contents with a couple of folders in it. These folders contain sample SageMaker models, but we won't look at these now. Instead, as shown in figure C.3, create a new folder to hold the code for this book by clicking New and selecting Folder at the bottom of the dropdown menu.

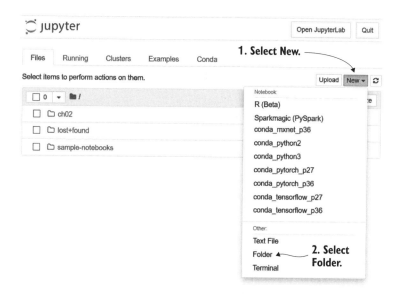

Figure C.3   List of notebooks available to you on your SageMaker instance

When you tick the checkbox next to Untitled Folder, you'll see the Rename button appear. Click this button and change the folder name to ch02. Then click the ch02 folder to see an empty notebook list. Figure C.4 shows the empty notebook list.

Just like we have already prepared the CSV data you uploaded to S3, we have already prepared the Jupyter Notebook you will now use. You can download it to your computer by clicking this link:

https://s3.amazonaws.com/mlforbusiness/ch02/tech_approval_required.ipynb

Figure C.4   Empty notebook list and Upload button

Then click the Upload button to upload the tech-approval-required notebook to this folder.

After uploading the file, you will see the notebook in your list. Figure C.5 shows your list of notebooks. Click tech-approval-required.ipynb to open it.

Figure C.5   Notebook list: tech-approval-required.ipynb

You are a few keystrokes away from your completing your machine learning model.

C.6   *Running the notebook*

You can run the code in one of your notebook cells, or you can run the code in more than one of the cells. To run the code in one cell, click the cell to select it, and then press Ctrl+Enter↵. When you do so, you'll see an asterisk (*) appear to left of the cell. This means that the code in the cell is running. When the asterisk is replaced by a number, the code has finished running. (The number shows how many cells have run since you opened the notebook.)

To run the code in more than one cell (or for the entire notebook), click Cell in the toolbar at the top of the Jupyter notebook, then click Run All.

That's it. You're now ready to dive into the scenario in chapter 2 and begin your journey in creating machine learning applications.

appendix D
Shutting it all down

The last step in getting acquainted with SageMaker is to shut down the notebook instance and delete the endpoint you created. If you don't do this, AWS continues to charge you a few cents per hour for the notebook instance and the endpoint. Shutting down the notebook instance and deleting the endpoint requires you to do the following:

- Delete the endpoint.
- Shut down the notebook instance.

D.1 Deleting the endpoint

To stop your account from being charged for your endpoint, you need to delete the endpoint. But, don't worry about losing your work. When you rerun the notebook, the endpoint will be recreated automatically for you.

To delete the endpoint, click Endpoints on the left-hand menu you see when you are looking at the SageMaker tab. Figure D.1 shows the Endpoints menu item on the Inferences dropdown.

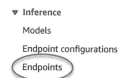

Figure D.1   Endpoints menu item

You will see a list of all of your running endpoints. To ensure you are not charged for endpoints you are not using, you should delete all the endpoints you are not using. (Remember that endpoints are easy to create, so, even if you will not use the endpoint for a few hours, you might want to delete it.) Figure D.2 shows a list of endpoints and what an active endpoint looks like.

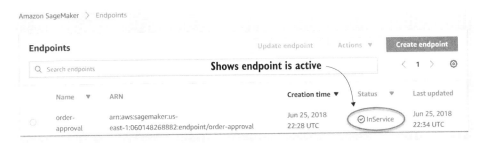

Figure D.2   Active endpoints are shown in the endpoint list. Delete any endpoints you are not using.

To delete the endpoint, click the radio button to the left of the order-approval name. Then click the Actions menu item and click the Delete menu item that appears, as shown in figure D.3.

Figure D.3   Dropdown option that allows you to delete an endpoint

You have now deleted the endpoint so you will no longer incur AWS charges for it. You can confirm that all of your endpoints have been deleted when you see the text "There are currently no resources" displayed on the Endpoints page as shown in figure D.4.

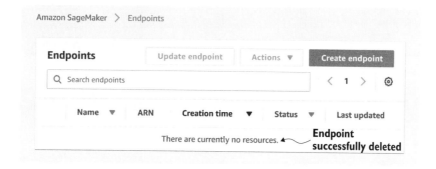

Figure D.4   Verifying that all of your endpoints have been deleted

D.2   *Shutting down the notebook instance*

The final step is to shut down the notebook instance. Unlike endpoints, you do not delete the notebook. You just shut it down so you can start it up again, and it will have all the code in your Jupyter notebook ready to go. To shut down the notebook instance, click Notebook Instances in the left-hand menu on SageMaker. Figure D.5 shows the Notebook Instances option in the SageMaker menu.

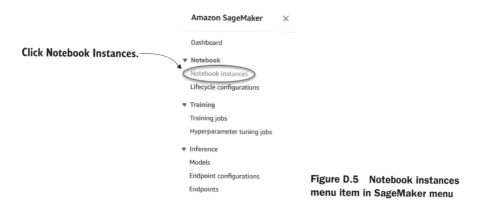

Figure D.5   Notebook instances menu item in SageMaker menu

To shut down the notebook, you just click the Stop link. SageMaker will take a couple of minutes to shut down. Figure D.6 shows the stop notebook action.

After it has shut down, you can confirm the notebook instance is no longer running by checking Status to ensure it says Stopped (figure D.7).

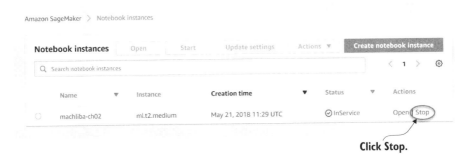

Figure D.6   **Shutting down the notebook by clicking the Stop link**

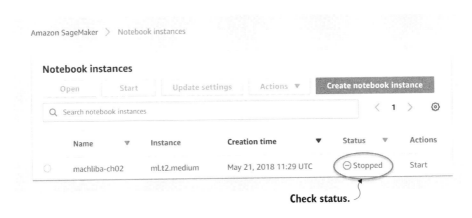

Figure D.7   **Verifying the notebook instance is stopped and shut down**

Congratulations. You have successfully shut down your SageMaker notebook instance(s) and endpoint(s). This will allow you to avoid incurring unnecessary costs.

appendix E
Installing Python

Installing Python on your computer has gotten much easier over the past few years. If you use Microsoft Windows, you can install it directly from the Windows Store at this link:

https://www.microsoft.com/en-us/p/python-37/9nj46sx7x90p

For the purposes of this book, you can accept all the defaults.

If you are using a macOS or Linux machine, you probably already have Python installed, but it might be Python 2.7 rather than Python 3.x. To install the most recent version, go to the Download Python page at

https://www.python.org/downloads

The website will show you a Download Python button that should be set for the operating system version you need. If it does not detect your operating system, there are links to the right versions lower on the page. Again, for the purposes of this book, accept all the defaults, and head back to chapter 8.

index